# BACKYARD BIRD SECRETS FOR EVERY SEASON

## ATTRACT A VARIETY OF NESTING, FEEDING, AND SINGING BIRDS YEAR-ROUND

# SALLY ROTH

Best-Selling Author of *Backyard Bird Feeder's Bible* and *The Backyard Bird Lover's Field Guide*

RODALE®

Rodale books may be purchased for business or promotional use or for special sales. For information, please write to: Special Markets Department, Rodale Inc., 733 Third Avenue, New York, NY 10017

Printed in the United States of America

Rodale Inc. makes every effort to use acid-free ♾, recycled paper ♻.

Book design by Christopher Rhoads

For photography credits, see page 326.

**Library of Congress Cataloging-in-Publication Data**
Backyard bird secrets for every season : attract a variety of nesting, feeding, and singing birds year-round/ Sally Roth.
     p. cm.
Includes bibliographical references and index.
ISBN-13 978-1-59486-910-5 hardcover
ISBN-10 1-59486-910-3 hardcover
ISBN-13 978-1-59486-911-2 paperback
ISBN-10 1-59486-911-1 paperback
1. Bird attracting  2. Gardening to attract birds.  3. Birds—Feeding and feeds.  4. Bird feeders.  I. Title.
QL676.5.R66835  2008
639.9'78—dc22

                                     2008035337

Distributed to the trade by Macmillan

2  4  6  8  10  9  7  5  3     hardcover

2  4  6  8  10  9  7  5  3     paperback

We inspire and enable people to improve their lives and the world around them

For more of our products visit **rodalestore.com** or call 800-848-4735

In memory of

American naturalist

**Thomas Say**

(1787–1834)

An original member of the utopian

community of New Harmony, Indiana


I am humbled to walk the woods and rivers in his footsteps.

# CONTENTS

# ACKNOWLEDGMENTS

WHEN MY CHICKADEES fly down to a handful of peanuts I just put in their tray, chiming out *dee-dee-dee,* it's not hard to guess what they're trying to tell me.

"You're welcome," I say. "Thanks for coming."

Kindness makes the world a happier place, whether you reach out a helping hand to birds or to people. And that's one of the main reasons I returned to New Harmony, Indiana, after a few years out West.

My small town is known for its history—but its people are the reason I came back. I feel grateful every day to live in a place where helping each other is a way of life. Thank you, one and all, for welcoming me home with warm smiles and open hearts.

Speaking of helping each other, here's a big thank-you to everyone who worked so hard on bringing this book to life. Don't let my name on the cover fool you—this was a group effort.

Editor Anne Halpin White groomed my words and helped me stay organized, even when I moved from one end of the country to the other in the middle of this project ("Which box did I put that in?"). But even more important, she supplied a healthy dose of good humor. Work goes a lot easier when you're laughing, and so does daily life.

Thanks to copy editor Erana Bumbardatore, too, whose eagle eye caught my typos, fixed those dangling participles I'm so fond of (ahem), and made sure that my sentences made sense. And to the ever-attentive indexer Lina Burton whose thorough review of final pages helps to make a better book.

Chris Rhoads, who designed this book, made me feel like I'd just been on one of those total-makeover TV shows. He figured out how to arrange my words on the pages so their best side is showing, and he added nifty details that spotlight the four seasons. Thanks to Faith Hague, too, who took care of the technical layout of the pages.

The book really came alive when photo editor Marc Sirinsky rounded up the right shots. Taking a good picture of a bird isn't easy—those little guys just don't sit still, at least for my camera!—and I'm grateful to the talented photographers whose work fills these pages.

Project editor Nancy Bailey was in charge of shepherding this book from start to finish. Did I say shepherding? More like rounding up a bunch of cats, especially with an author who's more likely to be outside sneaking up on birds than sitting by the phone. Thanks, Nancy, for keeping your herd of cats moving forward, without losing your cool.

Another big thank you goes to the marketing and creative team, Katrina Cwitkowitz, Sheila Dorney, Barbara Sheetz, and Heidi Wells. Their work was so appealing that I almost forgot I wrote the book they were talking about—I wanted to jump right in and order a copy.

And, finally, thanks to all of you, dear friends, for sharing the joys of birds and nature. I wish I could hear all your stories, too—I know you've got plenty. Aren't we lucky to have birds to watch, every day of the year, right in our own backyards?

# ATTRACT A VARIETY OF NESTING, FEEDING, SINGING BIRDS YEAR-ROUND

**C**OMPARING notes on the weather is a natural when we're talking to friends who live far away. "It's been really hot here," or "Had a killing frost last night," or "We're having a blizzard!"—I've heard just about every variation on the weather report, and no doubt so have you.

I quickly learned to tone down my reports when I lived in the Pacific Northwest. The climate is mild there—USDA Zone 8, for you gardening types—and the weather is usually way better than what other parts of the country are experiencing. (Well, except for the rain: From fall to spring, the skies are mostly gloomy with a good chance of showers.)

In summer, when friends called to complain about the heat, I changed the subject when my turn came around. How could I tell someone who was living through 100° heat and 90 percent humidity that I was reaching for a sweater at night on the patio and slathering on moisturizer because the air was so dry?

Same deal in winter. Blizzards? Ice storms? Frigid cold? Howling winds? Um, "It went down to 30° last night" sounds laughable, even to me.

The Pacific Northwest lacks the climate extremes of most other regions of the United States. The major seasonal shift is from the rainy season of fall, winter, and spring to the dry season of summer. Eventually, I got used to seeing tan, dormant grass in June and lush green lawns in January.

Southern California has an even more regular climate, with temps staying near 70° year-round. And, as the song only slightly exaggerates, "Seems it never rains in southern California."

I liked being able to get by all winter with nothing more than a fleece jacket. But I did miss the rhythm of four distinct seasons.

Temperatures don't swing nearly as much in that region as they do elsewhere. Frozen soil is a rarity in the part of Washington state where I lived, and so are sweltering summer temperatures. Humidity? Nonexistent, at least in that smothering sense those in the East, South, and Midwest know well. As for snow, fuhgeddaboutit, as a New Yawker might say.

Even the woods in the Pacific Northwest are pretty much the same from one season to another because they're almost entirely coniferous. Locals exclaim over the fall color of the vine maples and poison oak that dot the openings, but to someone who grew up with the flaming color of red and orange maples, golden hickories, purple ash, and all the other trees in a mostly deciduous forest . . . well, I bit my tongue every October.

Still, there is a seasonal cycle to the natural world, even in that little Eden. Birds migrate in spring and fall, just as they do in deep-freeze country of Wisconsin or Pennsylvania. Nesting takes place in early summer. Feeder traffic picks up in fall and stays heavy in winter, even though hummingbirds might be nectaring right beside suet-eating chickadees.

I learned to look for the subtleties of seasonal change in the Northwest, and I loved the years I spent there.

But, boy oh boy, was I happy to return to the Midwest. I've just finished my first full year in New Harmony, Indiana—Zone 6, in case you're wondering—after a six-year break, and it has been a joy to relearn the cycle of the seasons. The gradient between summer and winter temperatures is a big one, so the changes are dramatic, too. Plants, insects, birds and other wildlife all have ways of coping with the cold and the heat, and it's a constant pleasure to see how they change from season to season.

This book was inspired by my observa-tions of birds in all parts of the country, over all four seasons. Though our climates may be wildly different from one another, the habits of birds follow the same general pattern in spring, summer, fall, and winter.

# GETTING CONNECTED

"Where's that gigantic ball of string? I know you must have one around somewhere," joked a friend last spring.

I was working at untangling a rat's-nest of white cotton string, a prize I'd come across in the trunk of my car during a long-overdue cleaning.

"I wish!" I laughed. "But nope, no big ball. String doesn't seem to last around here very long."

I picked up a few of the loose pieces of twine, walked a few steps from the little brick patio where we were visiting, and draped the white strings over a nearby bush.

"Watch," I suggested, as we settled back into our chairs and picked up our conversation.

It was one of those beautiful May mornings that makes you feel glad to be alive. Hummingbirds zipped in and out from the feeder beside us, purple martins swept the sky overhead, and at least a

**all-season secret** Bird behavior is closely tied to the seasons, because those changes in weather patterns affect the cycles of the plants and insects that birds depend upon for food, nesting material, and cover.

# Marking Time by the Bird Calendar

We humans mark the beginnings of the seasons according to astronomical movements. We wait until the moment of the solstice (when the earth's axis is tilted directly toward or away from the sun) to declare summer or winter, and the moment of the equinox (when the sun is directly over the Equator) to mark spring or fall.

That timing seems somewhat off in many parts of the United States. By the time our calendar declares it officially winter, trees are long bare and Vermonters may already be shoveling snow. By the time we declare it summer, air conditioners in Georgia have been humming for weeks.

In the bird world, seasons aren't defined by the dates on our human calendar. "Bird seasons" tend to begin earlier than those official start dates. Each section in this book includes a timeline at the beginning, so that you can see where that season begins and ends according to bird behavior. The transitions between seasons are smudged, where birds are concerned: Some species adopt the typical behavior of that cycle earlier than others.

Timing also varies according to where you live: Spring migrants, for example, arrive in more southerly states days or even weeks before they make it to the northern tier. Watching for the signs of seasonal behavior will help you develop your own sense of the seasons in your particular region, often by tying it to other signs of the season. When the oaks are dangling with catkins, for instance, I start watching for migrating wood warblers.

dozen other species of birds were going about their business in the yard.

My friend and I were catching up after not having talked in a while, so we weren't paying much attention to the birds. And we almost instantly forgot to keep an eye on the string.

Until a flash of bright orange feathers stopped her in mid-sentence like someone had thrown a switch.

"Did you see that!?" she cried, pointing to the sycamore tree where the bird had flown. "What in the world was that?"

"Oriole," I said. "Male Baltimore. Isn't he gorgeous? Watch—he'll be back."

We didn't have long to wait. In a minute or two, the shocking-orange and black bird returned to grab another piece of string.

"Okay, what's he doing?" asked my nonbirdwatcher friend. "Why does he want string?"

"The female's up in the sycamore." I pointed to the branch where the yellow-orange bird was working. "She's weaving a nest."

The next trip, it was the female who came to choose her own string. She sorted through the pieces, taking her time making a selection.

Watching orioles work on a nest is enough to make a birdwatcher out of just about anyone. The connection we feel when the gorgeous birds accept our offering is just the start. That connection grows through the season.

We learn to listen for the proudly singing male.

We're thrilled when we hear the first faint chirping of newly hatched babies.

We get in the habit of looking for the parents, hard at work feeding their family.

Before long, we're telling our friends and coworkers about our orioles.

We put up an oriole feeder for nectar, and another one for fruit and jelly.

We're sad when we realize that the orioles have disappeared, when fall rolls around.

We get to know orioles. And it all starts with a piece of string set out at the right time.

Timing is important with birds because their lives follow a seasonal cycle. Put out a piece of string in October, and it will lay there unwanted because early summer, not fall, is nesting season.

# WHY FOUR SEASONS OF BIRD SECRETS?

In this book, you'll learn the seasonal rhythm of bird life and how their habits are connected to other events in the natural world. When caterpillars are at their peak in summer, for instance, bird nests are filled with hungry babies hollering for food. What are they clamoring for? Caterpillars!

If you take advantage of the natural cycle to plan your feeder offerings and your garden, your yard will quickly become an irresistible haven for birds—and you'll get to know your friends better as they live the cycle of the seasons.

Each of the four sections in this book includes dozens of secrets suited for that season. You'll discover how to adjust your feeder menu to suit the season. You'll find interesting plants that offer advantages at particular times of year. You'll uncover little extras that are quick and easy to add to

## Seasonal Snapshot

Each season brings a new activity to the forefront among our backyard birds. Here's a shorthand version of how it stacks up:

**Spring:** migration; early nesting

**Summer:** summer residents; breeding territories; nesting; molting

**Fall:** migration; increasing feeder traffic

**Winter:** winter residents; winter feeding territories; prime feeder season

your yard. And you'll meet some of the birds that are most likely to turn up in your backyard at that season.

Here's what you can look forward to in the chapters to come.

# Spring: Big Changes

Did you know that just by waiting until spring to cut back your flower garden, you can attract at least a dozen different species of birds? Or that a humble mud puddle may attract elegant swallows?

In this section, we'll look at the excitement of migration arrivals, and the poignancy of migration departures; courtship and mating and the earliest nesters; the foods to offer at the feeder and why; the changing natural menu and how to boost its potential in your yard/garden; special birds that are likely to show up in spring, and specific tips for them.

# Summer: Family Time

Did you know that insect life cycles coincide with bird nesting time, resulting in abundant food for nestlings? Did you know

that water is a bigger draw than feeders in summer?

In the summer section, we'll examine nesting at its peak; nest materials; dramatic change in feeder scene as natural foods become abundant; foods to offer at the feeder and why; the changing natural menu and how to boost its potential in your yard/garden; the vital role of water; special birds that are likely to show up in summer, and specific tips for them.

# Fall: Moving On

Did you know that being a lazy leaf-raker is a habit that will win you friends among thrushes, thrashers, catbirds, golden-crowned sparrows, and lots of other birds? Did you know that learning to appreciate weeds can boost your bird population? Did you know that fall is prime hummingbird time?

The fall section provides a look at departing summer residents, and fall migrants that begin to filter in; hummingbird traffic picks up; feeder customers increase; the foods to offer at the feeder and why; the changing natural menu and how to boost its potential in your yard/garden; special birds that are likely to show up in fall, and specific tips for them.

**all-season secret** It's not only fabulously beautiful orioles that can get us hooked on birdwatching. Creating a connection with any bird—even the English sparrows that squabble over a scrap from your lunch—makes us feel good. No wonder lonely folks like to feed pigeons in the park.

# Winter: Well-Fed and Safe Shelter

Do you know that water is a never-fail secret to attracting birds in winter—a temptation that's not food? Did you know that wild foods are even more nutritious than feeder seeds? Did you know that a roost box can save bird lives on frigid nights?

The winter section focuses on survival in harsh conditions; the highly nutritious foods to offer at the feeder and why; the natural menu and how to boost its potential in your yard/garden; the wonder of fresh water; special birds that are likely to show up in winter, and specific tips for them.

Thinking about the "why" behind bird behavior in each season is the best way to fine-tune your backyard to suit your favorite birds. It's also a great way to gain an understanding of the way we're all connected—from microscopic soil life to creepy crawlies to backyard birds to those who fill the feeders.

As the seasons cycle 'round, you'll discover which secrets work best for you and your birds. The stamp of success is easy to see: It will be a yard alive with all kinds of interesting birds, in every season. Enjoy!

# PART 1

# SECRETS FOR SPRING

## SPRING: A TIME OF TRANSITION

Long before the first daffodils trumpet the season, weeks before the vernal equinox that marks the start date of calendar-year spring, our yards are full of signs that the season has shifted. Early spring is all about anticipation, as anyone who's ever kept an eye on her daffodils knows. I watch for the swelling brown buds of pussy willows, growing fat before they burst out in sleek silver fur. I listen for the froggie chorus of spring peepers and watch for toads out and about on rainy nights. And I listen hard for the first love song from a chickadee—the two-note *fee-bee* that means a couple is courting. Watching for these early signs helps me enjoy the anticipation of the coming season, which brings so many fabulous birds to the foreground.

Once the changes of spring get underway, things happen fast—especially with the birds. Migration is the big news of the season, and the changeover from winter regulars to spring birds in our backyards makes us really sit up and take notice, as our old faithful friends are joined by a bunch of bright new characters.

In the bird world, spring runs mainly from February through April, with a few early birds showing spring changes as early as January and some latecomers spilling over into May. The actual dates will vary depending on where you live. Those 3 months will bring big changes in your backyard, with courtship and migration happening all around. In this section, you'll learn how to target your efforts toward the birds of this season and their springtime habits.

# CHAPTER 1

# BIRDS ON THE MOVE

**M**IGRATION is the headline news of spring. The cast of characters in our backyards shifts dramatically during this season. Instead of the same old faces day after day, we suddenly notice new friends at the feeder, new voices in the trees, and new colors in the yard as robins, wrens, tanagers, and other spring birds migrate north. Old winter reliables, like the juncos and white-throated sparrows that have added life to the backyard scene for the last several months, will be moving on, too.

Meanwhile, our year-round friends are shifting places, too. Many "year-round" birds do relocate with the seasons, though perhaps by only a few hundred miles or less, rather than by the thousands of miles that many migrant species put under their wings. The jays we've fed all winter may move on to nesting territories, while other jays move in to scout our yards for possibilities. It's the same with cardinals, goldfinches, and other birds we think of as year-round residents.

## CHANGING FACES, CHANGING PLACES

My good old dog, Duke, has eaten pretty much the same thing, day after day, for all of his 14 years. Dry dog food can't be very exciting, but he doesn't complain. Still, just rustle the bag of treats or let him get a whiff of that cheese sandwich, and all of a sudden old lay-about Duke comes to life. With all 70-some pounds of his wriggling body, he lets me know that he's ready for something new. Oh boy! Excitement! Something different!

That's how I feel, too, when spring arrives.

Migrating yellow-rumped wood warblers may turn up just about anywhere—including at your nectar feeder!

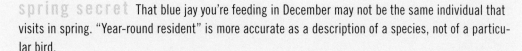

**spring secret** That blue jay you're feeding in December may not be the same individual that visits in spring. "Year-round resident" is more accurate as a description of a species, not of a particular bird.

While I love my winter birds—what a gray day it would be without chickadees to brighten breakfast time—the anticipation of what spring has in store makes me start to wriggle, too.

Spring, to me, is all about the old adage for brides: *Something old, something new, something borrowed, something blue.* Since anticipation is the best thing about spring, let's start by taking a look at that "something new" first.

## Something New

"Let's go on vacation for a couple of weeks this April," a friend suggested many years ago. We'd go to fabulous places, see exotic things, eat unusual food, have a ball.

"Sounds great," I told him, "but no thanks. That's when the warblers are coming through."

Warblers? Birds? How could I say no to an exciting trip to stay home and watch birds?

Talk about excitement. Foreign places can't compare to the thrill of migration, as far as I'm concerned.

Watching for the first robin is still a big deal to lots of us. But that's just the start.

Does "scarlet tanager" make your little heart go pit-a-pat? How about the thought of a rose-breasted grosbeak in full tricolor glory? An indigo bunting? A dozen indigo buntings? A dozen lazuli buntings? A hun-

Vivid indigo buntings often drop in at feeders during migration, before they move on to nesting territories.

dred goldfinches? Now we're talking. And let's not forget those wondrous wood warblers—dozens of tiny mites traveling through the trees.

After a winter of mainly gray and brown birds, with a dash of jays and maybe a sprinkling of cardinals, the cheerful color of spring birds is a delight worth staying home for. Many of these orange, red, green, or blue beauties are, sad to say, only temporary pleasures. Their visits last from a few days to a few weeks, either because they're just passing through or because they will soon be moving away from our yards and feeders and back to their natural nesting and feeding

spring secret Bone up before the birds arrive. Review a field guide (may I recommend *The Backyard Bird Lover's Field Guide,* by yours truly—see Sources, on page 320, for info) so you have an idea of who's who before the real thing arrives.

spring secret Technology has provided you with some bird-watching aids that old-timers (like me) didn't have. Try the bird ID cards with embedded microchips that play a snatch of birdsong (such as the "Identiflyer"; you'll find sources on page 320), or download audio files to your MP3 player or cell phone, if it's capable of playing them, for quick access in the field. You'll find a sampling of Web sites with recordings in the Sources section on page 320, or you can do a search for them on your computer. Or do what I do, and follow your ears to the singer.

grounds. Since I never know how long any of these visitors might stay, I spend a lot of time looking at my feeders when the season shifts.

Just as Duke hurries to see what goodies are in my hand, I rush to the feeder window on spring mornings to see who's new. Then it's a quick glance around the yard to check for surprises under the bushes or in the trees. Finally, it's time to get dressed, start the coffee, and go outside to fill the feeders with treats that will tempt any birds that might be flying by. My feeder menu changes in spring, along with the cast of characters, because I want to make sure I have something that will please them all. (You'll find tips on spring feeding, so you can do the same, in Chapter 3.)

## Spring Treats

The high point for most of us bird lovers is not birds in the bush, but birds at our feeders. What a thrill to spot a flash of sapphire from the first indigo bunting, or the flaming red of a tanager. Even those sunflower hogs, the evening grosbeaks, are a welcome treat in spring.

Here's a sampling of the newbies you might see at your feeder in spring—and you could add others to the list, since even birds that were previously standoffish about visiting feeders seem to be getting more used to the idea of investigating them. Check a comprehensive field guide, such as *The Sibley Guide to Birds* (see Sources on page 320) to see which ones have a possibility of passing through or alighting in your area.

Male birds, like this Audubon's warbler, migrate first, with the duller females following a week or two later.

## Something Old

All of that excitement over the new and different means that some old reliable friends of ours barely get a second thought at this time of year. Yet they, too, deserve some special notice, because this may be the last chance we get to enjoy their company until next fall. Depending on where you live, you may lose your juncos, your white-throated sparrows, and even your chickadees when they depart for nesting season elsewhere. For those birds, spring is the time for us to say "Good-bye, good luck, see you next year."

The only trouble is, it usually takes a few days before we even notice they're gone. Seems like every April, for years, I'd be looking out the window at the feeders when it suddenly dawned on me that I hadn't seen a junco in a while. When did they go? I hadn't been paying attention. Suddenly, I'd miss those juncos and sparrows I had taken for granted until they were gone.

Rose-breasted grosbeaks were once a rarity at feeders. Now they're a regular springtime treat.

## Snazziest Stars

- Bluebirds
- Indigo buntings
- Lazuli buntings
- Goldfinches, including American and lesser
- Grosbeaks, including rose-breasted, evening, and western
- Orioles, including Baltimore and Bullock's, at nectar and fruit feeders
- Tanagers, especially scarlet
- Wood warblers, including Cape May, yellow-rumped, and black-and-white

## Supporting Cast

- Brewer's blackbird
- Red-winged blackbird
- Rusty blackbird
- Catbird
- Grackles
- Robin (more often at birdbath, rather than feeder)
- Sparrows, including chipping, tree, and field
- Brown thrasher
- House wren

## A Vision in Red

Is there a redder red bird than the male scarlet tanager? Only the male cardinal comes close, but the tanager's color is even richer, and his black wings and tail add extra zing.

Scarlet tanagers are real standouts when they deign to drop in at a feeding station, which I think they've been doing more often in recent years. Look for this beauty in later spring, when oak leaves are that beautiful spring green color. Other tanager species may also visit feeders on occasion in spring, depending on where you live.

Don't expect crowds: A single male may be all you get. It's enough.

## Keeping Track of Changes

After a few decades of that "Huh? Where'd they go?" approach, I finally learned a little trick that gives me time to say good-bye—or to get out the welcome mat when it's time for new arrivals. You'll find details in "Red-Letter Days," below.

Even our year-round birds undergo a change of habits in spring. Once the hormones that govern courtship and nesting kick in, you'll notice that jays, cardinals, and other old faithfuls begin to dwindle. Instead of 10 cardinals cracking sunflowers at your tray, you may have only a single pair—those that have claimed your yard as their territory for the nesting season.

To really fill in the gaps, I depend on my local chapter of the Audubon Society. Many chapters keep records of first-sighting dates and sometimes of departures, too. (And if your chapter doesn't, why not suggest it at the next meeting? It's a great way to get

## Red-Letter Days

I'm worthless at keeping a journal of migration notes, but I've found that I can be at least somewhat disciplined about jotting entries on a calendar for quick reference. A big advantage of that system is that I can see at a glance who will soon be coming or going.

Around Christmastime, when I buy a new calendar for the upcoming year, I set aside an evening to look ahead. On those still-blank pages, unmarked by doctor appointments and other reminders, I make the important notes (with a red pen, so they don't get lost in the shuffle) of when to expect new bird arrivals and when to start getting ready to say good-bye to juncos and other old friends.

How do I know what dates to write down? Well, some of that is from my own unorganized record-keeping over the years. If I'm lucky, last year's calendar will hold at least some scribbled notes: "Juncos still here," say, on an April date, or, a couple of weeks later, "First indigo bunting at feeder." So I start by transferring those notes to the same dates on the new calendar, with variations: "Check juncos," and "Watch for indigo buntings."

## Make a Date with Spring Birds

Here's a quick cheat sheet for spring migration, with common species arranged in approximately the order in which they arrive or depart, from earliest to latest. Use this to get a general idea of comings and goings; the actual dates (and the species you see) will vary with where you live. I jotted these dates down for my backyard birds in southern Indiana; they match pretty well with the birds I hosted in Bethlehem, Pennsylvania.

| ARRIVALS | |
| --- | --- |
| Grackles, blackbirds | February–March |
| Phoebes | March |
| Robin | March |
| Meadowlark | Late March–April |
| Swallows, purple martin | April |
| Catbird | April |
| House wren | April |
| Wood warblers | April–May |
| Indigo bunting | Late April–May |
| Vireos | Late April–May |
| Thrushes | May |
| Orioles | May |
| Rose-breasted grosbeak | May |
| **DEPARTURES** | |
| Tree sparrow | Late March |
| Fox sparrow | Mid-April |
| Slate-colored junco | Late April |
| White-throated sparrow | May |
| Pine siskin | May |

members more involved.) If you have a nearby nature center, they may have some migration-date records, too.

On my bookshelves are some old volumes that include similar info for the regions those books cover. I like to compare that information with my calendar, once I have my notes down. The dates may not exactly match up with my area, but the seasonal time frame is pretty close, and the order of migrating species is still right on the money. I've included a shortened version here, covering some popular backyard birds, so you can set your own appointments with the birds of spring.

When a late snow buries the daffodils, you can bet that hungry migrants will soon swarm the feeder.

## SOMETHING BORROWED

Spring brings its share of surprising weather—cold snaps when we least expect them (cover those tomato plants!), snow that buries the daffodils, ice storms that crack branches.

We hate to see birds having a hard time. And it's frustrating to try to keep feeders cleared during a sudden snow, or to slip and slide out there after an ice storm.

When bad weather hits, an easy source of food—whether it's lingering rose hips on your hedge or feeders brimming with seed and suet—is an instant attraction for any birds in the area.

And some of those birds can really surprise you.

These are the "something borrowed" birds, the ones that don't typically visit feeders or that rarely show up in a particular area.

## Lost in the Storm

The front that drives that storm toward your yard can also sweep up birds along the way, disorienting them until they drop down, a few miles off course or a long way from home. One of those landed at my feeder years ago in Pennsylvania: A red-shafted flicker that should have been heading for the center of the country, not

spring secret Snap a picture or do a quick sketch when you spot an unfamiliar bird. The bird may not linger, but you'll have valuable clues to examine later, when you try to figure out who it was.

Got an extra can of tuna? Spring storms may cause even a great blue heron to check out your feeder.

he died soon after I found him. Today, he reposes in a drawer of specimens at the American Museum of Natural History in New York City, a rarity that research assistant John Bull was happy to accept for the collection.

The story of another "borrowed" bird that showed up after a storm had a much happier ending. He was also far more dramatic a presence. That'd be the great blue heron that settled down in my tiny fenced backyard in the midst of a spring blizzard, to dart out his snaky neck and scoop up vast beakfuls of whatever he could find. Seed, chopped suet, nuts; it all went down the hatch.

That was way back in the days of film cameras, and mine was empty, so you'll just have to imagine the scene: A 3-foot-tall bird standing at the seed tray, with the usual crowd of white-throated sparrows and juncos scratching near his big chickeny feet, and cardinals—who suddenly looked very small—nervously alighting within inches of that dagger beak. I wish I'd had the presence of mind to fix him a tuna sandwich.

Great blue herons are year-round residents in my area, so that guy wasn't off-course like the flicker. But my fenced backyard was definitely not his normal habitat. I only "borrowed" him until the fickle spring weather moderated, and then he flew back to his haunts at the river.

the eastern seaboard, where the golden-shafted race lives.

The blizzard that blew that bird in, and the bitter cold that came after, took their toll on the poor flicker, I'm sorry to say. Despite the high-calorie suet and seeds at my place, he never regained his vigor, and

spring secret Experiment with taking photos of your regular birds at the feeder or birdbath until it becomes second nature to adjust the lens, switch to macro, or make other adjustments. That way, you'll be practiced at the settings you'll need when a special spring bird drops by.

## Something Blue

Ahh, blue. My absolute favorite color. In fact, some might say—and have—that I seem to have a slight, yes, I'm sure it's only slight, obsession with it.

Not just any blue, of course. Nope. What tickles my fancy is blue-blue, or as most call it, cobalt.

When I recently moved back to New Harmony, Indiana, after a 5-year sojourn in the West, my good friend Beth stopped by with an armload of welcoming gifts. The fragrant lavender plant in a simple clay pot was wonderful, and so was the bottle of wine from the vineyard where Beth and friends had played music for a wine-tasting harvest party. But the gift that made me say, "Oh, wow!" was a small, simple, glass tumbler—in cobalt blue. It immediately claimed a place of honor on my kitchen windowsill, where I can enjoy it many times a day.

I don't know why "something blue" is part of the bride's mantra, but I'm all in favor. I'm even more in favor when that mantra is applied to springtime birds.

Sure, we have jays all winter, in various shades of blue. But only spring brings us the bluest of the blue—the fabulous indigo bunting.

### A Real Gem

The indigo bunting is often described as "sapphire," but the actual gemstones vary widely in color, from pale gray to deep, rich blue. To see for yourself what "sapphire" means when applied to the indigo bunting, you might want to plan an excursion to the Smithsonian Institution in Washington, DC. There you'll find the Logan Sapphire, a 423-carat whopper—nearly the size of a Ping-Pong ball!—donated by Mrs. John Logan in 1960. The Logan Sapphire is the same stunning color as a male indigo bunting—although I happen to think that the bird is even more beautiful than the gem, because of how its color shifts and deepens as it moves in the sunlight. (Maybe if I borrowed the Logan whopper for a while, I could make a better comparison!)

Or you can travel farther afield to England, where you can compare your

He may look like a living gem, but the indigo bunting has hamburger taste—white proso millet is a big hit with them.

## Bunting Pleasers

Indigo buntings have fancy feathers, but their tastes are simple. Inexpensive white proso millet is number one on their list of favorite seeds at the feeder, though they'll also peck at expensive finch mix, niger seed, and other small seeds, as well as sampling the occasional black oil sunflower seed.

In your yard, it's the most common weeds that suit their tastes—those that have gone to seed just as the buntings arrive. Once you see a vivid male bunting plucking seeds from a dandelion puff, you may get a whole new appreciation for those ubiquitous flowers. Tiny chickweed seeds, probably covering the ground in your vegetable patch, are another favorite.

**Every dandelion puff holds hundreds of seeds for buntings, goldfinches, and white-crowned sparrows.**

mental image of the indigo bunting to two fabulous sapphires in the Imperial State Crown, which the Queen wears when she presides over the annual opening of Parliament. The crown is part of the Royal Crown Jewels, which are transported in their own carriage to the Queen's dressing room. The Imperial State Crown is decorated with the incredible Stuart Sapphire, a huge oval stone, and St. Edward's Sapphire, which flashes from the center of the cross atop the crown. That one comes from the ring of Edward the Confessor, who wore it at his coronation in 1042. Edward gave away his ring, so the story goes, to a beggar—who just happened to be St. John the Evangelist. Years later, St. John gave it back, and it was buried with Edward. Not to stay, though: According to lore, the tomb was opened and the ring removed for the next king in line. It probably would've been less trouble to get an indigo bunting to perch on that crown.

## Blue of a Different Hue

Indigo buntings move through or nest in a large part of the country, so check your field

Small flocks of lazuli buntings, the western counterpart to the indigo species, descend on feeders in spring.

guide to see if they're a possibility at your feeder. If not, you may be in an area where you'll get another "something blue" spring treat—the related lazuli bunting.

Not quite as flashy a living gem as the all-blue indigo, the lazuli is still a bird that's worth watching for in spring. Blue on any bird is a wonderful color, but we can become jaded when a blue-feathered bird is a daily visitor. (Oh, hi, Mr. Blue Jay, didn't realize you were listening! What beautiful feathers you have!)

When a blue bird is only a fleeting pleasure, here today and gone tomorrow, it's way more special. Just like indigo buntings, lazulis drop in for just a brief visit in spring, before the tribe fans out to their nesting homes in fields with scattered bushes.

The indigo bunting tends to be a loner, showing up singly, although more than one may eventually arrive. But lazulis often visit in a small flock of half a dozen or more, delighting those who live in the right region with a bigger splash of blue.

## Best Blue in the Box

My young friend Lily was the reason I bought my first big box of crayons in more than 20 years. But I was just as thrilled as she was when we opened the lid and saw all 64 colors arrayed in pointy-tipped glory.

"What color do you want?" Miss Lily graciously asked, before she grabbed her own.

"Blue." Didn't even have to think about that one, of course.

"Which blue?" asked Lily, whose experience with crayons is much more up-to-date than mine. "Sky blue? Cerulean? Turquoise blue? Blue-green?"

"Just blue. Isn't there one that's just called 'blue' anymore?"

"I like sky blue," said Lily, laying that crayon to the side and pulling another out of the box.

"Here's your blue," she said, handing me the unexcitingly named color with a pitying look.

"Thanks," I said. "It's just what I need for what I'm going to draw."

"What are you making?"

"Bluebirds. See? I need plain old blue for that."

Bluebird blue. No crayon in the box can capture that color, a blue so pure that it makes us react to bluebirds like we do to fireworks: an involuntary "Ooo," "Ahh," or "Ohhh," when we get a glimpse of those celestial feathers.

Spring is prime time for bluebirds at the feeder, if you live anywhere within range of their feeding forays.

Insects, the birds' natural foods, are still hard to come by in early spring, and bluebirds are definitely early birds. They get started raising a family as early as February. By the time those baby beaks are gaping wide, the parents are working hard to find enough to fill them.

That's when a feeder tailored just to their tastes may quickly draw them in. Check Chapter 2 on page 44 for more tips on bluebird feeding.

## Moving On Up

Oh, look, it's the first robin, right there in your yard. Must be spring! But wait a minute—isn't that another one by the hedge? And what's that all over your neighbor's yard? Why, robins—lots of them.

You've no doubt noticed a similar scene. Sometimes migrants arrive in a loose group, like those wood warblers chipping as they work through the trees in your yard. Sometimes the first bird of a migrating species—a robin, a grackle, a wren—shows up alone. But it isn't long before you're seeing more.

When spring migration comes and it's time to move on, songbirds follow a strict order of gender. Instead of "ladies first," it's the gents who start things off. Adult males depart first for nesting grounds, then adult females, with immature birds—those hatched the year before—bringing up the rear like a bunch of dawdling schoolkids.

You can see this at work right in your yard and at your feeder. In spring, you'll spot the male red-winged blackbird first, as he spreads those flashy vermilion shoulder patches and practices his skreeky love song. By the time the nondescript brown females arrive a few weeks later, he's ready to put on quite the show.

## Timing the Takeoff

When my son David graduated from high school several years ago, he got the exact same "Congratulations!" card from six different friends and family members, which says something about the sense of humor we share.

The outside of the card began with typical Very Serious graduation-card language, something like, "As you head out on the journey of life . . . "

Inside: "Don't forget the snacks!"

If you've ever taken a long trip, you know how vital, and how universal, that advice is. Change of clothes? Check. Reading material? Check. Map? Check. Snacks? Check, check, check.

Birds pretty much do the same. Their migration maps are in their heads, or so science surmises: some sort of incredible method for keying in on the earth's magnetic field, so that they can follow the right path in the sky, even at night. No change of outfit is needed, of course, except for the occasional molted feather, and no reading material, either.

But those snacks are all-important to birds. They can't carry snacks with them or stop at a roadside café, so they need to make sure that there will be food all along the way.

Different birds follow a different schedule at migration, spreading out the arrivals of various species over several weeks, from late March to mid-May in many areas (or later or earlier, depending on where you live).

They haven't told us exactly why they migrate on different dates, so scientists and bird watchers like me have come up with our own theories. Common sense is the basis for that guesswork, and that puts food as the foundation.

It boils down to this: Birds need eats along the way.

The first migrants to start moving are the seed eaters. Unlike the insect eaters and fruit lovers, who follow along a little later, birds that mainly eat seeds can make do with leftovers along the way—the seeds that they can still glean from roadsides, fields, and your backyard.

## Seed Eaters Take the Lead

My garden seed collection has expanded over the years until it now fills a good-size plastic storage tub. Sorting through that hoard always makes me feel rich as Midas. My stash includes countless unopened packets that I bought when the price was right (20 for $1! Who could resist?), or because I thought I was going to plant them, but haven't quite gotten around to it yet. I also have envelopes or papers of seeds passed along by friends or gathered from wild plants—most of them labeled, I'm happy to report.

But at the bottom of the container rattles a thin layer of miscellaneous seeds that have escaped their packages. Some, like the fat, wrinkly seeds of nasturtiums or the flat arrowheads of zinnias, are easy to identify, although I have no clue what color flowers those treasures hold. But others—well, let's just say that the older my eyes get, the more those teeny brown and black seeds look alike.

## Slumbering Seeds

A fascinating experiment, colored with the romance of history and hope, has been going on for more than 100 years at Michigan State University.

In 1879, botany professor William J. Beal buried glass bottles around the campus, each containing 50 seeds each of more than 20 different plants. (Yes, he did leave a map!)

At first, some of the bottles were dug up every 5 years to test viability; in 1920, that interval was changed to 10 years; and in 1980—101 years after the bottles were buried—it was lengthened to 20 years.

One bottle was dug up in 2000, 121 years after it was buried. The moth mullein (*Verbascum blattaria*) seeds in that bottle still germinated.

What a testament to the superior storage package that is a seed!

Male red-winged blackbirds arrive in a mob in spring, but they're easy to satisfy with cheap cracked corn.

Petunias? Poppies? Evening primroses? Who knows? It's still fun to toss a handful into the garden, just to see what will come up.

In my—gulp—half a century of gardening, I've learned that seeds can last a long, long time. Just this year, I planted seeds my mother had saved some 20 years ago; the hollyhock seedlings that came up are doing fine. Want more proof? Just turn over a shovelful of soil and watch the crowd of long-buried weed seeds spring to life.

All of those long-lasting seeds mean that, for seed-eating birds, breakfast (and lunch and dinner) is everywhere they look. Seeds, with their nutritious oils and carbs packed inside, are all over the place, even in earliest spring.

- Seeds are still hanging on dead plant stems: on those coneflowers in your garden, on the goldenrod in fields, and inside withered berries and fruits.
- Seeds are buried in leaf litter: the winged seeds of maples, box elders, and elms; the sticktight seeds of enchanter's nightshade, smartweed, and other weeds of wild places.
- Seeds are still on trees: the cones of pines, hemlocks, and spruces, plus the seeds of tulip trees, alders, and others.
- Seeds are lying there for the pecking along every roadside and field: the great multitude of grasses, plus dandelions, chicory, Queen Anne's lace, and other plants of open places. Even though the dead stems of the plants may have fallen over during winter, those seeds are still on the ground, waiting for birds to discover them.

That's my guess as to why the seed eaters are the first songbird migrants to wing our way. There are plenty of snacks, everywhere they stop.

## Awakening Insects

After the swell of seed eaters—the blackbirds, grackles, grosbeaks, meadowlarks, horned larks, buntings, finches, and sparrows—comes the finale of migration: the beautiful tanagers and orioles, the little

spring secret  Remember to look *up* in spring. Many birds, including insect-eating vireos, tanagers, and orioles, stick to the treetops, and you may miss them altogether if your eyes are on the ground.

Seed-eating migrants are quick to zero in on leftover coreopsis and other flower seeds in garden beds.

dancing, or an early mourning cloak butterfly, even a mosquito or three, during those first mild days of sunshine. But the bugs don't begin to really burgeon until spring arrives in earnest.

That's when the last big rush of migration takes place. The glory days, as I think of them, when any walk outside is bound to yield fabulous birds. Now's the time when my field guide, open to the wood warbler pages, is always at the ready. When my ears are getting confused trying to recall songs I haven't heard in the last 9 months. When I wish there were more hours in the day, more days in the week, that I could spend outside, drinking in all that feathered life and beauty.

## Hey, It's Cold Out Here!

Cold weather makes me feel alive. I love a biting cold day, when I'm swaddled in scarves and sweaters and a heavy tweed coat, and only my nose and cheeks are out there on their own.

Some of my dearest friends, though, don't share my nature. No matter how warmly they dress, they still complain—and I don't think it's just because they like to whine. I believe they truly feel as if the cold "sinks into their bones," just as they say. And feeling chilled isn't much fun. Especially when there's a cozy house beckoning with warmth and cocoa and maybe even popcorn.

Popcorn? Let me just get these gloves off and I'll be right there! Hmm, there's another odd thing about my physiology—my hands rarely get cold. Often I don't wear gloves in cold weather; an occasional few minutes'

wood warblers, the loud-singing vireos, the shy thrushes and proud thrashers, the amiable catbird, the chipper little wrens, and the graceful aerialist swallows. Oh, and let's not forget the piece de resistance: the hummingbirds!

Is it just that the best always comes last? Not the way I see it. I figure that these birds wait until later to migrate because their natural food supply follows a different timeline than that of the seed eaters.

All of these birds depend heavily on insects. And while seeds are available year-round unless buried under ice and snow, insects don't awaken until weeks later.

Oh, sure, you may see some gnats

## Natural Reminder

Pay attention to the flowers in your area to make an educated guess about when hummingbirds will arrive. Early azaleas in bloom? Wild red columbine (*Aquilegia canadensis*)? Red horsechestnut (*Aesculus pavia*)? Any red or orange flowers at all? Put out that feeder!

If you want to note a more exact date on your calendar, ask your local chapter of the Audubon Society or a nearby nature center. April is arrival time for hummingbirds in many regions here in southern Indiana; it was April 15, give or take a day or two, when I last lived here 5 years ago. I'm curious to see if that has changed in the interim. Migration dates seem to be getting earlier, right along with the shift in wildflower bloom; climate change may be the culprit.

warm-up in my pocket is all my fingers need.

I figure I'm more like a hardy chickadee, swinging merrily on pinecones on a cold day, than I am like an exotic Baltimore oriole, wishing it had never left Florida when those late-spring cold snaps strike.

That built-in tolerance for cold, or the lack thereof, seems to vary from one species of birds to another. You'll find more on this topic in Chapter 13. For now, though, I'm guessing that the chance of cold weather may be another reason that some birds delay their migration while others show up early, ready to endure.

### Cold Snaps

Cold can have deadly effects on birds. In itself, cold can kill birds just as it can kill any warm-blooded animal—us included—who is outside in it. All birds, even those that spend the winter at your place, can be killed by exposure to extreme cold. During a

## Emergency Cold-Snap Menu

When weather arrives that feels more like winter than it does spring, high-fat foods may save the lives of backyard birds. At the least, these foods will make it easier for warm-weather birds to be comfortable during a cold snap. Any or all of these foods may be sampled by orioles, robins, catbirds, wrens, and other birds that aren't accustomed to severe cold. Serve them in a feeder that perching birds can easily access, such as a tray feeder.

Chopped or ground suet

Lard

Cream cheese

Bread dipped in bacon drippings

Bread drizzled with corn or peanut oil

Doughnuts

Peanut butter mixed with flour or cornmeal to form a crumbly dough

Chopped walnuts, pecans, or peanuts

Mealworms

Swarming gnats spell food to flycatchers and other insect eaters, so they arrive after bugs take to the air.

cold snap in spring, some birds may die no matter how generously our feeders are filled. Extreme cold is generally more of a problem for birds in winter.

In spring, cold weather affects birds more by "collateral damage," as the Pentagon might say, than by exposure. Long before a bird drops dead of cold, those low temperatures have already killed off countless numbers of insects.

That's the big problem with spring cold snaps—especially cold that comes in late spring, when migrants have already arrived or are passing through. To birds that depend heavily on insects, a spring cold snap can be a double whammy: Their bodies need more calories (food) to stay warm, but suddenly there's no food to be found. No food means dead birds, no matter how hardy their constitution may be.

Bluebirds, catbirds, wrens, and the swallow tribe (including purple martins) are especially vulnerable to spring cold.

We can't do anything to control the weather, but we can make sure provisions

are in place should a cold snap sneak in. You'll find simple ideas in "Emergency Cold-Snap Menu," on the opposite page, and more suggestions for emergency feeding in Chapter 2 (see page 43).

## Shrubby Shelter

Whenever I go afield after a snow or ice storm, I head for the bushes. Why? Because they're bound to hold birds. Even on sunny days, when birds seem to be everywhere, the "brush" along a field or the occasional shrubs dotting a meadow or roadside are apt to be alive with birds.

Staying safe is at the top of any bird's agenda, and shrubs are perfect for providing that vital protection. It's easy to carry that lesson into our own yards by creating brushy areas where shrubs can grow undisturbed,

Break up big stretches of lawn with shrubs, and you'll see your birdlife increase because of the extra cover.

## Add Some Evergreens

Dense conifers, with lots of little interior spaces where a bird can make a cozy hideaway, are one of the most helpful things you can add to your yard. Evergreens shelter birds from rain, snow, ice, and wind, and they provide good protection against predators, too.

or even better, mingle with naturalistic grasses and, dare I say it, weeds.

If you're not a fan of the wild look, go for a group of shrubs. Make sure they're planted close enough to one another that their branches touch or overlap at the tips and that they're underlaid with a bed of mulch or groundcover. That's essentially a short hedge. A longer hedge is even better, because it creates a twiggy corridor that birds can travel through. Birds can forage, nest, or roost within the hedge without exposing themselves to predators—or to the wild weather that spring often surprises us with.

Purple martins have lots of fans who eagerly await their arrival. Track their progress via Web site reports.

## Comparing Notes

"See any interesting birds lately?" is one of my favorite opening lines when greeting an acquaintance in spring.

Bird-watchers love to talk to each other about what they're seeing in spring, when exciting birds are everywhere. Bragging, you say? Of course! And that's part of the fun.

In the old days, local or regional bird clubs were the only way to go. Those groups are still great fun to join, because nothing beats talking to people in real life.

But nowadays, thanks to the Internet, we can also share our sightings and stories with folks from all over—without ever leaving our armchairs. I like to track hummingbird migration, for instance, by keeping watch on online sites where users across the country post the date they first saw the zippy little birds. Wood warbler fans and general birders do the same, for all kinds of species.

It's simple to find such sites. Just do a search for "bird sightings [YOUR STATE]." You'll get a list of links that can take you in many directions.

If you want to exchange info with birders closer to home, you can refine your online search by adding your city or county. Or you can meet real-life bird lovers by joining your local chapter of the Audubon

spring secret Check with your local bird hotline or nature society weekly—or daily, if you're inclined—to get the scoop on exciting birds in your area. There's nothing worse than reading about a local sighting of a rarity in the newspaper just days after it's gone.

Society or a nearby nature center. Newspapers often print calendar listings for such groups, or you can find a contact number in your phone book. One phone call is usually all it takes to get hooked up with a group in your area.

## Love Is in the Air

Friends are always accusing me of jumping the gun when I announce, "It's spring!" Which I tend to announce a lot, once I start to see the signs.

"Spring? What do you mean, spring? It's freezing out here," groused one of them a few years back, snuggling her fuzzy scarf a little tighter around her throat.

I was so full of enthusiasm, I plowed right over her objections. "Sure, it's still cold," I agreed, "but look over there. See how the willows are getting yellower?"

Still grumbling, my friend looked in the direction I was pointing, and reluctantly agreed. "Okay, so maybe they look a little brighter. So what?"

I didn't relent. "And see, over there, that hill with the woods? See how the trees look reddish? They didn't look that way a few weeks ago. Remember how gray they were?"

My pal, who'd lamented to me how depressingly drab the brown and gray winter world was, was beginning to get interested now. She just wasn't ready to admit it yet. "Okay, so the woods look reddish. They still don't have any leaves, though. So what does that have to do with spring?"

"Well, I don't really know," I admitted. "I just know the bark is changing color. Maybe because the sap is moving again? Those leaves are gonna be coming out, so I figure the tree has to get ready by pumping up the juice. And maybe that's what makes the bark turn color?"

I was guessing wildly, right on the spot. No Google available to check my theory, no scientist near at hand for me to buttonhole. I figured it didn't much matter anyhow, because the reason behind the color change

## Caught on Camera

Rare birds are de rigueur in spring, when wings are flying across the country. Be ready with your camera, so you can snap a shot if an unusual bird turns up in your yard or at your feeder. You'll have a valuable aid for identification purposes. You'll also have documentation, especially if you're using a digital camera that records the date you took the picture, which can serve to substantiate a sighting of a rare bird.

Pay attention to the natural world, and you'll soon notice that spring starts way earlier than most people think. Subtle changes in color signal new growth, and birdsong—instead of simple *chips*—means that courtship is beginning.

wasn't my point. The change itself was all I wanted her to notice, because it was definitely a sign of spring.

"Huh, how about that. You know, my mom used to talk about the willows changing color. Guess I just never noticed."

She was hooked, despite herself. "What else? Is anything else going on?"

## Spring Singers

"Listen," I said, and we did. "Hear that far-off noise like crickets? Those are chorus frogs. They start up way early—end of January, February—soon as it starts to warm up a little."

"They're only this big"—I held out my thumb and pointed to the nail—"but boy, do they make a racket. You should hear 'em up close."

"Oh, wait—hear that?" A loud, clear, two-note whistle had sounded from a tree beside us. We waited, and the whistle came again.

My friend feeds birds, but she hasn't paid much attention to them when they're not eating the seeds she puts out.

Both of us watched for movement in the tree.

"You see anything besides that titmouse?" she asked, trying to see around the trunk.

"Nope," I said. "But keep your eye on

him, you'll get a surprise."

Mr. Titmouse was so full of himself it took only a few seconds before he opened his beak and whistled again: "Pe-ter!" We both whistled back.

"Cool," she laughed. "They're at my feeder all winter long. I didn't know they sang."

"This one's a male," I told her, although I couldn't have discerned that from his looks, because male and female tufted titmice look pretty much alike.

Time for the coup de grace. "Know why he's singing?" I asked.

She looked at me and laughed. "Let me guess. Because it's spring?"

"Yep. And he's in luvvvv."

## MORNINGS MEAN MUSIC

Spring mornings sound different than fall, winter, or late-summer mornings. Why? Because the birds are singing. Step outside anytime after dawn's early light, and you are bound to hear robins regaling the neighborhood, or cardinals whistling, or any other birds in your area singing their signature "Here I am" carols.

Songs are the way a bird announces its presence. That's important when you're proclaiming territorial rights to a certain area. Like an explorer's flag planted atop a mountain or on the moon, the song alerts other birds of the same species that this place is no longer up for grabs. It's mine now, all mine, says the singer.

Claiming a territory is a vital part of bird life only at nesting time. In other seasons, birds roam freely, sharing rights to the food, water, or shelter they find. But when it's time to raise a family, birds drive away any others of their same species. That ensures that the brood in that nest bears their genes, not those of interlopers.

## Choose Your Partner

Many songbirds mate for life, or so some scientists surmise. But even those committed couples still go through the ritual of courtship each time spring rolls around. And, since a bird's life may only last a year or two in the wild because of all the hazards they face, selecting a new partner is a regular part of the equation even for formerly longtime lovebirds. New birds on the block—those that are just reaching their first

## Early Singers

Depend on these birds to get the party started. While migrants are still winging their way northward, year-round backyard birds are already in gear, courting their mates, claiming territories, and setting up housekeeping. Or, in the case of juncos and some sparrows, they may be singing even before they leave your feeder to reach their nesting territories. As with all other singing birds, their vocalizations are a reaction to the increasing daylight, which drives their hormones. To every thing there is a season, and spring is the time to sing.

| | |
|---|---|
| Chickadees | **Of the migrants, these fellows are the earliest** |
| Doves | **arrivals; you may hear them singing in February.** |
| Juncos | |
| Owls (great horned is earliest, hooting in winter) | Brewer's blackbirds |
| Song sparrow | Red-winged blackbirds |
| White-throated sparrow and other native sparrows | Rusty blackbirds |
| Titmice | Grackles |
| Towhees | Eastern meadowlarks |
| Woodpeckers (who both drum and call) | Western meadowlarks |
| | Robin |

When you hear birdsong, simply follow your ears to find out which of these early birds is singing. You can also buy recordings of specific birds' songs to listen to on CDs or on an MP3 player, or you can listen to recorded songs on the Internet. (See Sources on page 320 for more information.) Once you learn to recognize the sound of a bird's call, you may discover that you have more visitors in your yard than you can see.

breeding season—get into the act, too, when spring sets those hormones perkin'.

You'll see this seasonal behavior at your feeder and in your yard. Here are courtship moves to watch for beginning in early spring.

- Male birds first begin to show interest in females by showing off. Singing, posing, and chasing away competing males are the opening moves.

- Next comes the male's direct approach: Closely approaching a female, offering food to her, billing and cooing, and just generally acting besotted.

- Often, the initial moves are rejected by the female, who hasn't quite made up her mind which male to choose. As with all animals—including us—she's looking for the signs that show good genes and a mate that can offer protection for the brood to come. In the bird world, those signs of health and vigor may be flashy feathers, a protective disposition, or the ability to eliminate competition.

- Once a female accepts a male as her partner, she will show it. She'll be receptive to his overtures, accept the tidbits of food he presents, touch his bill with her own, bow and flutter her wings, or stay close instead of sidling away when he approaches. Congratulations to the new couple!

- Actual mating is a rare thing to witness. Apparently, even birds need some privacy.

## EARLY NESTERS

Birds nest at various times from February to July, depending on the species and its habits. Some species nest only once a year, while others raise two, three, or even more broods of babies.

Many early nesters, which begin raising their families in spring, are "cavity nesting" birds—better known to backyard bird lovers as birdhouse birds. They're the species that seek a secluded niche in a dead tree, or in a wooden box, to call home. In this section,

Mourning doves mate for life, reestablishing their connection every spring with billing and cooing.

you'll find lots of secrets for successfully hosting these birds.

Birds that nest in trees, shrubs, or on the ground may also get started in spring, but many of them wait until May or June (late spring to early summer, by the bird calendar) to begin those responsibilities. Some are migrants, which have to allow time for the flight home, plus the ritual of courtship, before they get started. Others depend on later plants for nest materials, or later natural food sources for their nestlings. You'll find plenty of tips for these birds in Part 2, Secrets for Summer, beginning on page 83.

## Maintain a Mud Puddle

You can always tell whether spring has come by taking one look at the shoes left by the doorstep inside my back porch. In winter, it's ski boots and hiking boots parked by the back door until the last of the snow or ice melts off. But come the spring thaw, the word is mud: An ever-growing pile of muddy sneakers, muddy boots, muddy slippers, muddy anything that I pulled on to step outside.

Mud and spring go together like spring and robins—or like mud and robins, shall we say? In March or April, depending on where you live, robins pair up and get serious about raising a family. That's when Mrs. Robin Redbreast goes in search of mud.

The robin isn't a cavity nester, but it is an early nester. So are the Eastern phoebe and swallows, which get started homemaking within a couple of weeks of returning from migration. All of these birds use mud to plaster their nests to supports and to give them sturdy foundations for an inner lining of soft materials.

It only takes birds a few days to build a nest, but they'll make many trips to a mud puddle, since they can only carry a small pellet of mud at a time. It's fun to see how determined they are when gathering it. And, if your eyes are quick, you might be able to see where they take it—revealing the location of a nest you can keep a discreet eye on.

In case you've forgotten how to make a mud puddle from the days when you were 4 years old, here's how.

1. Choose an area with open space around it. This is most appealing to birds because it allows a good view of approaching predators, as well as easy access.

2. Select a spot where water is already naturally slow to drain: where puddles form and linger after a heavy rain. Remove all vegetation from that spot.

3. If you don't have such a spot, scrape out a depression about 6 inches deep, 2 to 3 feet long, and 1 to 2 feet wide.

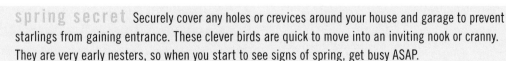

**spring secret** Securely cover any holes or crevices around your house and garage to prevent starlings from gaining entrance. These clever birds are quick to move into an inviting nook or cranny. They are very early nesters, so when you start to see signs of spring, get busy ASAP.

## Table for Two

Once nesting season kicks in, birds dwindle at the feeder for several reasons. One biggie is territorial rights: If a pair of cardinals claims your yard for nesting, other cardinals will be quickly escorted off the premises. The same thing may happen with your jays, robins, song sparrows, chickadees, or any other species that nest in your area. Instead of a pack, you're likely to host only a pair.

Make the sides sloping, like those in a natural puddle, so that birds can approach the wettest parts of the puddle safely. Stomp around in the hole to pack down the bottom, compacting it as hard as you can to slow down drainage.

4. Fill the depression or low spot with water from your garden hose. Let it drain, then refill. Repeat until the soil is muddy.

5. Rewet the puddle as often as is needed, so that birds can easily carry bits of mud away. That may be every other day, every day, or even a couple of times a day, if the weather is dry and warm.

6. Maintain the moist soil until birds no longer visit. Your mud may also attract home-building mud dauber wasps or other insects, which are also great fun to watch as they roll up mud like a snowball and carry it away.

## Birdhouse Birds

The nurturing instinct is just as strong in us as it is in birds raising a family. Happily for both birds and us, those nurturing instincts can dovetail nicely in spring. We nurture the birds by building or buying nest boxes, and birds nurture their families in the boxes. To attract the birds you want, you'll need to pick the right size box. And unless you're planning an all-starling apartment complex, you'll need to choose a box that has the right size entry hole. You'll find advice on those measurements on page 28.

Flickers and other birds that nest in cavities often adopt a birdhouse almost as soon as you put it up.

## Possible Tenants

Bluebirds are the first species that comes to mind for most of us when we think of birdhouses. They're a special case, though, because most of us aren't lucky enough to live next door to their natural habitat, or to have the kind of large yard with scattered brush or a wood's edge that they prefer, and house sparrows will provide fierce competition for your birdhouse.

If you can get bluebirds, great; if you can't, set your sights on less particular tenants, which will still give you plenty of pleasure. You'll find that even a pair of ordinary house sparrows can make fascinating neighbors, as they fill the box with whatever they can find and sit on the roof, chirping proudly.

Most cavity-nesting birds readily take to life in our backyards. Exactly which tenants

## Build or Buy?

Birds won't care whether you buy or build the nest box; their main concern is whether it will fit their needs. If you decide to buy, buy the best birdhouses you can afford; you want them to last for years. Some manufacturers are endorsed by birding groups, such as the National Audubon Society. Or you can determine solid construction yourself by looking closely at how the box is made. Commercially made nest boxes usually have a helpful label that identifies the bird they're designed to fit.

You can build a nest box cheaper yourself—maybe. But there are other considerations, too, when it comes time to decide which way to go.

### Homemade

- If you have tools and scrap wood, you will save money by making a box yourself—it's free! You'll need a circular saw or jigsaw and a drill with a hole saw attachment to make the right size hole.
- You'll get a big sense of satisfaction out of hosting birds in a house you made yourself.
- Kids love to help with assembly, which will give them a sense of pride and a sense of ownership, too. Even very young children can turn a screw or two.
- Building birdhouses is a great activity for that "what's next?" stretch after the winter holidays.

### Store-Bought

- It's instant gratification—buy a solid wood nest box labeled for the bird you want to attract, mount it, and you're done.
- A commercially made house will put more of a dent in your wallet—you'll pay at least $20 for a sturdy, well-made nest box.
- You may be able to find less-expensive but well-made boxes at craft shows or benefit sales; scout troops sometimes make and sell boxes, too.

you attract depends on what kind of natural areas are nearby, what kind of nest boxes you put up, and what your backyard habitat is like. Here is a list of the likely tenants for backyard nest boxes.

Bluebirds

Chickadees

Flickers

Ash-throated flycatchers

Great crested flycatchers

Nuthatches

House sparrow

Tree swallow (if you live near water)

Violet-green swallow (if you live near water)

Titmice

Downy woodpecker

Hairy woodpecker

Red-bellied woodpecker

House wren

## Keep It Simple

You can tailor-make your birdhouse to exact dimensions, or you can do what birds do in the wild—use a general rule of thumb, sort of "one size fits most" guidelines.

- Entrance hole: 1½ inches in diameter (will keep out starlings but allow cavity nesters to enter).

## Three Sizes Fit Most

Before you acquire an arsenal of drill bits or hole saws to bore birdhouse entrances of exact-to-the-least-fraction sizes, keep in mind that natural cavities have a lot of variation. Birds seek a size that will permit them to enter, and that's often a bit bigger than the hole size your birdhouse-building instructions may call for. (Or a bit smaller—I've watched birds squeeze through a hole that was as snug as my skinny-day jeans.)

Whether you're building or shopping for birdhouses, you can simplify things by satisfying just three general sizes of entrances: small, medium, and large. That should keep everybody happy! See the table below.

| BOX SIZE | HOLE SIZE | BIRDS THAT MAY USE IT |
| --- | --- | --- |
| Small (about wren-house size) | 1 to 1⅛ inches in diameter | Chickadees, red-breasted nuthatch, house wren; too small for house sparrow |
| Medium (about bluebird-box size) | 1¼ to 1¾ inches in diameter | Bluebirds, white-breasted nuthatch, titmice, tree swallow, downy woodpecker; 1½-inch or bigger holes allow house sparrow to enter |
| Large (about flicker-box size) | 2½ inches in diameter | Flickers, great crested and ash-throated flycatchers, starling, red-bellied and other larger woodpeckers |

- Floor size: about 4 by 4 inches.
- Entrance: about 5 inches above the floor. (That height will allow the fledglings a fairly easy exit when the time comes to leave Home Sweet Home; a too-deep box may have unfortunate effects when young are trying to leave, trapping them inside.)

## Purple Martin Housing Hopes

The big, beautiful swallows known as purple martins are different than other cavity-nesting birds because they nest in a group, or colony. Each bird has its own apartment (or gourd, or birdhouse), but the whole gang lives within the same small area. Commercial or homemade martin houses are generally constructed like a human house, with "floors" of entrance holes. Many even resemble our own houses, with pillars, porch railings, and slanted roofs that look like the ones over our own heads. Some handy do-it-yourselfers make martin houses that match their own houses, from the general style right down to the details, such as the color of the trim. Martin houses usually have at least 8 separate nesting compartments under the same roof, but they can run to palace-size, too, with room for 24 pairs of birds! You can even buy an expandable martin house that allows you to add on as your colony grows. Because of their size and complexity, martin houses aren't an impulse purchase for most of us. Well-made models start at about $150 and go up from there.

Attracting purple martins is a matter of luck, habit, and habitat. They prefer to nest within easy reach of water, so if you live near a river or lake or have a good-size pond, not a garden pool, you're in luck. You'll also need an open area without trees or utility wires that would impede their swooping flight.

That's the crucial habitat part. The rest is a matter of luck and of getting the birds to spread out from other colonies and adopt your new setup. Entire books have been written about the martin mystique, and groups of fans have formed societies, so at least you'll have encouragement while you wait. You'll find a sampling of purple martin aficionado groups in the Sources on page 320, or you can search for "purple martin societies" online.

## Tenant Timing

Birds begin looking for nest sites long before the vernal equinox marks the official start of spring. Tufted titmice and bluebirds may already be settled in by February. That's why it's a good idea to get your boxes up in late winter, so they're ready when the homemaking urge kicks in.

If you get a slow start, or if you get a beautiful birdhouse as a Mother's Day gift, say, put it up anyway. Nests often fail; predators can destroy eggs or nestlings, or spring cold can wreak havoc, especially on early nesters. And many backyard birds raise more than one brood a year. Your Johnny-come-lately nest box may be just the ticket when a pair of chickadees is looking for home site #2.

**spring secret** Don't be surprised if smaller birds move into larger homes; house wrens nested for years in my bluebird box—and the feisty little birds successfully kept the house sparrows at bay.

## Choosing a Location

Specialization is the name of the game for bird species. They seek different kinds of food, in different places—and at nesting time, they do the same thing. If all birds nested in the same locations and built the same kinds of homes, competition for materials and home sites would be fierce.

Natural cavities occur in all habitats, at all heights, and in all kinds of trees, and each cavity-nesting bird species has its preferences. Chickadees, for instance, nest surprisingly low, often choosing a cavity (or nest box!) that's just a few feet from the ground. Great crested flycatchers and flickers, on the other hand, will quickly adopt a hole or a birdhouse that's so high you'll need an extension ladder to mount it at 15 feet or more. Your job, when supplying additional housing, is to try to mimic those locations as best you can. (See "How High to Mount the Box," below, for some guidance.) The good news is that birds aren't too fussy when they're presented

## How High to Mount the Box

These general guidelines will help you target your box to the right tenant.

| DESIRED TENANT | BEST BOX HEIGHT |
| --- | --- |
| Bluebirds | Low; from 3 to 5 feet |
| Chickadees | Low; from 3 to 6 feet |
| Flycatchers | High; about 15 feet and higher |
| Nuthatches | Medium to high; 10 to 20 feet |
| House sparrow | Low to medium; from 4 to 15 feet |
| Tree or violet-green swallow | Low to medium; from 4 to 10 feet |
| Titmice | Low to medium; from 4 to 15 feet |
| Woodpeckers (incuding flickers) | Medium to high; from 8 to 20 feet |
| House wren | Low; from 3 to 6 feet |

## Hole in One

Some cavity nesters are so fixated on finding a cavity that they investigate just about any hole they come across, whether it's a knothole in the siding of your garden shed or a rust hole in a hanging bucket.

One year, I brought home a slab of slate with a perfectly round hole bored through it from the blasting process. I leaned the slab at an angle against a tree, intending someday to find the perfect spot. Boy, did that confuse a pair of home-site–seeking chickadees: They spent hours going into the hole and out the other side. You could practically hear their little brains trying to figure it out.

Recognizing compulsive behavior when I saw it, I removed the slab and mounted a nest box on the same tree the slate had been leaning against. You could almost hear them saying "Whew." Guess who moved in the very same day?

with a desirable, ready-made home: They'll adjust to the location because of the appeal of the nest box.

Keep three things in mind when you're putting up birdhouses: Where, how high, and toward which direction the box is oriented.

### Where to Mount the Box

Use common sense when you decide on a location for your box. Birds appreciate the same things we do at home: They like it not too hot, but not too cold; they want a secure foundation, and they like plenty of privacy.

- Keep the box out of direct midday or afternoon sun, if possible, so that it doesn't get too hot inside.

- Do place the box where it gets morning sun, if possible, to warm up the family after a cool spring night.

- Keep the hole facing away from prevailing winds, so that the winds that come in with a cold front won't chill the children.

- Attach the box securely to the post or tree; cavity-nesting birds prefer stability during those quick entrances and exits.

## Anti-Predator Protection

Feeling guilty isn't much fun, so you'll want to make sure that the birds that use your nest boxes are as well protected against danger as possible. That means a little more work or expense for you at the start, but it will pay off in peace of mind.

A box full of yummy eggs or nice plump babies spells late-night snack to raccoons, cats, opossums, snakes, and other predators. Raccoons may rip off the entire box to get at the contents; snakes may slither inside and help themselves.

Take a few precautions to help guard against the dangers:

- Protect the box with a collar that prevents predators from reaching it at spring secret  Place the nest box in an area that's relatively undisturbed, where the comings and goings of family or pets won't disrupt the birds. Choose a location well away from your feeding station, too, so that other birds don't interfere.

**Keep your tenants safe by mounting a no-nonsense baffle to block cats, coons, and other predators.**

all. If the box is on a post or tree, you can install a store-bought or homemade collar that flares out from the support. You can also wrap a 2-foot sheet of metal around the support midway up the post to help keep snakes and climbing creatures from getting to the box.

- Protect the nest inside with an anti-predator extension at the entrance. This is a tube that fits into the hole and extends outward, so that raccoon paws can't reach inside as easily.

- Rethink your plan altogether if stray cats are a problem in your neighborhood. Even if cats can't get at the box, they may be waiting when those babies leave the nest. For more on cats, see page 105.

# CHAPTER 2

# THE FEEDER SCENE
# IN SPRING

A FINE RESTAURANT in my small town of New Harmony, Indiana, keeps a constant menu of the most popular dishes. But each month, the chef adds a small selection of "seasonal specialties" prepared from local ingredients that are at their peak. It gives customers a sense of connection to the natural cycles of fruits and vegetables—tender asparagus in April, juicy peaches in July—and it perks up the palates of regular diners. Yes, I may still order my favorite year-round entrée of roast chicken, but my salad will have fresh greens in spring, my summer dessert may include just-picked berries from a local patch, and my fall entrée may be accompanied by homegrown squash.

Birds appreciate seasonal variety, too, which is one of the reasons that feeder traffic tends to drop off in spring. As insects and other foods become more available, the usual menu at your bird café becomes less enticing. And as new birds arrive on the scene, the standby seeds may need some augmentation with foods that appeal to the palates of those newcomers.

## DRAWN TO THE FOOD

A feeding station is a huge attraction for birds, as so many of us already know. While the winter menu stays constant to suit those winter birds, the spring season calls for an expanded menu to appeal to the changing clientele.

In this chapter, you'll find plenty of details on how to stock your feeder in spring. Here are the main considerations to keep in mind.

- Keep feeding the basics that you've offered all winter, to suit your year-round residents as well as spring birds that share their tastes.

- Add more "soft foods" for spring birds, which often depend heavily on insects.

Suet, peanut butter dough, and other soft foods are a hit with insect-eating birds like this Carolina wren.

Spring cleaning in the house isn't my cup of tea, but I do spruce up the feeder area when the weather warms up. It feels good to shovel up a winter's worth of shells, along with the buildup of droppings—and cleanup helps keep my birds healthy by reducing potential disease-causing organisms.

- Add fruit to the menu for late-spring arrivals.
- Be ready with nectar when hummingbirds arrive.
- Keep reserves of basic foods on hand, in case of sudden storms.
- Stock up on suet and other high-fat foods so you can feed generously if there's unseasonably cold weather.

## The Basics

The birds that live year-round in our neighborhoods are the day-in, day-out customers at the feeding station. In most areas, these are the species that depend heavily on seeds. Although they begin including insects and fruits as spring turns to summer, they'll still show up for the staples. Keep that part of your menu the same, and your jays, cardinals, native sparrows, doves, and other regulars will keep coming back.

Many spring birds also seek out seeds. The basics will suit them just fine, although you may want to adjust the mix, depending on which seeds your friends are most fond of.

These foods are the foundation of my feeding station year-round, including spring.

- Black oil sunflower seed is the staple for larger birds, including jays, cardinals, grosbeaks, and woodpeckers.
- White proso millet is eaten by smaller birds such as native sparrow, juncos, buntings, and others.
- Niger seed, beloved by goldfinches and other finches, makes my setup more tempting than others on my block, which offer a less-appealing birdseed mix.
- Cracked corn is very cheap, and it's a real draw for cardinals, doves, and a few other birds.
- Nuts, served sparingly
- Suet

To quickly create crushed nuts that will suit all of your feeder guests, fill a zipper-lock bag about one-third full of walnuts or pecans. Roll over the bag with a rolling pin, pushing down with force as you roll. You'll end up with a variety of sizes of nut pieces, from extra fine to big chunks. Pour the nuts into an open tray, unless squirrels are interested in your feeders. If that's the case, don't waste your money by offering nuts in anything but a Fort Knox–type feeder—those sold as "squirrel-proof." And see page 188 for more tips on dealing with squirrels.

spring secret Year-round birds and many spring guests find foods to their liking from the basic birdfeeder menu. But some prefer soft, fatty foods, either alone or as another course. A block of suet will keep your wrens, chickadees, woodpeckers, titmice, nuthatches, brown creepers, and bluebirds busy through all four seasons.

# Swarms of Finches

American goldfinches and other finches are gregarious birds that congregate together in flocks. Depending on where you live along their route, you may see a dozen finches, or you may see hundreds of finches.

Finches are fun to host at the feeder; they may stay for weeks in spring, in ever-growing numbers. Below, you'll find some tricks for tempting them to stop off in your yard, with more details in Chapter 3 on page 46.

## Goldfinches Galore

Get ready for the gold rush! Spring brings migrating American goldfinches to feeders in big numbers. And I do mean big—how would you like to host a hundred or more energetic gold nuggets at that thistle feeder? And at that seed tray, and all over the ground—wherever they can find a bite of sunflower seed or niger seed.

## Social Siskins

Like goldfinches, pine siskins are social birds that travel together in a group. They, too, can build to big numbers in spring, when migrating groups may descend upon your backyard to swarm the feeders. Often they pal around with goldfinches, and in some years, crossbills may join the burgeoning flock—which can reach 1,000 birds!

Usually, though, the group stays at a much more manageable hundred or two.

At first glance, siskins look a lot like female house finches—streaky brown "nothing special" little birds. Take a closer look at their wings and the bases of their tails, though, and you'll spot a wash of pretty yellow that sets them apart from those plainer house finch females.

## Sounds Like a Siskin

Once siskins start vocalizing, you won't be able to overlook them. All finches seem to have a lot to say, and these little guys do

Investing in niger seed pays off big-time in spring, when the high-priced seed attracts a living gold rush.

**Look closely to see the yellow-tinged feathers of the pine siskin—or listen for its frequent buzzy, rising call.**

sounds of siskins, you'll find you can pinpoint the movements of the flock as it travels around your yard or your neighborhood. *Zhreee . . .* must be siskins in that tree. Better fill those niger seed feeders!

## Royal Purple

Biggest and, many agree, prettiest of the finches, the beautiful male purple finch is a bird to watch for in spring.

The similar house finches are year-round birds across the country, but purple finches are usually just a seasonal treat, except for on the West Coast, in New England, and around the Great Lakes, where the birds live year-round. For most of us, though, spring is when we're most likely to get a good look at them, usually when a pair or small group visits our backyard for water or food during migration.

You'll spot the females right away because of their dramatic white eye stripe. That little accent stands out sharply against their brown-streaked bodies, giving you a clue that these aren't house finches you're looking at.

Male purple finches may cause you to wonder, for a minute, whether you're simply

more than their share of singing—if you can call it that. Their voices sound badly in need of a soothing throat lozenge. The signature note is a harsh, buzzy *zhreeeee,* trailing upward at the end. Get 100 siskins vocalizing at once in a cacophony of mismatched tempos, and you may find yourself wanting to holler "QUIET!"

The other siskin sound is the call note, sung out from bird to bird while the flock is in motion. It's a sudden high, sharp *kdeew.*

After you become familiar with the

## Time for a Change

You can see it's spring just by taking a look at a male goldfinch. In early spring, the boys begin to shift from their dull olive winter plumage to vivid yellow and black. You can watch the change as the birds linger in your yard for a few weeks in spring. Pay attention to the head, as well as the brightening body—it's fun to see that dapper black cap grow back in.

By the time spring dandelions have hit their peak, goldfinches are mostly finished with the molt. They'll blend right in with the sunny flowers as they reach for those tasty fluffy seeds.

## Backyard Bruins

Brown thrashers, tanagers, and other songbirds that previously didn't visit feeders have learned to take advantage of our largesse, delighting us with their visits.

A less delightful possibility that's also learned about feeders has fur, not feathers: the black bear.

In the Northeast and some other areas of the country, black bears have learned to head for feeding stations in spring, when they're looking for a fast fix after hibernation. Some regions have passed laws requiring bird lovers to take feeders down in spring; other communities have simply made it known that removing the feeders is a good idea.

It doesn't take much coaxing to get feeder keepers to follow through: One visit from a big ol' bruin is motivation enough.

seeing a better-than-usual house finch. Male house finches vary a lot in color, from pale to deeper hues, and some are pretty, indeed. But the purple finch goes past pretty to beautiful. They too have a distinct eye streak that's visible under that reddish purple wash.

Purple finches are more robust than the similar house finch, with a slightly stouter body and rich red-purple coloring. Watch for the male to partly raise his head feathers in a sort of modified crest effect. House finches rarely look so regal.

## A Slew of Sparrows

As a teenager, I spent more hours than I like to admit trying to tame my curly hair into submission so that I, too, would look like a California girl. I couldn't come close. (We won't even talk about the blue eye shadow!) It just didn't seem fair that personality should take a backseat to appearance, but I still tried my best to measure up.

I gave up that plan a long time ago. For decades, I've just been me, frizzy hair and all. My clothes are usually nondescript. But I do wear jewelry—a way-too-big collection of pieces that appeal to me, from a celluloid cicada pin to a necklace made of iridescent beetle wings.

In other words, I'm a lot more like a sparrow than I am a scarlet tanager: No one gasps in wonder when they see me coming. But they do seem to appreciate my personality, and eventually many of them notice the little bits of ornament I wear.

Maybe that's why I have a soft spot for sparrows, which I think are just as fascinating as any backyard bird. They don't have

**spring secret** Sorting out one sparrow from another can be tricky because they're all basically little brown birds. Pay special attention to their head markings, and you'll have—dare I say it?—a head start.

Subtle clues are the key to identifying native sparrows, so check for details like the eye ring of a field sparrow.

the knock-your-eye-out beauty of some songbirds. You have to take a closer look and get to know them to appreciate their friendly, interesting personalities—and their interesting bits of "jewelry."

## Sorting Out Sparrows

Spring brings a slew of interesting sparrows to our backyards and feeders. Luckily, their favorite food is white proso millet—an inexpensive staple that you can feed them generously, without worrying about your budget.

At first glance, you'll see just a bunch of little brown birds, busily scratching beneath your feeders and bushes or in your garden. The challenge of identification is part of the fun: I like to think of it as looking for each bird's signature piece of jewelry.

## Backyard Sparrows

| SPARROW | ADORNMENTS |
|---------|-----------|
| Chipping | Petite, with reddish beret |
| Field | Pale eye-rings for a look of surprise, and plain gray breast |
| Fox | Biggest, stoutest sparrow in the bunch, with heavily streaked breast |
| Golden-crowned | Yellow-gold stripes on crown of head |
| Song | White breast with brown streaks and dark "stickpin" blotch in center |
| Swamp | Looks like a song sparrow that's had a henna dye job on its feathers |
| Tree | Dark stickpin on unstreaked breast, with a reddish cap |
| White-crowned | White stripes on top of head; plain gray front; and erect, "proud" posture |
| White-throated | White bib at chin, striped head, and yellow splotch between eye and beak |

## Migration en Masse

Sparrows are gregarious birds during migration. They travel northward in flocks that include a mix of species. Since all sparrows feed on or near the ground, they share the same kinds of habitats during the journey.

In early spring, the flocks flow into backyards, where they often linger for several weeks. New arrivals come in to swell the numbers, while others disperse or depart when they're ready to move on.

Keep a good supply of white proso millet on hand in spring, so that you're ready when they get here. Sparrows are ground feeders, so you can lightly scatter some seed right on the ground, as well as in tray feeders.

You'll need to take a close look to find out who's who. So grab your binoculars, and let's see which widespread sparrows might be in our yards in spring.

### Not a Native

The bird that comes to mind first when we think "sparrow" isn't really a sparrow at all. It's the English or house sparrow, which is actually a weaver finch that hails from Europe and Asia. No use trying to correct its name—to everyone, it's simply a sparrow.

House sparrow numbers seem to be dwindling these days, both here and in England and other places. No one's really sure why. Still, there are more than enough to go around, so you're bound to see some of these small brown birds in your backyard, too. Males have a dashing black bib and face during breeding season; in winter, most of the bib disappears. Females are plain, without black markings.

These plump sparrows are social birds, hanging out in small groups of up to about a dozen birds. They're generally noisy, with lots of chirping, and they tend to squabble a lot. In summer, they delight in taking dust baths anywhere they can find a likely spot. They're fond of splashing in birdbaths, too.

If hordes of house sparrows are regulars at your feeder, you can distract them with an offering of cheap cracked corn. Scatter it on a flat rock or lightly on the ground, and they'll peck at it until it's gone. Stale bread and other bread-based scraps are welcomed, too—these birds are opportunists that often patrol parking lots at fast-food places, hoping for a stray French fry.

## Sheer Bribery for Special Guests

The special birds of spring offer a great incentive for adding "seasonal specials" to your regular menu. Tanagers, orioles, and other beauties eat mostly soft foods, rather than seeds, in the wild—and that means insects and fruits.

To tempt these birds, add some alternatives to your standard menu.

- In recent years, the feeder scene has been taken by storm with the introduction of mealworms and related insect foods. Give them a try (see below for details).

- Suet is also a big hit. Serve it in a feeder that less-agile birds can access, such as one that is firmly fixed rather than dangling. I chop suet and scatter it in my open tray feeders, too.

- Oriole fruit feeders have been around for a while, and they're worth every penny, because the brightly colored birds have become accustomed to seeking them out. Since orioles are a

## Eggs-Tra Added Attractions

I had no idea when I helped my mother tend her canaries 50 years ago that taking care of caged birds would teach me so much about feeding wild birds.

It makes perfect sense, of course. My mom was supplying all the needs of her canaries, since they couldn't fend for themselves. And of course she wanted to keep them healthy and happy. So the birds ate a carefully balanced diet, with whatever little treats my mom could dream up.

I loved taking care of the birds—keeping their seed cups full, washing their water dishes and bath, and replenishing their special foods as they needed them. In springtime, my mom's singing canaries got a treat of egg wafer—a flat, cracker-like treat formed from egg yolk—which they pecked at eagerly. Year-round, they had a cuttlebone wired to their cage, to provide the calcium they craved.

You can still buy egg biscuits and cuttlebones at caged-bird supply stores, but it's a lot easier to make a homemade version for wild birds. Just hard-boil an egg now and then, and you're set.

It seems a little odd to think of birds eating eggs, but hard-cooked eggs are a favorite treat for many birds. Both the egg white and yolk are high in protein and vitamins, and the yolk is high in fat, too. Cholesterol? I don't think birds keep count.

Here's how to offer eggs to birds as a feeder treat.

- Start with a small amount, about a tablespoon, of chopped, hard-boiled egg sprinkled into an open tray feeder.

- It may take a while for your birds to sample it, but once they do, you may find wrens, catbirds, mockingbirds, robins, thrushes, finches, jays, and others enjoying an occasional high-protein treat.

Save the shell when you peel that egg. Crushed shells are a good source of calcium for birds.

- Let the eggshells dry. Crush the shells with a rolling pin, or crumble them finely with your hands. Store in a zipper-lock bag and sprinkle the crumbled shells in an open tray feeder.

- Purple martins and possibly tree swallows may come to your feeder for crushed eggshells in spring, when nesting season is in gear.

- House finches, American goldfinches, crossbills, doves, and grosbeaks may also nibble on crushed eggshells, perhaps as a mineral supplement or as grit for grinding seeds.

later migrant, you'll find details about feeding them and other fruit feeders in Chapter 6 on page 116.

## Wild for "Worms"

The bait shop in my small town is run by a man named, very appropriately, Bill Fish. He sells all the enticements needed to catch a crappie or lure a catfish—and a couple of his offerings make darn good bait for songbirds, too. You'll also find the same items in slick bird-supply catalogs, and recently they've been added to the array of foods at bird shops.

We're talking about some simply luscious . . . larvae.

Conquer that queasy stomach, because if you like feeding birds, you're gonna love larvae. Caterpillarlike mealworms, wireworms, and waxworms are major magnets for birds. They're a hit year-round, but spring birds are especially fond of them.

These aren't the usual earthworm wigglers you'd put on a fishhook. They're whitish or tan grubs, about $\frac{1}{2}$ to $\frac{3}{4}$ inch

Mealworms are a huge hit with bluebirds, who'll bring the family to chow down on the tempting larvae.

long. Mmm . . . sounding better and better, aren't they?

It's not our prissy palates that they need to satisfy, though. And to birds they're simply irresistible.

Mealworms and similar larvae are fast becoming big business because feeder-keepers who try them can't believe the results. It may take birds a while to discover your offering, but when they do, you'll be stunned.

Think orioles. Bluebirds. Tanagers. Wood warblers. Vireos. Robins. Catbirds.

## Larvae Lovers

A multitude of birds, including the most striking birds of spring, eagerly eat mealworms or wireworms. You may attract any—or all!—of these.

| | | | |
|---|---|---|---|
| Blackbirds | Brown creeper | Nuthatches | Towhees |
| Bluebirds | Flickers | Orioles | Vireos |
| Buntings | Jays | Robin | Woodpeckers |
| Cardinal | Juncos | Native sparrows | Wood warblers |
| Catbird | Kinglets | Tanagers | Wrens |
| Chickadees | Mockingbird | Thrashers | |

## Shopping for and Storing Mealworms

Finding, buying, and storing mealworms and other larvae takes a little education. Here are some tips that I've learned.

- You can buy mealworms and other larvae at bait shops and bird supply stores, through catalogs, or online. See Sources on page 320 for some possibilities.

- Buy small mealworms, about ¾-inch long or less. Bait shops sometimes stock whoppers, which are less appealing and harder to contain.

- If you're using lots of mealworms, shop around to get the best deal; you can expect to pay between $10 and $20 for a couple of thousand live larvae.

- You'll find both live and roasted larvae for sale at bird suppliers. Birds are attracted to both, although live ones seem to be more highly desired at my feeder.

- Roasted larvae work fine to get your birds acquainted with this new feeder food, and they're easier to experiment with.

- Roasted worms are easier to store, usually less expensive when bought from bird supply stores, and won't make a break for it when you serve them.

- Live larvae will try to escape their container at the feeder. Be sure the sides of the container or feeder you use are high enough and slippery enough to deter escapees.

- Store roasted mealworms in a cool, dry place.

- Store live mealworms in a refrigerator in a container with a secure lid; punch a few air holes, and add a halved apple to provide moisture. Label the container and warn your family, to avoid an unsettling surprise.

Thrashers. With clientele like that, you'll want to add these lovely larvae to your spring menu right away.

### Serving Up Insects

Offering mealworms and other larvae will be a learning experience for both you and the birds. You'll soon find out what works best for your habits and your birds.

Here are some hints on how to get started with this alluring new food.

- Let the birds see those luscious larvae. Offer them where birds can get an unobstructed view—such as in an open tray feeder, not in a roofed feeder.

- For roasted worms, a foam supermarket tray (from meat or veggies) nailed to the top of a post makes a simple feeder.

- A small, hanging feeder with a clear plastic dome works well for live or roasted larvae; for wrens and other small birds, try a stick-on window feeder.

- Punch holes through either side of a tuna can, add a dozen mealworms, and suspend it from a tree branch to catch

Slippery glass dishes keep live mealworms from escaping—or you can offer roasted ones, instead.

the attention of kinglets, warblers, and vireos.

- Once your birds become converts, you may want to try a commercial feeder made especially for mealworms.

- You can even buy a mealworm feeder for bluebirds and other small birds. It has a side entrance hole that keeps out larger birds and a clear plastic panel so you can watch the birds inside.

## Feeding Fruit

Fruit eaters are some of the flashiest birds of spring. Orioles, which are late-spring arrivals from migration, are among the easiest to attract. They seem to be quickly learning that a feeding station may hold a special treat just for them. Tanagers, cedar waxwings, catbirds, thrashers, and even vireos may also stop by.

Oranges are the big draw for orioles, but you can also experiment with any other fruits you have on hand: bananas, other citrus, apples, and even melon. A serving of grape or other jelly is also a hit with orioles.

Fruit feeders are available commercially,

or you can improvise your own: Just push a halved orange, cut side up, onto a large nail, so that the fruit is held horizontally, and the bird can perch to eat.

## In Case of Emergency

Spring storms make life difficult for birds: They can't easily find food, and the cold makes them hungrier than ever.

Offer extra fats along with the usual menu during tough times. Birds will appreciate the extra calories to help keep their bodies warm.

Here are some quick ways to pack in the calories.

- Scatter finely chopped suet in trays and on the ground for sparrows, juncos, and other birds that can't cling to suet feeders.

- Spread chunky peanut butter on tree bark.

- Make a crumbly dough of peanut butter and cornmeal for bluebirds, thrashers, thrushes, and anyone else who wants a bite.

- Offer crushed or ground walnuts, pecans, hazelnuts, or peanuts in trays, where small birds and soft-food eaters such as wrens and catbirds can eat these high-calorie foods.

- Offer larger pieces of nuts in trays or wire-cage feeders for nuthatches, chickadees, titmice, and jays.

- Provide mealworms for primarily insect-eating birds such as wrens, warblers, catbirds, and others.

## Stormy Weather

Spring has a habit of dropping nasty weather on us long after we've had enough of winter.

Cold snaps, bitter winds straight from the North, ice storms, and spring snows can wreak havoc on any bird, but bluebirds and Carolina wrens are particularly susceptible. This is probably because they're insect eaters, and also because they seem to have a more delicate constitution or maybe less insulation than, say, tough little chickadees.

Any of those bad-weather events can make food so scarce that the birds starve to death, or freeze when they can't take in enough calories to stay warm. Factor in a family of nestlings for bluebirds, and the situation becomes even grimmer. It's plain to see why our backyard feeders are a prime bird destination when stormy weather hits in spring.

## Foul-Weather Friends

During a bout of bad weather in spring, ample food in your bird-friendly yard may draw in birds that normally keep to other haunts in your region.

## Bluebird Preservation

After being caught empty-handed when bluebirds arrived during a spring snowstorm years ago, I've changed my ways. Now I keep a few jars of generic peanut butter in reserve. My kitchen shelves always have some kind of carbohydrate-rich food I can mix with it—cornmeal, crushed crackers, breadcrumbs, unsweetened cereal—to make it easier to swallow. In a pinch, I've even served cooked pasta chopped up and mixed with peanut butter, which the hungry bluebirds seemed to be grateful for.

During a spring storm, feeder filling and clearing keeps me hopping, so I don't even bother with a measuring cup. I simply take a great big bowl, dump in whatever carbohydrate source I have on hand (finally a use for that box of stale Cheerios!), scoop in generous globs of peanut butter, some raisins or currants, and a chopped-up block of packaged suet if I have extra. Then I roll up my sleeves and use my hands to mix it up. Yum! It's a high-calorie hit with hungry bluebirds—and wrens, thrashers, catbirds, and mockingbirds—after a storm.

**Serve up fruit, mealworms, and homemade peanut butter dough to tempt bluebirds, wrens, and catbirds.**

## Last Resort

Another bluebird food I keep on hand for desperate days is a small bag of high-protein dry dog food. Pour a single layer into a cake pan, add about a cup of warm water, let it soften for about half an hour, and serve right in the pan.

Starlings will zero in on it, so I give them their own serving, and I place the bluebird food much closer to the door or to where I'm standing. Starlings are shy about approaching me or getting near the door, but bluebirds don't mind. Sometimes one will even flutter down to perch on the toe of my boot to eat.

Look for a dapper towhee busily scratching beneath shrubs or below the feeder after a spring snowstorm.

Rufous-sided towhees, for instance, often leave the sheltering woods to scratch beneath a feeder or hedge when snow or ice moves in. Fox sparrows, black-and-white warblers, and other woodsy species may show up, too, and purple or Cassin's finches may leave the trees of the forest for the feast at your feeder. Meadowlarks, sparrowlike dickcissels, and other grassland birds may forsake nearby farm fields for your feeder.

Keeping your regulars well nourished is gratifying, and the surprise birds that show up only add to your pleasure. That's why it's so important to keep a good stock of food on hand, until the weather has mellowed.

# CHAPTER 3

# NATURAL FOODS
# AND COVER FOR SPRING

**M**Y SON DAVID is a great traveling companion, especially on road trips. When the miles get long, we gnaw on all kinds of ideas.

"What do you think, Mom," he asked on one recent trip. "Agree? Disagree? 'All human activities are governed by self-interest.'"

The idea had come up in one of David's philosophy classes at college. And my knee-jerk reaction was to disagree. Strongly.

At first, I argued that of course we do things for purely selfless reasons. Like charity, for instance. We give to help others.

So why do they publish the names of donors, then? asked David.

Touché. But what about anonymous giving, I countered.

Hmm, wait a minute—there's no denying it feels good to give. So there's still a payoff, even if we give anonymously.

And acts of charity may help society, by uniting us around a common cause. We might even be "buying" protection through charity, because desperate people might be more inclined to steal.

Before long, I'd given up trying to argue against the statement and started thinking about it from another angle: Self-interest? Not such a bad thing.

That's why I acknowledge that creating a welcoming yard for birds is important to their well-being—but, first and foremost, it's a lot of fun for us.

Self-interest is where the benefits of having a bird-friendly yard begin. In spring, migrating birds are likely to stop off at any

Native plants with red or orange flowers, like the flame azalea, signal nectar to arriving hummingbirds.

yard that holds the promise of a hearty meal and a place to rest a while. Good for them . . . and good for us!

## SPRINGTIME SERVICE

Not only will you benefit from seeing beautiful and interesting birds in spring—your yard will be a winner, too, because all of those birds means way fewer bugs.

In spring, the insects in your yard are just getting started. If every one of them made it to adulthood, your yard would be so unpleasant that you'd never want to set foot in it. Leaves would be eaten to the bare veins, veggies would suffer, and flowers might never get past the bud stage without being devoured. At the least, you'd be tempted to pour gallons of pesticides onto that yard to try to keep one step ahead of the bugs.

## Feathered "Pesticide"

Did somebody say bugs? Birds to the rescue! Insects are the natural food of nearly every bird on earth, and they gulp down gazillions of them.

In spring, both your year-round birds and the new arrivals will spend hours each day finding insects on your plants, in your soil, in the air, and every other place that might shelter a likely prospect.

As we gardeners eventually learn, it's a lot easier to keep up with weeds when you pull a few every day, before they take over the garden. It's the same deal with bugs. The relentless sunup-to-sundown patrol of the Avian Insect-Control Corps keeps those six-legged critters in check.

The numbers are staggering. A single sparrow may down a couple of hundred insects every single day; a wren, even more. Come nesting season, when insects serve as the main meal for hungry nestlings, the rate of destruction goes much higher. Some experts say that a bird eats roughly half its own weight in food a day! Did somebody say, "Supersize me"?

The actual number depends on various factors, including:

- The type of insects
- The type of bird
- What else the bird is eating
- Whether or not the bird is feeding a family

## A Chickadee's Appetite

A black-capped chickadee weighs 10 to 12 grams. That's about as much as 5 pennies.

Aphids are one of the insects that chickadees eat, and for the sake of our example, let's say this particular chickadee eats only aphids. (That wouldn't be true for a real bird, of course—those sunflower seeds, caterpillars, and hundreds of other food items are too delicious!)

Hefted any aphids lately? It would take tens of thousands to equal half a chickadee. And that's just one day's consumption. Multiply that times a 90-day growing season, and a chickadee might down a pile of insects the size of a Volkswagen—or a city bus!

## Insect Timing

Most of our backyard birds are specialists when it comes to finding food. That's why migration is timed to coincide with when spring insects become available (and I'm including earthworms and spiders in this category, even though they're not insects).

Each bird species has its favorite places to look for insects. That specific "niche" depends on the bird's style of hunting, its style of eating, and where it lives. Ground-dwelling thrushes, for instance, are suited to a much different menu than treetop tanagers are. Here's where to look for birds seeking bugs, and what kinds of birds you may find snacking on the critters.

### On the Ground

Once the weather nears 40°F, earthworms, beetles, and other ground-dwelling critters become active and available to birds. Lots of insects and other goodies are available on the ground, and many birds take advantage of that bounty.

**Earthworms.** Robin and American woodcock (a woodland bird that may show up in backyards during spring migration)

**Beetles, grubs, spiders, and other ground dwellers.** Blackbirds, grackles, bluebirds, thrushes, sparrows, towhees, wrens, starlings, and crows

### In Trees

As soon as the first tender green leaves emerge, insects hatch to feed on them. Migrating spring birds arrive right on time to catch the hatch. Each species has its favorite trees and its favorite part of the tree canopy

Tender new growth attracts aphids, and aphids attract kinglets, chickadees, and lots of other insect eaters.

to search: scarlet tanagers prefer leafy oaks; Nashville warblers scour the lower branches of trees, while cerulean warblers stick to the very tippy-top.

**Caterpillars.** Grosbeaks, cardinals, tanagers, orioles, many warbler species, and vireos

## In the Air

Mosquitoes may be our first guess when we talk about what kinds of insects are in the air, but many, many, *many* other insects are also active over our heads: gnats, midges, moths, bees, wasps, and a host of others. Birds who share the airborne eating habit devour them in quantity.

**Flying insects.** Nabbing an insect in flight takes special skills. Some birds scoop them up during hours of flying; others make a quick dash-and-grab. Some birds, such as swallows, swifts, and martins, are in the air most of the day; other birds, like flycatchers, phoebes, some warblers, cedar waxwings, and red-headed woodpeckers, hunt from a perch, flying out to snap up insects and then returning to wait for more.

## In the Water

Got a garden pool or pond? Maybe you even have a creek running through your yard. If you have water, you have water insects,

Cedar waxwings love fruit, but they also eat plenty of insects, flying out from a perch to "flycatch" in midair.

including larval forms of mayflies and other insects that spend their early stages in water, then move to the air. You can bet that these aquatic insects are another niche for some birds to specialize in. Most of these bird specialists are not common in backyards, but some backyard birds will also take advantage of aquatic insects when they can reach them.

**Water insects.** Ducks, shorebirds, killdeers, kingfishers, crows, robins, thrushes, sparrows, water pipits, flycatchers, phoebes, and some warblers

## Frequent Flyer Club

The lovely iridescent blue-green tree swallow—love that snow-white belly!—is a tireless flying machine. A single swallow can easily cover hundreds of miles a day in the air. No, it's not flying long-distance from Point A to Point B. It's generally covering those miles by making constant loops around an area.

## House Wren Habit

Diminutive house wrens raise some of the biggest families around—a typical brood will have seven or eight babies. No wonder the parents are always at work, scouring our plants for insect life. That's a lot of little tummies to fill, and a big assist for our gardens.

### In and on Tree Trunks and Limbs

Many of our most familiar feeder birds seek insects in the crevices or behind the flaps of the bark on our trees, or within the wood.

**Insects in tree bark.** Chickadees, titmice, nuthatches, brown creeper, wrens, black-and-white warbler, woodpeckers, and sapsuckers

Tree bark hides countless insects and their eggs, but nuthatches have a real knack for spotting them.

## WONDERFUL WIGGLERS

Earthworms are the main food for the robin, which can find and eat 10 to 12 wigglers in 10 minutes. In spring, robin migration moves according to the temperature because these birds are so dependent on earthworms, which become available only when temperatures reach a certain point.

## Robin Roundup

Migrating robins follow what is called an isobar, an imaginary point-to-point line of average temperature that stretches across the country. In spring, robins wait for the 36° or 37°F isobar before they make their move. Can you guess why that isobar is so important? That's also the temp at which worms begin to appear above the soil.

Want to predict the arrival of robins in your yard? Here's how:

1. Keep track of the daily high and low temps for a week; you can find these each day in your local newspaper or online (www.weather.com).

2. Find the average temperature for each day by adding high and low numbers together and dividing by 2.

3. At the end of the week, add up those seven average daily numbers, and divide by 7.

4. That number is the isobar your area is part of.

5. Is that number 36 or above? You're on the 36°F (or higher) isobar—robins will be coming soon!

## BOOSTING BUG POTENTIAL

The biggest secret to having a yard brimming with bugs is this: Stop using pesticides. Put away those sprays and shakers, and insects will be more plentiful in your yard. At least until birds discover them. Then, nature will reach its usual balance.

Even organic pesticides will limit the variety of insects available to birds—and thus limit the birds you'll see. The natural control called Bt, and its variations, all have drawbacks for backyard use. Although it's not toxic to humans, it's poison to insects. And it's all too tempting to dust entire plants, including shrubs and trees, with it. When you do that, you are killing off all of the insects that make their homes on that plant.

At first, that may sound like a good thing; after all, those aphids are causing

Robins time their migration to the temperature, arriving when worms move up from deep below the surface of the soil.

deformed leaves on your young tree, aren't they? True enough. But it's not just aphids that bite the dust when you use Bt: So do countless caterpillars, beetles, and other insects that inhabit the plant. And those are bugs that could be attracting and nourishing birds.

I'll never forget the first time I came across Bt, shortly after its introduction. The label said something like, "Kills leaf-eating caterpillars." That would be just about all caterpillars, I realized, from those of the fabulous luna moth to those of the myriad

## Patriotic Robins

Throughout the book, wherever the word "robin" is used, we're talking about the common and widespread American robin, not its much rarer cousins, the rufous-backed robin and clay-colored robin, which are sighted only occasionally in a very tiny area of the Southwest or Texas.

Tent caterpillars or gypsy moths infesting your trees? The black-billed cuckoo gobbles up fuzzy caterpillars.

tiny nondescript moths that feed so many birds, to tent moths and the notorious gypsy moth. Personally, I'd rather wait for cuckoos to come take care of my tent moth caterpillars than to take the chance of killing off some of the larvae of those nighttime beauties I love to see at my porch light.

## Put Aside the Poison

In all my 50-some years of gardening, I have never once reached for a pesticide of any kind. Wait, I take that back, I *have* reached for pesticides—but I've never used any. More than once, I've stood in the pesticide aisle of

a store, reading the label and considering using poisons to make my life "easier." Every time, I've put them back and returned to my usual ways of doing things.

I'm a big believer in letting everyone make her own decision about what to do in her own yard and life. But I do think it's important to know that alternatives to pesticides are available, and they're easy to put into practice. Here are the measures I use to stay chemical-free, insect-rich, and bird-happy.

- **Keep your eyes wide open.** I watch my yard for signs of trouble. At least once a day, I stroll around, keeping an eye out for signs of insect infestations. Since I don't have bird eyes or avian agility, I overlook most of the insects in my garden. But I do notice when the first Japanese beetles move in, or when the aphids have reached big numbers on my plants. Then I take the next step.

- **Snip, snip, snip.** A pair of pruners is always in my hip pocket, ready for remedial action. A few minutes a day takes care of removing any badly infested, aphid-caked branches, which I drop on the compost pile for ladybugs to find.

- **Tap, tap, tap.** Japanese beetles get the tap-and-die treatment: Early in the morning, when they're sluggish, I knock

When pests move in on your favorite plants, clip off badly infested stems and let birds clean up the rest.

them into a jar holding a few inches of ammonia.

- **Tuck them in.** Spun-fiber row covers go over my broccoli, asparagus, and other bug-tempting crops, to prevent egg-laying insects from getting at them.

- **Laissez-faire.** I don't bother removing caterpillars; I'm fond of butterflies and moths, for one thing, and I also know that caterpillars are prime food for birds. No matter what kind they are, they won't last long.

## CLEANUP CONSIDERATIONS

In spring, many of my neighbors spend days tidying up their yards. Every last winter leaf is raked up and removed, every bit of debris beneath hedges is hunted down and raked clean, every dead branch sawed off, every stray twig disposed of, every shrub scissored into a neat ball. Their yards look clean and orderly, all right. But their birds don't linger: They stick around only long enough to visit the feeders.

Why are birds so quick to leave a super-tidy yard? Because it offers very little that they can make use of for food. And, worse yet, it puts them at risk of being eaten. Birders know that the places to find the most birds are what we call "edge habitats"—where a forest shifts to a field, for instance, or a path borders a hedgerow. Edges attract birds because the mix of plant types offers more opportunity for food, both seeds and insects. Your yard can become an inviting example of edge habitat if you aren't too quick to clean it up. The winter-dead stems of your flower garden lead to your lawn, making an inviting edge where birds can scratch for seeds. The lawn leads to a hedge or group of shrubs, which supply a sheltered place for perching and an inviting layer of decomposing leaves beneath.

Getting food is a bird's all-day quest. Most birds don't sit around doing nothing for hours on end. Except for brief periods of singing or courting, birds are constantly occupied with finding the next bite to eat. The more food-rich places you can offer in your yard, and the more cover your yard offers, the more time birds will spend there. We may call a yard like that "messy," but birds will feel at home.

Birds prefer a little messiness, or as I'd rather call it, a little bit of the natural look.

Let your rhododendrons grow naturally, without shearing, and they'll be more appealing as bird cover.

Here's how the typical "spring cleanup" activities affect the birds.

- **Natural food.** Those dead leaves you might rake from under bushes are great places to hunt for food. They also contribute to better soil as they decompose, and they make it easier for sparrows, towhees, and other birds to scratch in the loose, moist, insect-rich humus.

- **Nesting material.** Stray dead twigs that get raked away might have been valuable raw materials for nesting. Jays, mockingbirds, doves, cardinals, and many other backyard birds use a multitude of slim sticks in their spring nests.

- **Safe cover.** The dead stems of flower gardens and veggie patches provide

excellent protective cover in early spring, as well as food for birds such as native sparrows, towhees, juncos, and quail. When they're cut down in very early spring, migrant arrivals and resident birds become more vulnerable to predators and bad weather.

- **Travel corridors.** Free-form shrubs and hedges are easier to move through or perch in than extra-dense balls. Regular shearing often causes such dense growth in the interior of a shrub that it's difficult for catbirds, mockingbirds, sparrows, and other shelter-seeking birds to move about freely—or without betraying their presence by making rustling noises.

## VARIETY ON THE MENU

You can further boost the bug potential of your yard by expanding your plant palette so that it includes a variety of shrubs, trees, perennials, and other plants. Different kinds of plants attract different insects, which attract different birds. Different plants also expand the possibilities for nest sites and roosting places, as well as eating possibilities.

The more plants you have, and the more kinds of them, the more birds you'll attract.

Birds eat other natural foods in spring besides insects. You'll find plenty of info on

**spring secret** Watch for tree seedlings sprouting in your flowerbeds or along fences—wherever birds may have dropped seeds. While they're young, transplant the seedlings into a hedgerow, if you have the room, or move your favorites to a place of honor. They'll grow fast.

seeds, fruits, and other natural foods in the other seasonal sections of this book. Spring is for planting, so check out the suggestions in those sections, too, if you want to bring more birds to your yard in every season of the year.

## Natives, Naturally

It's a great idea to include at least a few native plants in the mix because they're already familiar to the birds that live in or migrate through your area. Native plants evolved right along with native birds, so they are guaranteed to be perfectly suited. I still plant some nonnative flowers and shrubs (it wouldn't be spring without forsythia—which originated in China!), but most of the plants in my yard are natives. Birds seek them out because they already know how to make use of them.

- Native plants may host particularly appealing insects—such as the caterpillars on a native oak, which tanagers seek out.
- Natives often offer tasty fruits or berries that are timed to the habits of birds; think of the staghorn sumac, which has fuzzy clusters that are sought in spring by migrant bluebirds.
- Natives may provide nest materials or nest sites that native birds will eagerly adopt.

## PLANTING TIME

Spring is a really dangerous time of year for me because I simply can't resist carting home more plants from garden centers, nurseries, plant sales, and friends' yards. The soil is moist, the rains are reliable, the sun is

Lingering berries of staghorn sumac attract bluebirds and mockingbirds in early spring, when fruit is scarce.

Graceful, adaptable spicebush blooms with the first daffodils, attracting small insects for early birds.

warm—what could be better than spending an hour or two planting?

My bank account and my back may not always be happy with me, but my birds sure are. The more shrubs, trees, and other plants I add, the more opportunities I make for them.

Take advantage of spring planting time to add plants to your yard for all seasons. You'll find suggestions for specific bird-friendly plants in other sections of the book. Here are some general guidelines.

- Plant a hedge for birds to use as a travel corridor, perching place, and foraging spot.
- Plant a group of shrubs to break up big open spaces in your yard. You'll provide all-important cover and additional food among the branches and beneath the bushes.
- Plant flowers that produce bird-favored seeds and—say it with me—provide cover!
- Add hummingbird-attracting flowers and shrubs, which other birds will use for— yep—cover.

- Plant fruiting shrubs and trees, including a patch of raspberries or other brambles, for food and . . . cover, of course!
- Plant a grapevine on a fence, trellis, or arbor, for summer fruit, nesting sites, and year-round cover.
- Plant evergreens for winter roosting and year-round cover.
- Plant a butterfly garden to attract insects for summer birds to eat. (See Chapter 7 on page 131 for info.)

## CORRIDOR PLANTINGS FOR SAFE TRAVELS

Getting from Point A to Point B without being eaten is a continual concern for birds. They're always watching out for cats, hawks, and other potential dangers—including us and our pets.

Watch the birds in your yard, and you'll see that most of them travel from one spot of cover to another, each in their own way. As

## Plant a Tree

From a bird's perspective, native trees are among the most beneficial of all native plants because their features are closely tied to the needs of birds in the area. It will take a tree years to grow to its full potential, but even as a youngster, a tree is a boon to birds. As it matures, it'll continue to attract birds for many years to come.

A tree is a living cornucopia, providing multitudes of caterpillars, beetles, ants, and other insects on its myriad leaves, its bark, and its flowers. Its seeds add another ready food supply, whether they're acorns, pinecones, or the winged samaras (helicopters) of maples. Nest materials and home sites, whether in knotholes or on branches, are other attractions. And trees provide plenty of shelter from the elements and from predators. Tree leaves can even serve as birdbaths as well as umbrellas: Small birds, including warblers and hummingbirds, bathe by rubbing against a wet leaf.

spring secret  A casual mixed hedge is one of the best ways to attract birds, because they can travel safely within it. Plant a mix of shrubs, including some natives, for even more bird appeal.

you watch your birds move about your yard or other places, you'll notice habits like these.

- Orioles move from treetop to treetop.
- Chickadees travel from tree to shrub to feeder to tree.
- Sparrows flit from bush to bush, or make a mad dash from garden bed to weedy patch along the fence.
- House wrens hop from plant to plant in the veggie garden, then make a quick flight back to the birdhouse.
- Nuthatches, woodpeckers, and brown creepers go from tree trunk to tree trunk, covering the open space between as fast as possible.
- A catbird slinks through a hedge; a brown thrasher hops beneath bushes. Both stay out of sight as much as they can.

Sheltering plants spell safety to birds. Open spaces, unless you're a robin or starling, mean danger.

Help your birds feel safe, and make your yard more appealing to birds, by planting cover where they most need it.

- Plant a pussy willow or other small tree next to the birdbath, so that bathers have a place to alight when arriving or to preen after the bath. Don't surround the birdbath with shrubs, however: Cats can sneak up too easily that way.
- Plant a spruce, fir, or other evergreen near your feeder area, so that birds can

make a quick escape if a hawk swings through.

- Add shrubs, hedges, and flowerbeds here and there around your yard, so that birds don't have to cross large stretches of open space when moving from one part of your yard to another.
- Add shrubs or stout perennials along a fence. This might be the place to plant more aggressive perennials that spread by roots, but which appeal to birds, such as perennial sunflowers (*Helianthus maximillianii* and others), common milkweed (*Asclepias syriaca*), bee balm (*Monarda* species), or goldenrod (*Solidago* 'Fireworks' or other tall cultivars). Or why not a mix?

Plan travel corridors through your yard so birds can move under cover from one area to another.

# CHAPTER 4

# SPECIAL BIRDS
# OF SPRING

SPRING IS SO FULL of fabulous birds that it's hard to keep up with them. Glorious reds, blues, yellows, and oranges flit across the yard and among the trees. Quieter brown birds aren't flashy, but they fill our trees and bushes with song. Many of those birds appear in our yards only during migration. Then they disperse to living in pairs on nesting grounds, which may or may not include our backyards. You can find lots of tips for encouraging special spring birds to visit your yard in Chapters 1 through 3.

In this chapter, though, you'll get a closer look at three families of birds that show up in spring. I can almost guarantee that you'll see some birds from all three families in your own yard. You'll learn how to put out the welcome mat for these special backyard friends, so you'll be ready when they get there. If you have the right kind of habitat, you may even be lucky enough to host a nesting pair and watch them raise their family.

The joyful, bubbling song of the tiny brown house wren is one of the most welcome voices of spring.

## THE WRENS

A dear friend once gave me the best compliment I've ever received. I was enthusing about something I'd seen that day—a bug? a bird? a flower?—when he turned to our companion and said, "Every day is like Christmas to Sally!"

So true. When you spend time looking at things outside, you'll get little surprises every day. And aren't surprise gifts—whether you're giving them or receiving them—one of the best things about Christmas?

Spring is full of surprises. It's a super busy season, since many of us love our gardens as much as we love our birds. With so much going on—checking out the nurseries, sowing seeds, moving plants around, filling the feeders—I often forget to keep track of which birds are due back from their winter hiatus in southern climes.

One of my favorite surprise gifts in spring is to wake up to the liquid, gurgling song of a house wren outside my bedroom window. Oh joy, the wrens are back!

## Backyard Wrens

The wren family includes nine species, but only a few of them are likely to show up in our backyards.

- That exuberant waterfall of spring song I hear outside my window is the trademark of the little house wren, a backyard favorite for centuries. Old-timers and country folk still know the bird as "Jenny wren," as it's often called in children's storybooks. House wrens cover the entire country, so you have a good chance of seeing—and hearing—one at your own place in spring. This small brown bird, less than 5 inches from stem to stern, has a beautiful, complicated pattern of barring on its upper feathers (which you'll need binoculars to best appreciate) and a plain, pale belly. Like all wrens, it often holds its tail upright, giving the bird a jaunty look.

- Another widespread member of this family is the even tinier winter wren, a stubby-tailed mite that measures just 4 inches from the tip of its bill to the tip of its tail. It haunts the dim conifer forests of the Northwest, singing even

That bold eye stripe is the trademark of Bewick's wren, or of its eastern counterpart, the Carolina.

more explosively than the house wren. Winter wrens are common in the Northeast, too, and have expanded their range to now include most of the country. They often roam the woods but may also visit your backyard to drop in at a welcoming feeder or serenade you from the shrubs. If you spot one, it will look a lot like a house wren, but smaller and with a stubbier tail.

- The larger Carolina wren covers a huge area, too, with its similar western counterpart, Bewick's wren, filling in the southern half of the West as well as the western coast. These birds, with their noticeable eye stripe, often patrol backyards and stop at feeders for a bite of suet or another snack, even in winter.

Like other wrens, the Carolina is quick and agile, flitting from one perch to another as it looks for bugs.

## Now You See Them

With their sweet, long-lasting songs—they sound as if the bird is bubbling with joy—and their friendly personalities, wrens are a true treat in your backyard. You'll quickly get attached to these active, friendly birds.

The Carolina and Bewick's wrens are often year-round residents in many regions, and sometimes the winter wren is, too. But the house wren is a true migrant, spending its winters in the steamy South and returning north in spring.

Of course, like other birds, wrens sing in spring. So even if your Carolina wren has been around all winter, you'll still get to enjoy him in a new way: as a spring singer.

- For those of you in the Southwest, there's the cactus wren, a familiar and vocal bird of the dry desert—and its backyards. This wren is a lot bigger than its relatives and has a spotted breast.

The United States is home to other wrens, too, whose names give a good clue to the kind of homeland they prefer: the sedge wren, marsh wren, rock wren, and canyon wren. Unless your backyard includes one of those habitats, though, these wrens are not likely to drop in.

## Now You Don't

Wrens are intensely active birds, but lots of that motion takes place out of sight. They're attracted to dense vegetation, so expect to hear or see them moving through your shrubs, flowerbeds, veggie patch, and that—oops!—collection of weeds in the corner by the fence.

Low levels are the places to look for wrens. They're not birds of the treetops, but birds that generally stay below about 5 feet. As you can guess, abundant cover is the way to make a wren feel at home. Groups of shrubs, thickly planted garden beds, ground-

spring secret   When I hear an odd noise in my yard in spring, I think "wren" right away. They may be famed for beautiful songs, but loud rattles and churrs are also calling cards of these birds. The Carolina, in particular, has a habit of hiding out in a dense vine or shrub and sounding forth with short, loud bursts of unusual noises.

The big, loud cactus wren can go months without a drink of water. It gets its moisture from its food.

covers with shrubs, vigorous vines, and hedges make a prime wren habitat in the backyard. Supply enough plants to suit their hide-and-seek habits, and a pair may decide that your backyard is the place to call home. Another place to look for wrens is in your birdhouses! Most species are cavity nesters, and they may adopt your wren-size bird box.

## What's for Dinner?

A wren's long, thin bill is the big clue that wrens are insect eaters—and crevice-probers. They're built for picking bugs from cracks in rocks, from leafy litter, and from wherever they can reach in foliage. Fruit goes down the hatch, too—especially in summer, when wild berries ripen.

### In the Yard

- Your ample plantings will supply all the insects a wren could want. They're among the best birds at natural pest control, downing from hundreds to thousands of insects every day.

- A layer of dead-leaf mulch is a draw for wrens because it holds a multitude of spiders, millipedes, snails, and other tasty bites.

- Let leaves blow under shrubs and trees in fall, instead of raking them up, to improve the wren appeal of your yard.

### At the Feeder

- Caterpillars are hugely popular with wrens, so mealworms and other larvae are tops at the feeder, although it may

Escargot, anyone? Wrens seek out snails, sliding them right down the hatch without a garlic butter sauce.

(continued on page 64)

## Plants to Attract Wrens

| PLANT | TYPE OF PLANT | DESCRIPTION | HARDINESS ZONES |
|---|---|---|---|
| Autumn-blooming clematis (*Clematis terniflora*) | Deciduous vine | This vigorous vine forms a dense, tangled mass of stems and foliage; it has clouds of small, fragrant white flowers late summer to fall. Grows to about 15'. | 4–9 |
| Broccoli (any cultivar) | Annual garden vegetable | "Broccoli" is the buds of this cabbage-family plant; they open into large sprays of small yellow flowers. Grows to 2–3'. | All |
| Burning bush (*Euonymus alatus*, *Euonymus fortunei*) | Deciduous shrub | Fabulous fall color that lives up to its name; wrens are more interested in small, dangling berries. Grows to about 6'. | 5–9 |
| Cholla cactus (*Opuntia* species) | Bushy or treelike cactus | Spiny cacti with showy flowers and waxy fruit. Grows to about 6'. | 8 or 9–11 |
| Serviceberry (*Amelanchier* cultivars and hybrids) | Deciduous shrub or small tree | Graceful plants, often multistemmed; intense fall color of red, orange, and purple mixed together; abundant small white flowers in spring, followed by blueberrylike fruit. Grows to about 12'. | 3–9, depending on cultivar or hybrid |
| Strawberry (any cultivar) | Low-growing perennial fruit plant | A pretty plant with glossy leaves and sprays of yummy berries. Grows to about 6". | 4–9, depending on cultivar |

| USE | COMMENTS | OTHER BIRDS ATTRACTED |
|---|---|---|
| Cover, roosting, nesting | Fast-growing and trouble-free, autumn clematis is useful to wrens in all seasons; in winter, the thick stems provide shelter. | Catbirds, thrashers |
| Insect food, from caterpillars and adults of cabbage white butterflies | Snuggle a few plants into your flower garden for the birds. | Flycatchers |
| Cover, food from fruit, insect food from flowers and foliage | Use in a group or in a hedge to provide cover and a safety corridor. | Bluebirds, catbirds, robins, thrashers, thrushes |
| Nesting, cover, food from fruit | An excellent plant for desert gardens; beloved by western wrens. | Thrashers |
| Fruit | You can't have too many serviceberries! Plant in hedges or groups; plant tree-types in flowerbeds. | Bluebirds, thrushes, waxwings |
| Juicy red berries are irresistible to wrens | Strawberries make a pretty groundcover in sunny spots. | Native sparrows, robins |

## Home Sweet Birdhouse

House wrens are charming tenants for backyard birdhouses—if a persnickety pair decides to give yours the nod.

An entire block or neighborhood may share one pair of wrens, so do whatever you can to give your place the edge. Plant your yard with a mix of open lawn, garden beds, and shrubbery that spells home, and supply tempting feeder foods. A vegetable garden or a grape arbor that teems with bugs is sometimes all it takes to tilt the decision your way.

Don't get too excited when you see a wren maneuvering sticks into your alluring birdhouse. Males start more than one nest, then take the female on a tour so she can choose her favorite. If yours doesn't get the nod this time, there's always hope for the next brood—or next spring!

Before the female house wren arrives on the scene, the male starts a few nests to aid in wooing.

take the birds a few days to discover your cache.

- Suet is a hit, too, and wrens are agile enough to cling to a wire feeder and reach inside to grab a bite.

- Wrens also appreciate homemade peanut butter treats like the bluebird dough described on page 44.

- In winter, Carolina and Bewick's wrens may eat crumbled baked goods or millet.

## WOOD WARBLERS

Every once in a while the Roth family has a reunion—and what a gathering that is! It takes hours just to sort out who's who, thanks to big families and scads of cousins. During spring migration, the wood warbler clan comes pretty close to the size and scope of that Roth reunion. This extra-large collection of bird relatives, which join together in mixed flocks at traveling time, includes more than 50 separate species of warblers! Depending on where you live, you may see just a few species . . . or hundreds of birds representing dozens of species. Spring migration is practically a family reunion for these little birds, as they join together to follow a similar path back to their breeding grounds.

Considering that the nuthatch family includes merely four species—count 'em, four—you can see why warblers get so much attention from bird-watchers. Keeping track of how many species of warblers you've seen—in a lifetime, or in a year—can quickly slide into obsession. This is especially true in spring, when the whole giant clan is passing through, dressed in their most colorful plumage.

## Warbler Mania

Every spring and fall, waves of these migrating songbirds, a dozen to scores at a time, pass through backyards and wild places. At first glance, most of them look a lot alike. They're tiny yellowish green birds, and they rarely sit still.

Tiny birds. Always in motion. And basically look-alikes. No wonder I cry "These warblers are driving me crazy!"

If you do manage to get your binoculars focused on warblers, you'll see that these birds are beautiful. Each species has distinct markings—some subtle, some so bright it's hard to miss them. And once you start watching warblers, it's hard to stop. Ticking off the species you've seen is habit-forming. You'll want to "collect" them all!

The striking "flame throat" or Blackburnian warbler joins mixed warbler groups during spring migration.

Like other wood warblers, the blue-winged may move through any backyard along its migration route.

Watch a "wave" of spring wood warblers and you may catch the dramatic hooded warbler in their midst.

## Where Warblers Roam

Only a handful of species—the Nashville warbler, the yellow warbler, the yellow-rumped warbler, and the American redstart warbler—can be seen practically anywhere across the country.

The vast majority of this big family is found only in the eastern one-half to two-thirds of America. A few species, just enough to make life interesting, live in the West, Northwest, and Southwest.

## Spring Sightings

When I was a kid, there'd come a day in every April when my mom would return from a stroll around the yard and announce, "The yellow birds are here!"

We'd sit together on the front steps and strain our eyes to see the flow of motion in the oak next to our house. Its leaves were still just emerging, but dangling catkin flowers decorated every twig, and that's what drew the warblers. Even with bare eyes, we could tell they were picking bugs from the flowers.

Our family had never even heard of field guides, so guessing what these birds might be was part of the occasion.

"I don't think they're goldfinches," my mom would say. "Goldfinches don't act like that."

"And goldfinches would be brighter yellow," I'd add.

"Maybe they're all lady goldfinches," she'd suggest.

But both of us knew we were looking at something unique. "Yellow birds," we'd pronounce, as if naming a new species. Later, when I'd become the proud owner of a pair of heavy, cheap binoculars, my mom loved to take a close look at her yellow birds. She couldn't believe how different they looked through the lenses—why, some

## So-So Singers

As for the name "warbler"—don't you believe it. Only a few are musical virtuosos.

- Most warblers hold forth with high-pitched trills or buzzy songs. They often get lost in the background among the more noticeable songsters of spring, such as thrushes or wrens.
- Warblers are known for their "chips," too. Many species have a call note that's some variation on a short, sharp "chip" sound.
- Those who spend a lot of time watching wood warblers learn to tell the very, very similar chips apart—an incredible feat.
- Like many songbirds, warblers fly at night during migration. Speaking of unbelievable skills—some birders have such a fine ear for those chips that they can identify the species in a mixed flock flying overhead at night!

## Backyard Warblers

Any wood warbler species that migrates through your region may show up in your backyard in spring or fall, when the birds are on the move. But these are the species you have the best chance of attracting as regular visitors, or even nesters.

| WARBLER | WHEN TO LOOK FOR IT |
| --- | --- |
| Black-and-white | Nesting season (summer), in much of the eastern half of the country; winter, in Florida; also occasionally in winter across the country |
| Common yellowthroat | Nesting season (summer), across all of the country except for areas of Texas and California; winter, along a wide strip of much of the Gulf, Atlantic, and Pacific coasts |
| Orange-crowned | Nesting season (summer), in the West; winter, in the South and southeastern Atlantic coast |
| Palm | Winter, in the Deep South |
| Pine | Nesting season (summer), in the Northeast and Appalachians; year-round, in the South and Southeast |
| Yellow | Nesting season (summer), in all but the South and areas of the Southwest |
| Yellow-rumped: both myrtle race and Audubon's race | Nesting season (summer), in the West and Southwest; winter, in much of the southern half of the country and the Atlantic and Pacific coasts |

were even orange, and others had beautiful rusty trim, and while some had streaky breasts, others were as plain as Quakers.

The stream of birds would continue for an hour or more, new arrivals replacing those that continued northward. There'd be a lull, then another flock would arrive. The flight really was in waves, just as birders describe it.

## Family Habits

Once you start listening for the many and varied songs of warblers, you'll hear these birds a lot more often than you see them. Warblers stay well within the greenery, and their small bodies are exceptionally tricky to spot among all that foliage. Here's what to look for.

## Special Occasion

Plan a do-nothing day in spring, when you can set aside at least an hour to watch warblers. A whole morning is even better. The spring migration is a sight to behold, but it's easy to miss if you don't take some time to watch the warblers.

April through early May is prime time in most areas. Call your local chapter of the Audubon Society or ask a nearby nature center, and they'll gladly help you pinpoint the best date for warbler watching.

I look for a location where there's a hedgerow, a tree line, or a scattering of trees that funnels the birds past me. Golf courses, tree-dotted pastures, or your own backyard can be great. Just park yourself in a comfy spot, and wait to experience the wave.

- Warblers have a lot of nervous energy. They're quick, active birds, constantly on the move. Only the kinglet family beats them in the perpetual motion department.

- Their occasional pauses, often when they break into song, are your best opportunity to zero in on a bird.

- Fluttering and flycatching are trademark behaviors of many warblers. Like kinglets, bushtits, and other small insect eaters, they often flutter before a branch tip or leaf to home in on insects.

- Some species, including the northern parula and black-and-white warblers, also cling to tree bark, like nuthatches do.

- The painted redstart, a boldly marked black and red bird, has big white patches on its wings and tail, and it shows them off frequently by fluttering its wings and opening and closing its tail like a paper fan. The American redstart, with an orange, black, and white color scheme in the male and a green and yellow one in the female, also fans its wings and tail to exhibit the colored patches. It's quite a show, if you're lucky enough to catch it.

### In the Yard

- Cover is the watchword: If a small, greenish yellow bird could easily stay out of sight in your yard, you're on the right track. Low, thick growth, 5 to 8 feet tall, will make them feel at home.

- Give them some privacy. Plan an area that you won't be fiddling with and fill it

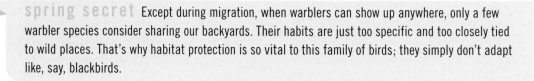

spring secret  Except during migration, when warblers can show up anywhere, only a few warbler species consider sharing our backyards. Their habits are just too specific and too closely tied to wild places. That's why habitat protection is so vital to this family of birds; they simply don't adapt like, say, blackbirds.

with stout, leafy perennials that can take care of themselves, such as mallows and goldenrods, and warblers are more likely to come to call.

- Hedges or closely planted groups of deciduous shrubs are great for warblers. I usually mix in a few small trees and some clumps of grasses, just to make it seem more like a natural "brushy" hedgerow.

- It's not the particular plants but the amount of cover they provide that counts. I'm sure my good luck has more to do with staying out of those areas than with the particular plants growing there.

## Infinite Insects

Bugs, bugs, bugs: That's what warms a wood warbler's heart. Warblers eat insects, and plenty of them. About the size of a chickadee but even more hyperactive, a warbler can easily down several hundred small insects every single day. Just watch a tribe of these flighty little birds move through your flowering crabapple in spring, when they're moving on migration, and you'll see that the insect-eating action is just about nonstop. Except for an occasional snatch of hurried song, it's gobble, gobble, gobble—and we're not talking turkey noises.

I've never seen the quantity spelled out by experts, so I'll take a stab at it from my

## Serious Specialists

Each warbler species has a distinct habitat preference, and they can be mighty picky. Some live in dark rhododendron thickets; others in sun-dappled willows on a riverbank. Some stick to swamps, while others head for clear, rushing streams. Some spend their time high in the tops of 100-foot conifers; others head for sunny pastures dotted with shrubs.

Kirtland's warbler lives in stands of young jack pine (*Pinus banksiana*). But forget trying to attract them to your yard by planting jack pines—Kirtland's warbler only nests in stands of pine that are greater than 80 acres in size. It's so specific that you can actually take a guided tour to this warbler's home grounds in Michigan, the only place where this habitat occurs.

Being so particular has turned out to be a losing strategy for warblers. Many species are declining in numbers, as their habitat is lost both in nesting grounds and wintering areas. And there's even more bad news: Warblers are one of the top targets of cowbirds, the parasitic species that lays its eggs in other birds' nests. As warbler habitat gets carved up by development or road building, cowbirds can more easily reach nests that were once safe deep in the wilds.

If you want to keep track of how the birds are doing or learn more about the ecology and conservation of warblers, a good place to start is the Audubon Society watch list, posted at http://audubon2.org/webapp/watchlist/viewWatchlist.jsp.

*(continued on page 73)*

## Plants to Attract Wood Warblers

| PLANT | TYPE OF PLANT | DESCRIPTION | HARDINESS ZONES |
|---|---|---|---|
| Bayberry (*Myrica pensylvanica*) | Evergreen shrub | Dense branches of small glossy leaves; barely noticeable flowers but striking whitish berries thickly studding the stems. Grows to about 15'. | 3–6 |
| Goldenrod (*Solidago* species and cultivars, such as 'Fireworks') | Perennial flower | Clump-forming perennials, with masses of small golden flowers. Grows to about 4'. | 5–9 |
| Hibiscus or rose mallow (*Hibiscus moscheutos* species and cultivars, such as 'Lady Baltimore', 'Lord Baltimore', and the Disco Belle Series) | Multistemmed shrubby perennials | Knockout flowers the size of a salad plate, in pink, white, or reddish pink; superfast growth. Grows to about 5'. | 5–10 |
| Pussy willow (*Salix discolor* species and cultivars; *Salix gracistyla*; not weeping pussy willow, *Salix caprea* 'Kilmarnock' or 'Pendula') | Deciduous shrub or small tree | Superfast growth, with erect branches hugged by silvery catkins in early spring. Grows to about 10'. | 2–9 |
| Red raspberry (*Rubus* cultivars, such as 'Heritage') | Deciduous shrub | Quickly grows into a large clump or thicket of arching, prickly canes that hold clusters of sweet red berries. Grows to about 6'. | 3–8 |
| Redtwig dogwood (*Cornus alba* species and cultivars) | Deciduous shrub | Multistemmed shrub with open branches; clusters of white flowers followed by white to bluish berries. Grows to about 8'. | 2–8 |

| USE | COMMENTS | OTHER BIRDS ATTRACTED |
|---|---|---|
| Berries | You'll need both a male pollinator and a female for fruit; shop for a plant that already has berries at your nursery, as well as a sparsely fruited male plant, to make sure you get one of each. | Thrushes, waxwings, and other birds; many birds use the multi-stemmed shrubs for cover, for shelter in bad weather, or as travel corridors |
| Insects; cover; possible nest site for common yellowthroat | Spreads fast by roots; may also seed itself. Plant in a mixed hedge with hibiscus and other tough perennials, where its pushy habits are appreciated by common yellowthroats. | Flycatchers, mimic thrushes, vireos, wrens, and other birds; stems used by mountain bluebirds and others as nest material |
| Insects may attract common yellowthroat; possible nest site low among the thick stems | Plant in an undisturbed part of your flower garden, along with other tall, easy-care perennials, such as goldenrod and Shasta daisies, to attract the common yellowthroat. | Orioles and vireos |
| Insects at maturing catkins; fluff for nesting material; Possible nest site for yellow warbler | The world of pussy willows is fun to explore; many native species of willow, such as Hooker's willow (*Salix hookeriana*), produce beautiful catkins, too. | Chickadees, orioles, titmice, vireos, and others |
| Fruit, eaten by some warblers; insects; cover | The hardiest or most cold tolerant of the brambles, this is a good plant for a wild corner or hedge in your yard. Let it go unpruned to provide nesting sites. | Catbird, thrushes, mockingbird, orioles, tanagers, thrashers, wrens, and other birds; catbird, mockingbird, and thrashers may nest in dense canes |
| Insects; some warblers eat berries; excellent for cover | Great fast-growing, wide-spreading plant for cover or hedges. Variegated cultivars are just as appealing to birds. | Mimic thrushes, thrushes, waxwings, and many other birds; may be used as nest site by native sparrows |

# Warbler Dining Spots

With 50-some warbler species roaming various parts of North America, there's a whole battalion of bug-eaters ready to exploit just about every niche. Here's just a small sample of preferred dining spots.

- Black-and-white warblers search tree bark.
- Blackburnian warblers have an affinity for hemlock trees in a mixed forest.
- Yellow warblers and Wilson's warblers patrol willow thickets near water.
- Hooded warblers often hide among rhododendron thickets along clear, rushing streams.
- Prothonotary warblers are fond of Spanish moss–draped cypress trees and other plants of the swamps.
- Worm-eating warblers seek dense, low- to mid-level vegetation, where they can find plenty of caterpillars ("worms").
- Grace's warblers head for pines in the mountains of the Southwest; bay-breasted and blackpoll warblers prefer spruce forests.
- Black-throated gray warblers prefer dry oak woods.

### In the Yard

- Nearly all warblers eat a diet of 100 percent insects. During spring migration, warblers may move through any leafy plants, searching for snacks along their way.
- They're also drawn to flowering crab apples, hawthorns, and other spring-flowering trees and shrubs because the blossoms attract small insects.
- If you ever needed another reason to avoid pesticides, warblers are it. As long as your yard is alive with insects, warblers may stop to visit. Caterpillars (the "worms" from which the worm-eating warbler gets its name) are always a hot item. Crane flies, mayflies, beetles, and other insects, as well as spiders, round out the menu.
- In fall and winter, the myrtle, or yellow-rumped, warbler seeks out bayberries (*Myrica pensylvanica*) to augment the insects. Visit the Atlantic Coast where bayberries are thick, and you're bound to see the little birds.

### At the Feeder

- Suet is a prime draw for yellow-rumped warblers; other species are learning its charms, too.
- Mealworms are gaining popularity with folks who feed birds, because they work like magic to tempt unusual birds to the table. And they're gaining popularity with birds, including warblers, who are learning to look for them at feeders.
- Cape May warblers, orange-crowned warblers, and some others sip sap in the wild. Now that they've figured out that sweet stuff is in our nectar feeders, they're showing up as customers there, too.

## Bayberry Bounty

Bayberry-scented candles are a staple in our homes at Christmastime, but on the bush, those waxy bayberries are ideal tidbits for tiny warblers. *Myrica pensylvanica* is an evergreen shrub that grows to about 15 feet tall, with leaves that are wonderfully aromatic when crushed. The flowers are barely noticeable, but the striking, whitish gray berries thickly stud the stems in fall and winter—and draw yellow-rumped warblers like the proverbial magnet. Palm warblers passing through to winter grounds in the South are fond of them, too.

You'll need both a male pollinator and a female plant for your bayberry bushes to bear fruit. Shop for a plant that already has berries at your nursery, as well as a sparsely fruited male plant, to make sure you get one of each. It's hardy in Zones 3 through 6. South of Zone 6, try wax myrtle (*Myrica cerifera*).

In addition to warblers, waxwings, thrushes, and other birds may also gobble up the bountiful berries. And many birds will use the multistemmed shrubs for year-round cover and as shelter in bad weather.

own observations: I'm guessing that 99 percent of the diet of all of the wood warblers, taken as a whole, is nothin' but bugs. The last little bit is an occasional sip of nectar (orange-crowned warblers and a few other species may sip sap or even visit a nectar feeder, on occasion), and a few bites of small berries (yellow-rumped warblers are the main berry eaters in the bunch).

## THE FLYCATCHERS

Next time you come across a cloud of swarming gnats, give yourself a little test: See if you can isolate one of the insects and follow only its movements with your eyes.

Like watching a snowflake in a blizzard, isn't it? Following a flying insect is just about impossible for us to do, but it's child's play for a flycatcher.

No wonder flycatchers always look so alert. They have to be, to zero in on a single flying insect. These birds are the bane of

mosquitoes, gnats, and plenty of other flying insects. They're fast and agile in the air, and they turn on a dime when they're in pursuit.

All of the more than three dozen species in this big family share the same style of feeding: perch, pursue; perch, pursue. A

The willow flycatcher looks just like the alder flycatcher, but its *fitz-bew!* call is distinctive.

The great crested flycatcher weaves a crinkly snakeskin into its nest. Why? The birds haven't told us yet.

flycatcher sits alertly on a perch, then darts after a flying insect, grabs it, and returns to a perch. Repeat until the belly is full!

## Perfect Posture

When I was in junior high, my most dreaded class was home economics, where a dragon lady of a teacher screamed at us over stitches that weren't fine enough or popovers that were soggy in the middle. Years later, when I came back to sewing and cooking on my own, I was surprised to find out that they were actually fun to do, even if the results were less than perfect.

I can't say the same for the posture lessons that were part of those classes. At the end of the class, we'd stand in a line and settle a heavy book just so on our heads. Then we'd walk around the room, gliding

like queens. Or at least that was the idea. My book invariably landed on the floor with a loud bang—until I figured out that if I wore my ponytail really high on the back of my head, I could cheat and rest the book against it.

What does perfect posture have to do with flycatchers? Every species looks as though it spent years under the tutelage of my home ec teacher, getting that regal bearing just right. Good posture for a flycatcher looks just like that ideal I never quite managed: An erect bearing, a straightened spine, and a head held high.

## Sorting Out the Species

Flycatchers can be small, medium, large, or extra-large, but all sit erect and alert when perched. Some species, such as the vermilion flycatcher of the Southwest and the lovely salmon-bellied Say's phoebe of the West, are spectacularly colored. But most are greenish or grayish, and many are so hard to tell apart by looks that birdwatchers listen for their voices to determine who's who.

- A few flycatchers, including the kingbirds and great crested flycatcher, are attention-grabbers, with sharp whistles or whoops.

- A few species, including the phoebes and the peewees, very kindly say their own names. (Well, they do if you use your imagination.)

- Most flycatchers have unexciting songs, often just a repeated pair of syllables that blend into the general symphony of birdsong. Careful listening to these calls

## Faux Flycatchers

Once you start looking for flycatching behavior, you'll notice that it's a habit with other birds, too.

When mayflies or other insects are hatching and rising from a stream or lake, a flock of cedar waxwings often settles in trees along the water, taking turns darting out and snatching a bite on the wing, and then returning to a perch until the next mayfly comes along.

Red-headed woodpeckers display the same behavior from the top of a utility pole or other perch. So do kinglets, warblers, gnatcatchers, bushtits, chickadees, hummingbirds, and others.

These birds are "flycatching." But they're not flycatchers.

True flycatchers depend on this style of feeding most of the time, while other birds flycatch only now and then.

can help you ID the look-alike species. Consult a field guide to learn the common calls of the species in your area.

## Backyard Flycatchers

Flycatchers flit across the country, showing up just about everywhere flying insects are found. Each species has its own range, with some covering half the country and others limited to a tiny corner of a single state.

But of all the many flycatchers, only a few species are likely to show up in backyards. The rest prefer wild places, such as woodsy spots along streams, or wide-open farm fields. The kind of habitat near your house affects which flycatchers you might see at your own place. If you live on a ranch in the West, or next to a forest, or beside a lake, your chances of seeing more flycatchers are way better than someone who lives in a city.

Most small species hang out in brushy areas, some haunt the woodlands, and many stick to the rich hunting grounds near water. Some are birds of open country, such as the dapper kingbirds and the incredible scissor-tailed flycatcher, who trails a deeply forked tail that's nearly twice as long as its body.

Look for these interesting birds sitting at attention in your yard.

- Ash-throated flycatcher

- Great crested flycatcher

- Kingbirds, including eastern and western

**spring secret** Among my favorite things about spring are the "surprise birds" that slip in when I'm not looking. The eastern phoebe falls into that category for me: While I remember to keep an eye out for martins, house wrens, and other noisy or flashy arrivals, such as orioles, I generally forget to watch for the phoebe. The phoebe reminds me he's back by saying his name, sort of: *fee-brr-reeep, fee-burr*. What a treat to hear that familiar burry whistle for the first time since the previous year!

- Phoebes, including eastern, black, and Say's

Flycatchers survive almost entirely on insects (with a small helping of fruit and berries on the side). So when cold weather nears, spelling the demise of their diet, the birds hightail it to warmer areas, from Mexico southward.

When insects are once again active in spring, flycatchers move northward.

## Sit Tight

Flycatchers aren't particularly secretive, but they're definitely "background" birds. Most species are easy to overlook, even though they usually perch in conspicuous places— on the tip of a tree, say, or on a dead branch. When you spot a perched bird with good posture, watch its tail: Most flycatchers have the habit of raising and lowering their tails while perched, and many species raise their head feathers when they get excited.

## At-Home Habitat

Where are multitudes of flying insects most likely to be found? Near water, when mayflies, mosquitoes, and other insects that have spent their early life stages underwater become adults and break through the surface into the air. Another good place is over grassy fields, where grasshoppers and crickets abound. Flycatchers are common in both places.

Flycatchers also patrol forests; that's where you'll find the ash-throated, brown crested, and great crested flycatchers. Desert species are found in sagebrush and chaparral; flycatchers of the Great Plains are found in fields or in trees or bushes along watercourses.

## Hot on the Trail

You know those chase scenes on TV nature shows, with the cheetah or lion tearing after big game, zigging and zagging close behind? I usually switch the channel on these scenes before the denouement.

A flycatcher chase has that same drama on a small scale.

When a flycatcher is catching flies—or bees, wasps, dragonflies, butterflies, or a horde of other flying insects—it's just as focused as any cheetah. Of course, it helps to have a mouth that works like a dustpan and broom—flycatcher beaks open w-i-d-e, and special short, stiff feathers around the beak help sweep the insects right in.

## Backyard Matchup

An ordinary yard, with a mix of trees, shrubs, and open spaces, suits most flycatchers, as long as there's plenty to eat. If you have a garden pool, you can fringe its edge with shrubby willows to recreate a smidgen of naturalistic habitat. Or you can plant a hedge of mixed fruiting shrubs and trees to supply food and create a good habitat. See "Plants to Attract Flycatchers" on page 78 for a few good candidates to add to your landscape.

## An Insect-Filled Menu

A smorgasbord of insects fills the beaks of flycatchers. Gnats, flies, bees, wasps, butterflies, moths, treehoppers: It seems like anything with wings is fair game. Spiders go down the hatch, too. Even giant cicadas aren't safe; the larger flycatchers are happy to make a meal of them.

When berries ripen, many flycatchers make a beeline for the fruity change of pace. Wild blackberries, elderberries, mistletoe berries, honeysuckle berries, and other small, soft berries are favored.

Flying insects are a little hard to provide at the feeding station—unless you have plenty of rotting fruit to nourish a happy colony of fruit flies. So you'll need to depend on Mother Nature to provide the temptations that will draw flycatchers to your backyard. A pond is a terrific tool, especially one that's large enough to support a hatch of mayflies or a few broods of mosquitoes.

On the other hand, mosquitoes aren't a backyard visitor I really want to see more of. Got plenty already, thank you! So I focus on attracting insects that I enjoy, too—butterflies.

## Perfect Perches

Ever notice how your eye goes right to the man-made objects in a garden? Flycatchers respond just as fast to man-made perches. In most cases, a tall perch—6 feet high or better—is preferable to a shorter one of only 3 or 4 feet, because it affords the bird a better view.

Add a few of these to your yard, and see if you get any takers.

- Iron shepherd's crook–type hooks
- Metal or wood arbors and arches
- Metal or wood trellises
- Stand-alone posts with decorative finials that are securely attached and a suitable shape for a bird to grip onto. A fleur-de-lis is fine; a ball is not.
- Bamboo teepees, such as bean towers
- Wire or twig structures, such as tuteurs
- Wash lines

## Plants to Attract Flycatchers

These plants either attract butterflies and other flying insects or supply fruit, nests materials, and perching places for flycatchers in your neighborhood.

| PLANT | TYPE OF PLANT | DESCRIPTION | HARDINESS ZONES |
|---|---|---|---|
| Thornless blackberries (*Rubus* × 'Chester') | Deciduous, suckering shrub | Fast-growing stems; bountiful, juicy fruit. Grows to about 6' tall. | 5–9 |
| Goldenrod (*Solidago* species and cultivars) | Perennial plants | Clusters of tightly packed, tiny yellow flowers. Many goldenrods are aggressive spreaders; best in a naturalistic garden. Most grow 3–4' tall. | 5–9 |
| Willow (*Salix* species, not corkscrew type) | Shrubs to medium-size trees | Long, thin leaves; deciduous; twigs become colorful in late winter; catkin flowers mature to fuzz. Grow from 6–50' tall, depending on species; choose one that fits your yard. | 3–9 |
| Milkweeds (*Asclepias* species) | Perennial plants | Varies by species, but all forms clump and many spread by roots. Flowers are complex and most are deliciously fragrant; mature into seedpods filled with silken seed "parachutes." Grow to 4' tall. | 3–9 |

Providing nectar-filled flowers and caterpillar host plants is a great way to attract flycatchers to—sorry, butterflies—a feast. A couple of other tricks may also help draw in flycatchers.

## In the Yard

- Plant a butterfly garden of nectar flowers and include host plants, such as broccoli (for cabbage whites), for butterflies in your gardens.

| USE | COMMENTS | OTHER BIRDS ATTRACTED |
|---|---|---|
| Fruit eaten by larger flycatchers, including great crested; stems supply perches | Thorny blackberry bushes are a favorite hideout for the brown thrasher and catbird, but perching flycatchers and human berry pickers will appreciate the smooth, thornless canes of this cultivar. | Catbird, jays, mockingbird, thrashers, thrushes, wrens, and other birds; catbird, mockingbird, and thrashers may nest. |
| Flying insects in spring | Stiff stems stand tall all winter for cover; cut them down to the ground in very early spring. | Vireos, warblers, and other birds; native sparrows eat seeds in wintertime; indigo bunting, common yellowthroat, or other small birds may nest in stems of a substantial clump of goldenrod. |
| Nest sites, nest materials | Experiment with species that are native to your region. | Chickadees, orioles, titmice, vireos, and warblers glean insects from catkins and foliage and may collect nest material. |
| Nest material; butterflies and insects for food | Collect common milkweed pods in fall and offer the fluff as nesting material in spring. | Orioles; hummingbirds seek nectar. |

- Install perches near flower gardens, such as a shepherd's crook or a stand-alone metal trellis.
- Plant an elderberry bush for small, juicy berries.

- Put up a nest box for cavity-nesting flycatchers, mounting the box at least 6 feet above the ground on a tree or post. The ash-throated flycatcher can use a bluebird house; give the great crested a

## Wobbly Wings

I saw my first scissor-tailed flycatcher in unusual conditions: He was hundreds of miles off course, and drunk as a skunk. The bird showed up in eastern Pennsylvania one autumn, far from its usual haunts in Oklahoma and Texas. He'd taken refuge in a roadside hedgerow that was thick with wild cherries. The fruit was past its prime—so far past that it had started to ferment, which didn't bother Mr. Flycatcher in the least. Although he was already a little too wobbly to fly, he kept on swilling down the fruit.

larger box with 6 × 6-inch floor, 9-inch-tall walls, and a 1¾-inch entrance hole whose top is about 8 inches above the bottom of the box. Provide soft, fluffy nest materials.

### At the Feeder

- No matter how tempting a spread I put out, flycatchers would rather find their own food, it seems. But I keep trying (and so can you)! I still hope to see a flycatcher sampling the mealworms someday.

## Home Decorating

Flycatcher nests are beautiful creations. The dainty, woven cups include many soft materials in the mix. And that's where you come in. Although these birds are perfectly capable of collecting their own building materials, they may also investigate treasures that you supply. Bird-supply stores and catalogs have made it easy by selling pre-filled containers of such materials, but I still like to gather my own fluffy materials, like these.

- Fresh moss—the long-fibered types that often grow in shady spots
- Dried sphagnum or Spanish moss
- Twists of cotton, from natural—not synthetic—cotton balls
- Short 6- to 8-inch sections of cotton twine that I've untwisted
- Milkweed fluff, from inside the seedpods
- Cattail fluff
- Soft feathers

Stuff an empty suet feeder with your offerings, so the birds can see what looks interesting and easily tug the material out

 **spring secret** A butterfly garden is one of the best ways to attract flycatchers to your yard. If you plant flowers and host plants that hairstreaks, skippers, and many other nectar-seeking butterflies like to visit, such as zinnias and common oregano, you'll have a good chance of catching the attention of a flycatcher, too.

through the grid. Keep in mind that birds only use a little bit of these materials in their nests. Your pile of goodies won't disappear overnight—in fact, you may barely notice that anything at all is missing. Somewhere, though, there may be a flycatcher family keeping cozy, thanks to you.

## Birdhouse Nesters

A few species of flycatchers—including the largest ones—seem to have an independent streak when it comes to nesting. Instead of building a nest in a shrub or tree, they seek out a cavity to call home—which means they may adopt a nest box!

The great crested flycatcher is your most likely tenant. But you may also have luck attracting an ash-throated, olivaceous, sulphur-bellied, or western flycatcher as a resident, if you live within their nesting range.

While the biggest flycatchers head for a birdhouse, others look for a ledge. The western kingbird, black phoebe, Say's phoebe, and eastern phoebe (all part of the flycatcher clan) often build their nests on or around houses and outbuildings, supporting the nest on a door sill or other small ledge, or plastering it to an eave. Try a simple small, flat shelf for these birds, 4 to 6 inches wide and 8 inches long, to which they can plaster the mud foundation of their nest. Nail the nesting shelf to an outside wall of your own house or an outbuilding, at about the height of the sill over the door. Choose a location that is not exposed to direct sun or to rain.

# MOVING INTO SUMMER

The spring season ends with the arrival of the last of the spring migrants, the beautiful, brightly colored "neotropical" birds that wintered in Central and South America. When orioles, tanagers, and grosbeaks arrive, summer is just around the corner.

In the next section, you'll learn how bird life shifts once migration is finished. As the days lengthen, the focus is completely on raising a family. Birds change their habits, and their diets, to match the new season. In Part 2: Secrets for Summer, you'll learn how to fine-tune your yard and your feeders to tie in with this new cycle.

## Home Sweet Home

Wrens are famous for picking odd places to build nests, but cavity-nesting flycatchers can be eccentric, too. House gutters often attract their efforts, and all you can do is keep your fingers crossed that there's not a deluge before the birds are done nesting. They've been known to build nests in the scoop of a bulldozer, in pipes stuck in the ground, in exhaust pipes of cars, and in pants hanging on a wash line. And we worry about whether our birdhouses are good enough?

# SECRETS FOR SUMMER

## SUMMER: FAMILY TIME

Summer means family life for birds. This is when you'll get a peek into how busy birds really can be. Between weaving a nest—try it sometime, using only your "beak"—and keeping a batch of babies warm, well fed, and safe from predators, birds have a lot going on these days.

Any bird you see in your yard during this season is a nesting bird. That means it's a species that raises its family in your region. By following the tips in this section, you can boost the chances of successful breeding, no matter where the birds nest. But—way more fun!—we can also encourage those birds to nest in our own yards and bring their fledglings to our feeders.

This season is also prime time for natural food—insects and berries are at their peak, so birds are much less attracted to your feeder, no matter how fine a spread of seeds you offer. No need to pack those feeders away, though: Just adjust your menu, and your expectations, to suit the season.

In this part of *Backyard Bird Secrets for Every Season*, you'll learn how to take advantage of this seasonal cycle. By offering nest materials that suit the needs of resident birds, adding plants with summer potential for nest sites and natural food, and shifting the feeder menu to better serve families, you can make your yard a destination for birds living the family life.

The summer season, which in bird land runs from May through July, also sets the stage for another easy way to attract birds. The hot, dry days of summer make water harder to find, so providing a reliable source will be a big draw. This is a great time to explore birdbaths, fountains, and other ways of offering water that will please you and the birds.

# CHAPTER 5

# SUMMER IS
# FOR FAMILIES

I T  S E E M S  L I K E just yesterday that you were delighting in the huge flock of goldfinches swarming your feeders and singing from the trees. You were accustomed to enjoying a half-dozen cardinals at one time, as well as a small flock of noisy jays. Juncos and sparrows were a constant presence on the ground below your feeder and beneath your hedge. Your lawn was alive with robins.

Then, in just a short time—it may seem like overnight, but it actually takes a few weeks—it all changed.

Your feeders and your yard are almost bare of birds now. The juncos are gone, and nearly all of the sparrows seem to have gone with them. Instead of a bunch of red cardinals, you have two. As for jays, you rarely even see them anymore.

Is it you? Has your seed gone bad? Where'd everybody go?

Try not to take it personally. It's just part of the natural cycle. In summer, birds switch their focus. Instead of spending their time hanging out, they're getting down to some serious parenting.

## IT'S THAT TIME
## OF THE SEASON

Before there can be a family, there must be a couple. Nesting season begins with earlier rituals that set the stage for a Mommy and a Daddy to get together.

In Chapter 1, we talked about birds that nest early, beginning in spring. Only a handful of species get an early start—mainly

Showing the world that they're a couple, the female cardinal begs for food, and her partner obliges.

## The Summer Bird Season

When does "summer" begin in your area? Since bird behavior is connected to the seasonal timing of natural foods, plants, and weather, the specific date for the start of "summer" varies from one part of the country to the next. Birds don't pay attention to the calendar date that marks the official start of summer. Just as with other seasons, the timing of the summer cycle for birds depends on the climate of your area.

The distance that migrating birds must travel to reach your backyard plays a big part in determining the date they arrive.

- For a large part of the country, summer—by the bird calendar—begins around mid-May and lasts until about mid-August.
- If you live in the northern tier of the country or at a high altitude, your backyard birds will get a later start on the season, and their nesting season will probably end sooner.
- If you live in the southern part of the country, your birds may begin showing summer behavior weeks earlier. Louisiana's robins, for example, may already be fledging their first batch of nestlings, while Michigan's robins are still on the wing heading north to their homelands.

the cavity nesters that choose a natural hole or birdhouse as home.

Many more species wait until around the beginning of May to start their breeding season. These are what I call the summer nesters, even though the solstice is still weeks away by the calendar.

## HOMEBODIES

As spring slides into summer, the scene changes dramatically in our yards and at our feeders. Our loyal friends that have been with us all through winter and early spring change their habits, and the new arrivals take up homemaking.

- Many of the most abundant feeder visitors—the flocks of juncos and native sparrows, the goldfinches that gather in growing numbers in spring—move along during migration to more northerly homes.
- Year-round birds—chickadees, titmice, jays, cardinals, woodpeckers, and other

**summer secret** Migration is over by now, so the orioles, thrashers, cardinals, and other birds we see in summer are the species that will be with us for the duration of the nesting season. Focus your efforts on those species, to encourage them to choose your backyard as home. See "20 Likely Nesters" on page 93 for some possible summer residents.

The male black-headed grosbeak is much flashier than his mate, who blends into the foliage when she sits on the nest.

regulars—desert our feeders, too. It's not because they suddenly decide they don't like sunflower seeds or suet. It's because they've paired off and dispersed to nesting territories in the neighborhood.

- Spring migrants that delighted us with a stopover for several weeks also move on. Some travel to farther reaches—such as purple finches and red-breasted nuthatches that move on to higher altitudes or northern homes. Some leave our yards to find a suitable habitat for nesting—indigo buntings to the fields, bluebirds to woods' edges, western grosbeaks to thickets near water.

- Some spring migrants, including hummingbirds and wrens, may simply move over to a neighbor's yard, if there's a more suitable spot there to make their home.

## COURTSHIP

I've never been lucky enough—yet—to have a Romeo sing me love songs from below the balcony, but I can completely understand why that would melt a woman's heart. Maybe those love-struck Romeos take lessons from the birds, because, after all, their courtship begins with music.

Many songbirds mate for life, although "life" in the bird world may be only a few years, depending on the circumstances that befall the birds in question. Still, each summer the ritual is reenacted, with males winning the females' favor through their singing abilities.

## Song and Dance Men

It's biology in action we're listening to: A male bird who boldly sings from an open perch is showing the female that he is a good choice because, first of all, he's healthy enough to have a vibrant song, and second, because he is capable of defending the family.

Bright plumage enters into the mating game, too. In early summer, male birds look their best. Duded up in their brightest colors, they engage in postures or dances that show off those flashy feathers.

## Tuning Up

The breeding season begins with courtship, a ritual that year-round residents begin in spring to early summer. When you notice that birds are beginning to sing, rather than simply chip or chirp, it's a sign that the breeding hormones are kicking into gear for at least some species. Chickadees are often the first to slip into songbird mode, with a paired-note call: *fee-bee, fee-bay.* Listen for the clear whistle of a cardinal or tufted titmouse, too, or the buzzy trill of a junco near the feeder.

Soon, those start-up soloists will be joined by every bird voice in your area. By the time migrants arrive on the scene, every bird on the block will be singing its little heart out. Instead of the whistle of a lone titmouse or the loud shouts of a flicker, either of which may have had center stage to themselves a few weeks earlier, you'll now hear a true symphony of songbirds.

Many of us, even the most dedicated

"Look what a great catch I am," the common grackle screeches, showcasing his fine feathers in the sun.

birdwatchers, have difficulty picking out individual voices or species from the crowd, because that chorus is so complex. I try to get to know each bird's voice as that species starts singing: That makes it easy to notice the new arrivals when they chime in.

Morning is prime time for the concert. Robins are often the earliest voice of the morning, followed soon after by wrens. Once birds start singing, you may hear a

## The Wall of Sound

Think back, rock 'n' rollers—or oldies-radio listeners: It's 1963, and the Ronettes are working to a crescendo in "Be My Baby." Instant hook, instant hit, thanks to producer Phil Spector's innovative "wall of sound," a richly layered background of echoing orchestral instruments joined with guitars.

On a June morning, when breeding season is at its peak, the full-strength chorus of birdsong has that same effect. At first, I find myself just getting lost in it, letting the combined voices wash over me while I revel in the "wall of bird sound." Then, having a brain that loves to sort and classify, I try to separate the blend of voices into species.

If you're a symphony-goer or a musician yourself, you can think of this little game as trying to pick out the clarinet, say, or following the musical line of the mezzo-soprano in a Bach choir—or of heavily mascaraed Veronica Bennett (later Ronnie Spector) on the radio.

summer secret Male birds sing to win the favors of a female. But they also sing to mark the edges of the land they've claimed. One of the main functions of a male bird's songs is to tell other birds of that species where the boundaries of his territory lie. He's singing a series of "No Trespassing" signs, in effect. If the warning isn't enough of a deterrent, the male chases and attacks invaders. Watch for such skirmishes to see who's nesting in your neighborhood.

snatch of song any time of day and another small symphony before sunset.

## Claiming a Territory

Sharing space is the name of the game in fall, winter, and early spring. Birds that are not nesting have no need to defend their territorial claim against possible competition for a female, so they forage together.

In the colder months, when food is scarce and mating hormones are not in gear, birds gather wherever there's a reliable food supply. Feeding territories are much larger than nesting territories, so you may host birds from a wide area in your bird-friendly backyard.

Come nesting season, that all changes. All of a sudden, birds switch from an attitude of "Come one, come all" to "Keep out!"

### The Big Backyard

That pair of robins in your lilac bush may seem like they're yours alone, but unless you

summer secret A short, fast, forceful burst of song seems like an unusual reaction to a predator or other threat—"Oooh! Don't sing at me!"—but I suppose it must work. Otherwise, birds would've stopped trying it, you'd reason.

You'll sometimes hear a quick few notes at night, when predators are prowling under the cover of darkness. It's as if the bird is hard-wired to respond with music whenever its partner or family needs protection.

The alarm note or call is used by both male and female birds. It's usually a short, loud "chip!" or a series of chatterings or chippings. It sounds agitated, nervous, excited—and it is. Birds use this call when a cat, snake, or other predator is anywhere inside the boundaries of their nesting territory, or when a human is getting too close to their nest.

Other birds in the same area rush to help when they hear an alarm call, no matter what species is making it. Banding together to drive away predators is a behavior that ultimately benefits all of the nesting species within that area, so they're quick to rush to each other's defense. That's why I go investigate, too, when I hear an alarm call: It's a great way to find out who has a nest in the area because you see which birds have gathered and where they disperse to when the danger has passed. I often lend a hand, too, shooing away the neighbor's cat or urging a snake to take another path.

## Still a Mystery

There are a lot of gaps in the scientific data on nesting bird territories because it's simply impossible to study so many birds in so many different habitats. No one yet knows what exactly it is that causes birds to claim a territory of a certain size—let alone just how big that territory is. So feel free to come up with your own theories as you watch your summer birds.

| BIRDERS BELIEVE | FACTS OF THE MATTER |
|---|---|
| The size of a species' territory is determined by the availability of food within it. | MAYBE. It may be a factor—or it may not. No one knows for sure, since it's mighty hard to count insects or otherwise inventory food supplies within a territory. |
| The territory size is the same, or nearly so, for all pairs of that species. | FALSE. Not so. In one study, one pair of chipping sparrows claimed 7.6 acres; another pair—in the same region—a mere 2.7; and four pairs of eastern kingbirds showed a spread from 14 acres to 35. |
| Experts know the sizes of various species' territory. Some sources, for example, note that a pair of bluebirds or titmice claim about 2.5 to 5 acres; a pair of nuthatches, 20 acres or more. | FALSE. Most of these published territory sizes are just guesses (or "crude approximations," as one researcher put it), and sources may simply repeat the info without verifying it. Different pairs of the same species, studies have found, claim territories of varying sizes—and, as we learned above, we don't even know what the "usual" size is for any bird. |
| The territory claimed at the onset of nesting—when the birds are building their nest and laying eggs—is used by the parent birds throughout the season. | FALSE. Territories shrink as parents turn to feeding the young. The territory actually used then is often much smaller. |
| The male bird defends the entire territory by singing around its boundaries and chasing intruders. | PARTLY TRUE. Species vary in this behavior: Some males defend only the area around the nest, while others defend the entire area used for mating, feeding, and nesting. |

The eastern kingbird is smaller than a robin, but it may claim a nesting territory covering several square miles.

have a really big backyard, chances are you share those robins with other neighbors. Birds don't pay attention to our property lines when they claim a territory, so there's lots of overlap.

Backyard bird species claim different amounts of home ground. A pair of house wrens, for instance, may need only one big backyard (and we hope it's ours!) to suit the needs of their family. Robins, too, often hold small territories. But a white-breasted nuthatch may claim a few blocks of the neighborhood, plus that city park down the street. As for a pair of pileated woodpeckers—you

may be sharing these big red-crested birds with folks a mile or more away.

## Where's the Best Place?

Summer nesters build their homes under the open sky, instead of in a knothole or nest box. Well, not under the sky, exactly—a sheltered site, tucked among branches or within a clump of tall grass, is chosen by nearly every nesting bird.

Those eggs and nestlings are precious. Selecting a site where they will be shielded from view goes a long way toward keeping them safe.

Birds seeking nest sites look for these features.

- Good-size shade trees, such as oaks, maples, and many others, to provide sturdy supports up and out of reach of ground-dwelling predators.

- Small, medium, or large conifers of any kind to hide a nest in and which are difficult to penetrate.

- Sheltering shrubs, especially in a connected group, including foundation shrubs, to help disguise the location of the nest as the parents exit and enter.

- Thorny shrubs, such as roses or barberries, to deter predators.

- Untrimmed hedges, where a nest won't be disturbed.

**summer secret** Planting a hedge interspersed with a few small trees along your property line may help keep birds within your yard. A male bird setting up territory may stop at that hedge, check out the singing perches, and make it part of the boundary line for his territory, too.

## Unexpected Exposure

I'm always on the lookout for bird nests, and over the years, I've sometimes seen a sheltered nest site suddenly became exposed to view. The parents are always highly uncomfortable and on full alert, but they don't desert the nest.

Here are some unfortunate circumstances that can suddenly put a bird's well-hidden nest right out in the open.

- Gypsy moth depredations, which can defoliate most or all of a forest or hedgerow, can reveal many nesting birds. I've spotted vireos, wood warblers, rose-breasted grosbeaks, and many others sitting on their nests in full view.

- Some of the saddest cases I've seen happened along roadsides, where maintenance crews sprayed herbicides. I say saddest because, to my way of thinking, the herbicides were unnecessary—or at the least, could've been timed to a later date, when birds weren't hatching a family. Those exposures included indigo buntings, lazuli buntings, many native sparrows, goldfinches, common yellowthroats, and others.

- I've seen grassland birds in farm fields suffer the same fate. The advent of "no-till" farming results in a full-sweep application of herbicide—right at nesting time. Left in full view were nesting meadowlarks, horned larks, dickcissels, and many native sparrows.

- Red-tailed hawks often use the same nest year after year. One pair I watched returned to their nest in a deciduous tree that had died over the winter—and used it anyway. Predators weren't the problem: The intense sun and heat were the danger. Both parents took turns shielding the nestlings with their outspread wings. You could practically hear them say "Whew!" when their youngsters successfully left the nest. The parent birds did not make the same mistake the following year.

- Dense woody vines, such as honey-suckle, sweet autumn clematis, or wisteria, with a tangle of stems and branches that make approach tricky for predators.

- Relatively undisturbed garden areas of ornamental plants, such as perennials or naturalistic meadow gardens, to give the family privacy.

- Strawberry beds or other low vegetation that can disguise a nest on the ground, such as a song sparrow's.

- Raspberry and other bramble patches, to deter predators and provide a food source.

## The Beauty of Birds' Eggs

I loved my new old house in southern Indiana before I got any farther than the salmon-pink sunporch, preserved just as it was painted back in the late 1950s. The mint green kitchen took some getting used to, but the bedroom was another instant hit: It's robin's egg blue.

The not-quite-turquoise blue-green hue of real robin eggs used to be so familiar that most people could instantly envision what color was being referred to. Nowadays, though, many of us don't have a clue what color a robin's eggs are, let alone those of a blue jay, cardinal, goldfinch, or any other common backyard bird.

The birds still nest in our backyards, but modern life has moved indoors for much of the time, and the old lore isn't being handed down much anymore.

Still, it's never too late to learn. Try these tips to get a general idea of which egg is whose.

- The easiest way to sort out the owners of those eggs is to see the parent bird at the nest. It's very tempting to sneak a peek into a bird's nest, but you can easily cause the family's demise if you aren't very careful. (It's also against federal law to interfere with nesting birds, in case your own conscience doesn't provide enough of a deterrent.) Always observe from a distance of at least 6 feet, and don't peek frequently, so that your scent doesn't alert predators to the nest's location.

## 20 Likely Nesters

If your yard gets the seal of approval as a summer nest site, you may get to host any of these birds. Most have very widespread breeding ranges; check a comprehensive field guide to find out for sure if they make their homes where you do.

These species build their nests in trees, shrubs, vines, and on the ground. For more info on backyard nesters that build in nest boxes or natural cavities, see page 26.

1. Cardinal
2. Catbird
3. House finch
4. American goldfinch
5. Grackles
6. Grosbeaks
7. Blue jay
8. Juncos
9. Mockingbird
10. Orioles
11. Robin
12. Chipping sparrow
13. Song sparrow
14. Brown thrasher
15. Hermit thrush
16. Towhees
17. Yellow warbler
18. Cedar waxwing
19. Carolina wren
20. Common yellowthroat

An undisturbed patch of prairie or meadow is an ideal home site for a pair of ground-nesting native sparrows.

## Unscrambling the Clues

Finding an intact bird egg on the ground is a thrill. We don't often get to hold such a small, perfect package. More frequently, we find broken eggs or empty shells in our yards. Whether they're whole or just an empty half, all "misplaced" bird eggs have a story to tell.

- Whole or broken bird eggs on the ground, or empty pieces of shell, don't necessarily mean the nest is near. On the other hand, it doesn't hurt to carefully look around, and down, and up—there may be a nest nearby.

- A few bird species can recognize the eggs of parasitic cowbirds, which sneak into another species' nest, lay an egg, and then leave it for the other birds to incubate and raise. Blue jays and brown thrashers give such eggs an unceremonious heave-ho.

- Somehow, it seems, parent birds can recognize a defective egg. I used to think that was just an old wives' tale until I put a fallen cardinal egg back in the nest a few feet above it. Within minutes, the female returned and deliberately maneuvered the same egg over the side again.

- Jays, grackles, crows, and occasionally mockingbirds or thrashers carry off and eat other birds' eggs. If an egg holds remains of the yellow yolk or is whole, it

- Color is another big clue, but many birds lay similarly colored eggs. You'll probably need to use other clues in addition to color.

- Small birds lay small eggs; larger species, larger eggs. A chickadee-size bird egg is about ½ inch from tip to end; a robin-size bird egg, a little bigger than 1 inch.

- All eggs are oval, but shape varies from one species to another. Some have wide bottoms and an abruptly pointed tip; some are nearly round, or gradually tapering; others are more uniformly oval.

summer secret  A good food supply can encourage birds to nest in the area, so stock your feeders with treats tailored to the tastes of your nesting birds. (See Chapter 7 for info.)

Birds are secretive about their nests because the eggs are tempting food for animals, snakes, and some birds.

## Nest Materials

An inviting yard with plenty of cover and available nest sites is a big enticement for birds to make their homes with you. If you already have a yard with established shrubs, trees, hedges, and conifers, you're halfway there. If you're just starting, though, it can take a year or longer to achieve that kind of habitat.

While you're waiting for birds to give your place the seal of approval, try another trick to sweeten the deal: Offer them a plenitude of nest-building materials.

## Construction Crew

Just as our feeders aren't strictly necessary for birds, neither is an offering of nesting materials. Birds are perfectly capable of finding their own twigs, fibers, and other construction materials.

But a collection of tempting materials may catch their eyes—and bring them to your yard to "shop." Even if they choose to build that nest at your neighbor's place, you'll get to enjoy watching the orioles, vireos, and other birds sort through the goodies you've put out for them, make selections, and carry them off.

may have been dropped by a feathered thief being hotly pursued.

- Other predators, including raccoons and opossums, may carry off eggs and drop them in transit.

- Parent birds remove eggshells when the nestlings hatch. They carry the pieces away from the nest before dropping them, so as not to betray the location of their home.

**summer secret** Starling eggs are easy to confuse with robin eggs. Starling eggs are paler blue and slightly bigger. Robin's eggs are a rich aqua shade, leaning toward greenish blue. Best bet: Peek into a robin's nest and see for yourself. Don't touch the nest, the eggs, or even the shrub or other support of the nest—your scent may draw a predator to the nest. And don't linger or disturb the family. If the parent birds are agitated, back off and leave them in peace.

# Egg ID Guide

Whose egg did you find in your yard this morning? Check this guide to eggs of common backyard nesters to find the answer.

| BIRD | EGG DESCRIPTION |
|---|---|
| Cardinal | Pale bluish white with reddish brown and lavender speckles and spots, which thicken at wide end |
| Chickadee | White or cream eggs with reddish or light brown speckles. |
| Brown-headed cowbird | White with flecks of brown and tan all over, heavier toward larger end |
| Crows | Huge greenish blue egg heavily splotched with dark brown |
| House finch | Pale blue with fine dark speckles at larger end |
| Blue jay | Greenish buff with sparse olive-brown spots |
| Scrub jay | Light greenish with olive spots at larger end, or grayish with brown spots |
| Slate-colored junco | White oval with band of reddish brown speckles at wide end; sometimes entire egg is speckled |
| Robin | Robin's egg blue (aqua) |
| Chipping sparrow | Like a mini robin's egg, but with blackish brown freckles at wide end |
| English or house sparrow | Whitish, heavily marked with gray and black splotches |
| Song sparrow | White or greenish white, heavily splotched with brown; much variation in amount of markings |
| Starling | Pale bluish green, similar to robin egg but slightly smaller |
| Brown thrasher | Whitish to greenish white, speckled with fine reddish dots |
| Carolina wren | White with pale reddish brown and purplish speckles, which thicken at wide end |
| House wren | Pinkish white heavily speckled with tiny reddish brown dots |

## Everlasting Mud

The American robin, eastern phoebe, swallows, and other birds that incorporate mud into their nests usually build their homes in spring. Their first homes, that is. Many of these birds nest a second time, and sometimes even a third.

Nearly all species of backyard birds build a new nest for each family, which means they need mud throughout summer, too. If your mud puddle is still moist and pliable, they may visit it dozens of times a day as they collect mud for their nests, one beakful at a time. Use your garden hose to refresh your mud puddle when it begins to dry out and crack. Don't be too generous with the water, though: You want to avoid creating a mosquito-breeding pond! Mud is what you're making, not a puddle of standing water.

## Treasure Hunt

Gathering possible materials from around your house or from a thrift shop or craft store is just plain fun. Enlist your kids to help; they're great at brainstorming once they grasp the simple concepts.

- Lengths of stringy things are one of the most appealing materials you can offer.

Horsehair is a prized commodity in the bird-nest market, so offer a handful of long tail hairs.

It takes a lot of work to strip fibers from plants, so orioles and other birds will be quick to take advantage of your generosity.

- Thin strips of cloth and paper are welcomed by orioles, robins, and other birds.

- Fluffy materials are very likely to draw the attention of chickadees, titmice, vireos, and other birds.

- Introduce yourself at the nearest stable and ask for combings from horse manes and tails—horsehair is better than gold to chipping sparrows and other species.

- Crinkly cellophane and crinkly plastic wrap appeal to crested flycatchers, indigo buntings, and other species that incorporate shed snakeskins into their nests.

- Twigs are a dime a dozen in almost any yard, but a tempting pile of slender dead sticks is worth a try to tempt cardinals, jays, grosbeaks, doves, and a long list of other birds.

## Fibers and Fluff

The most popular nest materials we can offer birds fall into two general categories: fibers, such as string; and fluff, such as tufts of natural wool.

Preferences for different materials stem from the way birds build their nests. Each species makes its own style of fabulous construction, but the general principles are shared among many types of birds. Understanding the reasons birds choose one or the other will help you tailor your offerings.

### Fibers

- Many birds are weavers. Lengths of fibers are the prime choice for birds that make their nests entirely of woven fiber (like orioles, goldfinches, and vireos) or that weave fibers in among the twigs (like robins and many others). Short lengths of string or twine, thin strips of fabric, and even the fibers from an old string mop are prized by nest-building birds.
- Nests often have a softer inner circlet of woven fibers or hairs. Many native sparrows eagerly accept horsehair, thread, dog hair, and other fine fibers for that use.

### Fluff

- The center of the nest often holds a soft bed for nestlings, such as the thistledown used by goldfinches or the moss incorporated by phoebes.
- Some nests incoporate soft, fluffy materials, such as fur or moth cocoons, as insulation to help moderate both heat and cold.

It's fun to know that you played a part in making a bird's nest, whether it's for an oriole or a chickadee.

## Creative Sourcery

Watching birds select items from your stash of nest-building supplies is just as much fun as watching birds at the feeder. It's even more gratifying because you'll know the bird will be adding that feather or bit of string to its nest—and that will make you feel like you had a hand in the building process!

Finding items that might entice birds will give you a whole new perspective on household objects—and on trash. You'll start looking at everything in a whole new light, asking yourself, Does this item have any possibilities for fibers or fluff?

The birds in my yard strongly prefer natural fibers to plastic, maybe because natural fibers look more like the plant material the species has used for ages. I offer a few pieces of green garden twine and other plastic fibers, but cotton string, jute twine, and other naturals get way more takers.

Here are a few nest material sources to get you thinking creatively.

- Your old or new string mop holds a lot of potential for oriole nest material, as well as for other birds that appreciate some string in their nest. Snip a few strands at the base, then offer them in 6-inch lengths, either as they are or unraveled into thinner strings.

- Artificial flower arrangements may yield dry sphagnum moss; craft items may have undyed raffia decorations.

- Save your used pieces of unscented, unwaxed dental floss. Offer them to nest-making birds by loosely draping several strands in a highly visible place.

- If your house leans toward minimalist decor, plan a Saturday morning of garage-sale shopping, or schedule a trip to your local thrift store, to see what you can ferret out that might work as nesting materials. Lots of possibilities at penny-wise prices!

- Save the natural burlap wrapping from your nursery trees. Even a small scrap interests nesting birds. Snag the scrap securely on a hook or a branch stub, so birds can tug out individual fibers. Plastic burlap isn't very appealing to birds, other than English, or house, sparrows, which may snatch it up for their big conglomeration nests.

## Making the Offering

Birds are surprisingly good at discovering bits of nest-building material, such as a lone feather under a bush. But I like to make it easy for them by setting up a centralized

## Pseudo Snakeskin

Birds are adept at finding just the right material for their nests, but some items are harder to hunt down than others. Twigs are easy; shed snakeskins—well, there aren't all that many to go around.

Indigo buntings and great crested flycatchers are noted for using snakeskin in their nests, but they will also adopt a reasonable facsimile.

Save plastic wrappings that are thin but crinkly—the kind that make noise when you crumple them and don't stay in a tidy ball, such as the wrap used on CDs. Cut it into strips about 1 inch wide, and presto, pseudo snakeskin!

## Grasping at Straws

Straw is a popular nesting material with bluebirds, house wrens, and some other species, including starlings and house sparrows, which I not only tolerate but enjoy watching. A bale of straw is inexpensive (usually just a few dollars), but if you don't have a pickup truck, it can be tricky and messy to transport.

Try these tricks when acquiring straw for your bird offerings.

- A few handfuls should be enough for starters; if you buy a bale, use the extra for mulch.
- Take a paper grocery sack along to a local landscaping firm or construction company; they often keep straw on hand to control erosion on job sites and will gladly give you a handful if you ask.
- Ask for clean, unused straw at a local stable or farm.
- Craft stores may stock mini-bales, especially during fall; the straw will cost a lot more that way, but convenience may be worth the trade-off. Read the label to make sure the bale has not been treated with chemicals or dyes.

location. Of course, I plan that site to be within easy view from my favorite window or garden seat, so that I can spy on the comings and goings.

Keep your nesting materials separate from the feeder, so that bird traffic doesn't dirty the offerings. Birds that are working on a nest prefer some privacy: They're more secretive in their actions than birds at the feeder because they are trying to keep the location of their nest hidden.

Try these quick and easy methods for getting your goodies to the construction crew in your neighborhood.

- Drape 6- to 10-inch lengths of white cotton twine over the top of a shrub or on the grass, in full view, to garner quick attention from nest-making orioles. They can't seem to resist it.
- Place nest materials in a conspicuous place, such as on the lawn, in the crotch of a tree, dangling from a clothesline, or draped over a shrub.
- An inexpensive suet cage makes a good holder for fluffy nest materials, but try not to let the stuff get wet, or it is likely to mold or mildew. Fashion a roof for the cage from an aluminum foil pie pan or another piece of foil bakeware, or hang the roofless holder under an eave to keep the exposed materials dry.

summer secret Keep an eye out for birds that are investigating twigs on the ground, strips of bark, plant fibers, grasses, or vines. Nesting is on the agenda, and if you pay attention, you can find the location of that nest by watching where they carry the stuff off to.

**summer secret** Don't offer dryer lint to birds. Although it looks fluffy, the fibers are too short for practical bird use. The lint absorbs moisture very easily, sticking to baby birds just like it does to your fingers when you clean the lint trap.

- Avoid placing string or other nest materials on the roof of a birdhouse. That's a sign to many birds that the box is occupied; apparently it looks like the tenants have just stepped out for a few minutes, leaving their work in progress. Birds may be reluctant to take the materials—or to move into the box.

## Quality, not Quantity

Most birds use these soft items as finishing touches for the inner lining of the nest, so they won't need much. A handful of material may be enough for all of the nesting birds in your neighborhood. A wire cage stuffed with nest materials may even last more than one nesting season, depending on how many nesting birds are in your area. Store it in a dry place over winter, away from mice, and put it out again next year.

Small, agile birds like chickadees and titmice will visit a wire cage stuffed with soft materials to pull out what they need. Robins and other larger songbirds aren't as adept; they'll have an easier time gathering the goodies from a more natural spot, such as on a bush or lawn.

Pack that nest-material holder pretty firmly, so that birds can tug at one fiber without everything falling out. If you don't have enough materials to fill it, use crumpled newspaper to add bulk in the middle.

## Now You See It, Now You Don't

The sooner birds see your nest materials, the sooner they'll investigate what you have to offer. Visibility is one of the best ways to attract customers. Birds have terrific eyesight, and even those that fly over your yard can easily spy the white string and other materials you have to offer—if they're visible from above.

Since most birds prefer to stay safely near cover, I put just a few decoy strings or white feathers on the open lawn. Then, like Hansel and Gretel did with bread crumbs, I mark the trail by dropping a few more goodies to lead the birds onward to the tree where my wire cage is stuffed full of soft materials.

## Grow Your Own

For eons, birds have depended on wild plants as a source for those treasured fibers they use in their nests. I've taken to growing some of them in my own yard so that I can watch orioles, vireos, warblers, and other birds hunting and gathering among my gardens.

My flowerbeds are definitely on the

Milkweed fluff isn't ready when nesting begins, so clip and store a few pods to delight your birds next June.

casual side, and my top three picks slip right into that style. Two have running roots, so if you like a neater look, try them in a strip along a garage or other out-of-the-way place, where they won't become a weeding problem. All are easy to grow and widely adaptable.

- **Common milkweed** (*Asclepias syriaca*) forms a spreading colony of stout, 3- to 4-foot stems with large, oblong leaves, and is topped with superfragrant clusters of interesting mauve flowers. Milkweed is a butterfly plant—the host plant for monarch caterpillars and a nectar source for many species. But it's also a source for fluff and soft fibers for nest linings.

- **Indian hemp** (*Apocynum cannabium*), a milkweed relative, forms a colony of plants about 2 feet tall, with clustered butterfly-magnet flowers followed by bundles of long, skinny seedpods. Like milkweed, the fluff from the pods is sometimes used by birds, and old, dead plant stems are stripped of fibers that are used to build nests.

- **Wild flax** (*Linum usitatissimum*), a beautiful native wildflower, has sky blue blossoms on delicate, wiry stems. It grows here and there from coast to coast; in Wyoming and other western states, it forms a river of blue along highways in summer. Herbalists have long used the plant as an aid to digestion; today, flaxseed and flaxseed oil are big business because of the heart-healthy properties of the omega-3 fatty acids in the seeds. Finches and sparrows eat the seeds, and dead, weathered stems are investigated for the long, soft fibers—which we humans weave into linen.

# FAMILY SAFETY

Keeping the family safe depends upon keeping them hidden—and plants provide the hiding places. Baby birds are highly

**summer secret** Puss in boots? Not likely, which is why fledglings often leave the nest when it's raining. There's much less risk of predators, whether it's a backyard kitty or a prowling possum.

## Rotting and Retting

"Retting" is the smelly process by which flax plants are rotted to release their fibers for making linen. My mom used to tell stories about a small DIY operation in the countryside near her hometown of Emmaus, Pennsylvania, in the old days, when she was a child: A horse trough full of rotting flax in stinky water, which they would tromp with bare feet to separate the long strands from the pulp.

I inadvertently discovered a much lazier way to free the flax fibers—by allowing the stems to weather and letting the birds do the work.

I buy flaxseeds in bulk for less than $1 a pound at the grocery store and scatter them throughout my gardens and on any other bit of bare ground. They quickly reach flowering size, creating a lovely sky blue filler among the other plants.

One year, I planted a 5-foot strip along the driveway entirely in flax. A friend who was helping with mowing in early fall cut down the entire swath, thinking it was weeds. No problem, I assured him, I'll just let them lay; the birds will find the seeds. And they did.

When the snow melted in spring, I raked up the soft, wet, dead stems and tossed them on the compost pile, where they continued to decompose. By the time the orioles returned in May, those flax stems were ready to supply fibers for every oriole in town. Day after day, I got to see brilliant orange orioles pull off long, tan strands of flax and carry them to the trees.

vulnerable when they leave the nest, too, so the more places to hide, the better.

Just who is after those li'l birdies? Here's a rundown of who might be on the lookout in your neighborhood.

- **Four-legged prowlers:** Cats, raccoons, squirrels, opossums, weasels, minks, dogs, coyotes
- **Two-legged fliers:** Owls, hawks, crows, ravens, magpies, grackles, jays
- **No-legged slitherers:** Black snakes, garter snakes, and many other snakes seeking bird eggs, nestlings, or even an incubating parent

You'll find plenty of suggestions for providing cover for nesting birds in "Cleanup

Scatter flaxseed among your perennials for food and nest fibers for the birds—and pretty flowers for you.

Even a slim little garter snake can unhinge its jaw wide enough to swallow delectable bird eggs and nestlings.

Plant shrubs under your trees so that fledgling birds can safely hide while they learn to use their wings.

Considerations" (see page 53) and "Corridor Plantings for Safe Travels" (see page 56) in Chapter 3.

Extras are built into the bird population, to balance out the birds and nests that are lost to predators. But that balance has tipped toward the negative side, and many species of birds are in trouble. One major cause is cats. Our pets and our feral felines destroy many nests and parent birds (see "Cats: A Grave Danger" at right).

Another major factor in the success or failure of bird nests? Us. We humans have wrought big changes in the world. Our

## Fledged but Not Flying

Most backyard baby birds leave the nest before they are fully capable of flying. Although they may have stood on the rim flapping those newly feathered wings for days, they haven't quite mastered the airborne technique.

That first "flight" is usually more of an awkward tumble as the fledglings leave the safety of home behind. They'll spend the next few days on or near the ground, laying low among sheltering shrubs, ground-cover, or garden beds, as their parents bring them food and keep an eye on them from a distance.

Soon, those vulnerable young ones are fluttering higher into the shrubs, then making short flights across open spaces. Eventually they are able to work those wings pretty well, and they follow their parents from perch to perch, still demanding to be fed. A highly dangerous time is over, for that family.

summer secret There's no way to keep predators out of your yard entirely, but you can help discourage the prowlings of at least the four-legged type. A "barbed-wire fence" of barberries, brambles, or shrub rose bushes around your boundary lines may help deter them.

pesticides, habitat destruction, and human activities have caused dramatic effects on insects and plants, as well as on the birds directly. Everything in the natural world is connected, and we've been wreaking havoc long enough to start seeing its effects.

# Cats: A Grave Danger

The cat problem is one that's not easy to talk about. We love our kitty. Okay, so maybe once in a while there's a sad mound of feathers on the porch. Or we might even catch her in the act of snatching a sparrow from the yard, or stalking the feeder. So maybe Kitty kills a few birds a year. That's not so bad, is it? Surely our dear pets can't cause all that much damage, can they?

Indeed they can. And they do.

Cats are by far the biggest threat that bird populations face. Scientists estimate that hundreds of millions of birds are killed by cats every single year.

Birds don't reproduce fast enough to keep surviving that kind of slaughter.

It's not only feral cats (strays and pets gone wild, or their offspring) that kill birds by the millions. The problem is just as huge with our own beloved pets.

## Doing the Math

Science is just beginning to focus more attention on the predations of cats, and studies are putting into numbers a problem that most of us prefer not to look at too closely.

More than 90 million cats are kept as pets in this country, and a 1997 study showed that only about one-third of them are wholly indoor cats. Count up all of the strays and feral cats that roam city streets and the countryside, and you start to see how huge the problem really is.

As you may have seen in your own backyard, cats kill common species such as cardinals, blue jays, house wrens, and many others. I don't know about you, but I'm pretty fond of my backyard friends, no matter how common they may be. So I take cats seriously.

Birds in the wild suffer because of cats, too. Habitat fragmentation, in which large areas of woodland and other wild places are carved up into smaller pieces by roads and housing, puts the birds that nest in those areas at much greater risk from cats, as well as from raccoons and cowbirds, which are reluctant to prowl far into deep woods but eager to investigate smaller patches. Wood thrushes, wood warblers, and other woodland species are suffering now that predators can reach their nests.

Cats also kill birds that are already in worrisome decline, including endangered species such as piping plovers, Florida scrub jays, and the California least tern.

## Indoor Vacation

Think it's hard to teach an old dog new tricks? Wait until you try to switch your cats from being indoor/outdoor pets to being indoors-only. You can expect wails of protest that all too easily cause you to weaken your resolve.

Try these tips to make it a less stressful process, for both you and your cats.

**Before you start:**

- Resolve to go cold turkey. Cats adjust more easily if you completely cut off outdoor time right from the start of training.
- Remember that if you let your cats out sometimes and make them stay indoors at other times, they will constantly test you to see if this might be a time they can go out.
- Keep your cats indoors year-round. If you let them out in winter, say, but not summer, you will have to train them all over again when the indoor season starts.
- Don't let them out at any time of day, either. Neither night nor day is a safe time for cats to be outside, if you are trying to protect birds.
- Remember that although nesting season is the absolute worst time for cats to roam free, no season is a good time for cats to be outside; they will kill birds whenever they can find them.
- Consider building an enclosure where your cats can spend some time out in the fresh air. You can see photos of how people have done it or buy a how-to-do-it handbook at www.just4cats.com.
- Consider training your cat to walk on a leash attached to a harness. It is possible, with patience.
- Putting a bell on your cat's collar has no effect on its hunting abilities. Cats quickly learn how to keep the bell quiet—until they are making the final leap toward their prey. By then, the warning of the bell is too late.

One scientific study found that the decimation of piping plovers is indisputably tied to cat activity. On New York beaches, where nearby homeowners keep many pet cats and where there are also lots of strays, cat tracks led to nests that showed a sad ending. Adult plover heads and wings were all that was left behind after the kill. Cats were observed playing with eggs by batting them around the beach. When enclosures were employed to try to protect the plovers, cat tracks wore a path around them, and the birds abandoned their nests.

### Responsibility Begins at Home

It's easy to point to habitat loss as the reason for the decline in birds—that's not our fault. But scientists say that cats are the second biggest danger to birds. They kill countless numbers of our feathered friends every year.

**During the training process:**

- Consistency counts. Training your pets is like teaching children that "no means no": If you are inconsistent and change your mind after you initially say no, they will only beg and whine more the next time you say no.

- Be sure the entire family, and any guests, know that the cat is not allowed outdoors. Put a sign on the door as a reminder. And be sure to guard the door when entering or exiting, to prevent a sudden rush for freedom.

- Give your indoor cats plenty of toys, either homemade or storebought, that it can play with on its own. Sock ball, anyone? Paper sack hide-and-seek? Playtime will help make up for the lack of free-roaming exercise and the pleasure of hunting.

- Give your cats more of your own time. Invent active games that will satisfy your pet's hunting instincts. Tie a crumbled ball of paper or a feather on a string and pull it invitingly across the rug. Make a "fishing pole" with an enticing toy as bait, and practice casting across the room.

- Train your cat to accept boundaries in play: No attacking your feet when you walk across the room, for instance. Stop the cat, and say a stern "No!" Then toss the cat one of its play-alone toys.

- And finally, don't reward bad behavior by offering food or petting when Kitty whines. Let your pet sulk alone, so that it doesn't learn that meowing or yowling will result in a treat. Tough love, I know, but a trained cat is a contented cat.

Cats kill birds year-round, but birds are at their most vulnerable during nesting season. Parent birds are reluctant to desert the family to save themselves, and young birds can't muster the fast getaway or confident flight that might keep them out of Kitty's clutches.

If you have cats, do the birds a favor and get your kitties accustomed (or at least fairly well resigned) to staying indoors. Every little bit does help.

## A HELPING HAND

Our first impulse upon finding a baby bird in the yard is to pick it up. Don't do it— that youngster may have left the nest under its own steam and simply hasn't learned to fly yet.

Consider these questions before you step in to help.

- Does the baby bird have feathers? A naked nestling on the ground is obviously

## Your Neighbors' Cats

Even if your cats are indoor cats, or you don't have cats, your bird-attracting backyard is likely to attract bird-hunting cats. After watching a neighbor's beautiful smoky gray cat systematically kill six goldfinches in quick succession at my feeders, I went over to have a talk.

My neighbor was sympathetic, but she wasn't willing to keep her cat indoors. So I invested in a device that hooks up to the garden hose and instantly shoots a strong spray of water at any animal that crosses its motion-detector sensor. That did the trick.

Another house I lived in had a fence around the backyard. Cats were reluctant to come inside, because my dogs were frequently in the fenced yard. At night, though, when we were sleeping and the dogs were in the house, cats did enter the yard; they killed my house wren and my song sparrow family, and they pulled down the robin nest. As soon as I could afford it, I added "cat fencing" to my picket fence. The black plastic mesh was easy to staple to the existing fence. You can explore this option at www.catfencein.com or www.catfence.com, whether you are trying to keep your own cats in your yard or trying to keep other cats out.

### The Feral Cat Problem

Feral cats are homeless cats. They may have been dropped off or left behind when owners moved, or they may be offspring of previously abandoned animals. Many live in city parks, where they come out at night to search the trash for food and to kill wildlife. Others roam farmland or other wild places.

A growing number of communities have instituted a spaying and neutering program aimed at feral cats. In my own small town of about 700, a dedicated couple set about trapping, neutering, and releasing the cats in all neighborhoods. There aren't as many kittens these days, which is a relief to us bird lovers. But the adult cats are still roaming. Still, the effort has helped reduce the problem, even if only somewhat.

Reducing feral cats seems to be a thorny problem. Public meetings quickly become impassioned, as cat lovers square off against bird lovers. I'm a cat lover myself, as well as a bird lover, so I'm hoping that somehow we can find a middle ground.

Meanwhile, as Bob Barker used to say at the end of every episode of *The Price Is Right*, please spay and neuter your pets. Some veterinarians and humane societies offer neutering services at a reduced cost, or even for free.

not where it's supposed to be. A baby that's mostly feathered, including stubby wings, may be old enough to be on its own.

- Can the youngster open its eyes? Older nestlings can open and close their eyes; very young birds have closed eyelids.

- Does the beak of the baby bird have yellow corners? Those soft corners persist even after the baby leaves the nest, so don't depend on this trait.

Birds invited for dinner shouldn't become dinner themselves, so keep your cat indoors and shoo away strays.

- Does the baby bird try to get away from you by floundering and flapping? It may be old enough to be out of the nest.

- Does an adult bird come close or answer if the baby bird squawks? It may be old enough to be out of the nest.

- Did you or your kids have to chase the baby bird to catch it? Definitely old enough to be out of the nest!

If the baby you have found is too young to be on its own, read on to find out how to help it. If it's feathered and old enough to be out of the nest, then corral those caretaking impulses and don't interfere with the natural process.

## Rehabbers to the Rescue

Summer is the busy season for bird rehabilitators. These skilled and dedicated folks put in many hours feeding and caring for nestlings that people find in their backyards—including many fledglings that should never have been picked up in the first place. Rehabbers often work with wildlife rescue centers or nature centers, while others work out of their own homes. All are skilled at caring for adult birds and animals, as well as babies.

Rehabbers are licensed so that they can legally care for birds. Some people also care for baby birds on an informal basis, even though it's not legal.

If you do come across a baby bird that needs help, here's what to do until you can deliver it to a caretaker.

**summer secret** Interfering with songbirds or their nests is a great big no-no. In fact, it's a federal offense. Nearly all backyard birds are protected by federal law. Keep your hands off unless it's absolutely necessary to rescue the bird to take it to a rehabber.

No need to "help" this baby blue jay—it's old enough to be out of the nest, even though it can't fly well yet.

underneath its body. Hold it firmly but not too tightly, so that it doesn't squirm and fall. Set the bird into the shoebox, nestling it near the bottle, with tissues between so that it's not directly touching the very warm bottle.

4. Phone your local nature center or chapter of the Audubon Society, and ask for contact information for a rehabber. Get two or more names, if possible, in case one of them isn't home.

5. Phone the rehabber and make arrangements to deliver the bird ASAP. Every minute counts with young animals, so be as efficient as you possibly can at getting the bird into good hands as soon as possible.

1. Fill a shoebox or other small box with crumpled facial tissue to make a soft, warmth-retaining "nest."

2. Fill a 20-ounce plastic bottle with very warm, almost hot water, cap it tightly, and dry it off; then nestle the bottle securely in the box to provide heat for the bird.

3. Don a pair of disposable plastic gloves and gently lift the bird, holding it

## Fast Food at Home

Baby birds need food frequently. If you can't reach a rehabber immediately, or if it will take an hour or more to deliver the bird, you may want to consider feeding the bird yourself. Calories from food help keep the baby warm, as well as being needed to fuel its ultra-rapid growth. Here are some quick and easy foods to feed the baby until you can reach an expert.

summer secret  The parasitic brown-headed cowbird often lays an egg in nests of birds much smaller than itself. That cowbird egg sticks out like a sore thumb among the smaller eggs of the song sparrow, yellowthroat, or other species—but most birds never recognize it as an impostor.

The clever blue jay almost always spots it, as do other members of the jay family. The American goldfinch, which nests very late in the season (beginning when thistles have gone to seed, usually in July), avoids the peak of cowbird activity, so it rarely has to deal with feeding an oversize impostor.

Do not attempt to give a baby bird a drink of water, milk, or other liquid. It's all too easy to spill some into their nostrils, which can be disastrous. Moist food will supply all the moisture they need.

- Tiny bits of hard-cooked egg white, about the size of a small split pea, are a good all-purpose meal in emergencies. It takes just 10 minutes to hard-boil an egg; cool it under running water and you're ready to feed.

- Soak a few pieces of dry dog food until it's very soft, then break off tiny pieces for feeding.

- Try bits of moistened unsweetened cereal, whole-grain crackers, or whole-grain bread.

- For older babies, try mealworms from your feeding station supply. Caterpillars are a familiar and popular food for all baby birds, including fledglings; mealworms are a reasonable facsimile. Even seed-eating species feed caterpillars to their offspring. (Doves are a rare exception; they require a special diet of partly digested seeds.)

Touch the bird on the top of its beak to encourage it to open wide, and drop the food down the hatch. I use my fingers, but you can try using tweezers for this operation.

If the bird is reluctant to open its bill, gently grasp the bill just before the softer corners, and very carefully pry it open. Be ready to immediately drop in the food when you do this. It takes some practice! And keep a soft tissue handy to clean the bird after it eats; hand-feeding can be very messy until you get the hang of it.

Baby birds need soft, highly nutritious food, and insects are the perfect choice. That's one of the reasons that feeder traffic drops off so dramatically in summer: Birds are busy seeking insects, not seeds. In the next chapter, you'll learn how to tweak the menu at your feeding station to entice birds back to the banquet, no matter how many juicy caterpillars are calling to them.

# CHAPTER 6

# THE FEEDER SCENE IN SUMMER

**H**AVEN'T SEEN YOU in a while," my usual checkout clerk at the grocery store commented to me one summer day. "Where've you been?"

Thanks to friends and neighbors, my grocery bills are delightfully small in summer. No, it's not that they invite me to share their supper—it's the summer bounty of their vegetable gardens that keeps me well supplied.

From early June through the dog days of summer, gifts of tomatoes, cucumbers, summer squash, sweet corn, peppers, and, of course, plenty of baseball bat–size zucchinis show up on my doorstep. For months, I make my meals of free food, adding only a little rice or pasta to round them out.

I still visit the supermarket, but not nearly as often as I do in winter. In summer, it's just the treats that inspire me to make the drive—frozen fruit Popsicles, nuts, and chocolate. Exactly what the checkout clerk was ringing up at that moment.

Summer birds work the same way. They usually fill their bellies with natural foods and just stop by our feeders for snacks.

## SUMMER FEEDING

The peak seasons for feeding birds are fall through winter. Why? Because natural foods are scarce, so birds quickly become regulars at a feeding station. You'll host lots of individual birds of a dozen or more species, day in and day out, during those seasons.

In summer, the scene is much different. Compared to the crowds of fall and winter, visitors will be few and far between. And instead of spending hours at your station, they'll dash in, grab a bite, and disappear.

Think about what's going on in the bird world at this time of year, and you'll understand why feeder traffic is so scanty in summer. First of all, there's an incredible bounty of insects in every nook and cranny of the natural world, ready for the taking. Butterflies at the flowers, caterpillars on the leaves, 'skeeters in the sky, ants trailing across the picnic blanket—it's hard to find a few bug-free inches of real estate outside in summer!

summer secret Suet is a vital high-fat food for winter, but it's a valuable summer food, too. It's popular with nesting birds because parents can grab a few quick bites for a fast snack. And it's a popular destination for families with fledglings. The suet feeder is often their first stop because the soft, fatty food slides down the hatch just like a juicy caterpillar.

Summer heat can cause suet to melt, so move your suet feeder to a shady spot, out of direct sun. Be sure the suet is not hanging over a deck or other wooden or paved surface, which it can stain if it should melt. Look for suet blocks labeled "nonmelting"; they cost about the same or only a little more than regular suet blocks. You can also switch to a homemade summertime mix that includes flour, cornmeal, and quick-cooking oats, which will hold the block together and still satisfy birds; you'll find a recipe on page 120.

Ample insects are a big reason why you don't see as many birds at your feeders. But there's another big shift taking place, too: Birds are now living on their breeding territories. The gangs of sparrows that livened up the feeder scene a few months ago have dispersed to nesting grounds, two by two. Instead of a host of cardinals, you may have only a single pair, if you're lucky. So instead of daily backyard visits by maybe 100 birds, you're down to, oh, perhaps a dozen—and they're mostly eating insects, not hanging out at the seed tray.

Birds can thrive perfectly well without us in summer. But if you keep your feeder going, you'll have an opportunity to host some fabulous birds—a vivid oriole is a distinct possibility. You'll also get to enjoy the first visits of fledglings. A lineup of young chickadees, titmice, or nuthatches, begging Mom and Dad for a bite of suet, is utterly charming. Of course you'll want to keep nectar feeders in your yard, too, because summer spells hummingbirds.

# KEEP STOCKING STAPLES

My kitchen cupboards hold a supply of rice, pasta, Scottish steel-cut oats, beans, and other basics. These are the staples I like to keep on hand, so they're ready when I want them. Your cabinets no doubt hold the same sort of essentials, whether it's boxes of your kids' favorite cereal or a supply of tuna. Open the cupboard at any time of year, and we're likely to see the same items.

Certain staples remain the same at our feeding stations, too, no matter what the season; birds eat them year-round.

- Sunflower seeds
- White proso millet
- Suet

These three basics form the backbone of the feeder menu through all four seasons because they are widely accepted foods eaten by birds year-round. Start with these three staples, and then add some goodies to

## Year-Round Clientele

Bird species that live with us year-round are the ones most likely to visit in summer for more of that same-old, same-old fare. Sunflowers still attract house finches, goldfinches, cardinals, nuthatches, chickadees, titmice, and jays. Millet still is popular with song sparrows, English or house sparrows, and any other sparrows you may host. Suet is still a target for woodpeckers, nuthatches, chickadees, and titmice.

My nature is somewhat the same. While I love trying out new recipes or sampling interesting dishes at trendy restaurants, I still tend to fall back on my old favorites: "Mmm, that crab omelet sounds delicious . . . but I think I'll have scrambled eggs, thanks."

That's the way it works with birds, too. They may dip into the fruit feeder, but they'll want some of those old favorite sunflower seeds, too.

**Year-round birds like this tufted titmouse enjoy the same basic feeder foods in all seasons.**

get the attention of summer birds and to make adjustments for summer eating habits.

## SUMMER SPECIALS

Think of yourself as a world-class chef, getting ready to cook for a special group of friends. Your apron is neatly tied, your toque in place, your knives and sauté pans at the ready. There's a whole wall of cookbooks at your fingertips and a wealth of knowledge in your head. Where do you begin?

Well, unless you're an egomaniac who just wants to show off, you start by considering the tastes of your friends. Sure, you may want to tempt them out of their comfort zones—but you'll do that by offering variations on their usual preferences, not by serving, say, sliced tongue to vegetarians.

That's the approach to take with summer birds, too. Offer them feeder foods that are similar to their usual diet, and you're likely to win rave reviews. Ready, chefs? Let's look at some specials for the summer menu.

## Delightful, Not Disgusting

Like millions of other TV watchers, I also tuned in to various reality shows to watch contestants or hosts try to eat unusual foods. Okay, so let's just say those foods are "gross," because to our culture and palates, dining on grubs, grasshoppers, and other insects is reason for revulsion. Other people around the world know that these natural foods are highly nutritious, and they eat them with relish. But most of us Americans react with rapt disgust.

Bugs may not be our cup of tea. To birds, though, they beat just about any other summer food. And bird-supply companies are finally catching on to what bird-watchers have known forever. Nowadays, you can buy a variety of insect foods for birds. Here's a look at what's out there, but explore for yourself because the list keeps growing.

## Make Your Own Bugged Suet

If you don't mind working with dead insects in your kitchen, you can easily make your own enriched suet. Here's how I do it.

1. Buy a container of insects-only turtle food from a pet supply store; read the label or ask a clerk to find one that contains only insects. You may also find insects-only fish food.
2. Unwrap a commercial block of plain suet (without seeds or other additions). Remove the suet from the plastic mold. Set the mold aside.
3. Place the suet in a microwavable bowl and partially melt the suet in the microwave on high; try 20 seconds, and adjust as necessary for your oven. You're aiming for melting about one-third to one-half of the block.
4. Use the back of a tablespoon to mush the unmelted suet with the liquid part, so you end up with a thickish "stew."
5. Pour in a generous amount of insects; I use about 1 cup per suet block.
6. Use the back of the spoon to "cream" the suet and insects together.
7. Scoop the insect-enriched suet back into the plastic mold, and pack it in with the back of the spoon.
8. Cover the suet with plastic wrap and place it in the freezer until it's hard.
9. Slide the frozen block into a suet feeder and serve. Or wrap snugly in plastic wrap and store in a zipper-lock freezer bag in the freezer until ready to serve.

In summer, you may spot house wrens, Carolina wrens, myrtle warblers, brown creepers, and thrashers—as well as the usual titmice, nuthatches, woodpeckers, and chickadees—taking a taste of your buggy suet.

**Mealworms.** These brown or whitish larvae were the first insect foods to make the commercial-birdfeeding big time. Mealworms and similar waxworms and wireworms are a huge hit with birds, and in summer they can draw neighborhood tanagers, orioles, grosbeaks, wrens, vireos, warblers, and a slew of other cool birds to your feeder. You'll find details on buying, storing, and serving them on page 41.

**Insect-enriched suet.** About 15 years ago, I sent away for suet blocks from a small Oregon company that added houseflies and fruit flies to the fat. I was living in the Northwest at the time, and my varied thrushes, hermit thrushes, wood warblers, and myrtle warblers quickly discovered the treat. All was well until a pileated woodpecker showed up and polished off the pricey block of bugged suet in 2 days.

Young starlings are fond of mealworms. Try moist dog food to distract them, or use an anti-starling feeder.

Within a couple of weeks, my entire supply was eaten, and I switched back to regular beef-fat trimmings from the butcher. The special birds still came to nibble, but not nearly as often. Today, insect-enriched suet is more affordable and available.

## Fruit at the Feeder

Fruit attracts orioles and other summer birds, but it also attracts insects—and some of them have stingers. That's why I keep my fruit offerings well away from the rest of the feeders and out of the path of passersby, myself included. Bees and wasps are usually not aggressive, but if you get too close to their food supply, they may sting. Ever since a close friend had a terrifying, life-threatening reaction to a wasp sting, I don't take chances.

Now that you're thinking, Hmm, maybe I don't want fruit at my feeders at all, let's shift from gloom and doom to happier thoughts: Wait till you see the birds that a fruit feeder may attract. It reads like a who's who list—the cream of the crop.

- Bluebirds
- Catbird
- Great crested flycatcher
- Grosbeaks
- Mockingbird
- Orioles
- Robin
- Tanagers

- Thrashers

- Thrushes

- Vireos

- Warblers

- Woodpeckers, especially downy

- Wrens

Fruit feeders have spikes onto which you can firmly push a piece of fruit; that way, birds can peck and pull at it without knocking it to the ground. I used to find it odd that the photos in catalogs and online, and on the boxes themselves, almost always showed a bright orange-and-black oriole eating an orange at that feeder. Didn't matter what design or what price range the feeder had—it was oranges. And orioles.

I'd been feeding fruit myself, without benefit of a classy feeder, and I already knew that lots of birds came for the offering. I also knew that oranges aren't a popular fruit with many other species. Apples are way more popular—and much cheaper—than oranges.

Orioles often winter in citrus groves when the crop is ripening, so oranges are a food they're familiar with.

So why the orioles and oranges? Here's what I figured out.

- The beauty of an oriole, as well as the cheerful color orange, are hard to resist, so the usual picture makes sense from a marketing standpoint. Show a starling eating an apple, and your sales wouldn't be nearly as high.

- The flesh of a cut apple turns brown quickly. By the time the birds arrived for

## Mass Appeal

Whenever I take a long road trip, I know I can depend upon my favorite fast-food franchise for a meal that's just what I expect. Maybe I'll try that roadside barbecue joint later tonight, after I've freshened up, but generally I just want a filling meal that's enjoyable to eat and holds no surprises.

Apparently I'm not alone in that thinking, since McDonald's and its ilk have made billionaires of their owners.

I follow that same guideline when I choose the menu for my birds. Sure, I'll add an out-of-the-ordinary item now and then, for the birds that are adventurous enough to try it. But usually I stick to the tried and true.

Fruit feeder? Apples and oranges are the Quarter-Pounders of my menu. Birds know them, like them, and eat them.

## Small-Bird Fruit Feeder

Grab a pair of pliers, a piece of sturdy wire, and your creativity, and you can design a fruit feeder for small birds in less than an hour. No wire on hand? Untwist a coat hanger. You'll find directions below for a figure-eight fruit feeder, but why not make your own design? The only design criteria are a prong on one end (to skewer the fruit and hold it securely while birds perch and peck at it) and a hanger on the other end.

This quick project, which accommodates wrens, warblers, chickadees, and other small birds, is fun for kids to help with. Once they get the hang of it (yuk-yuk), it may even discourage starlings from gobbling your apples lickety-split.

Start by untwisting a wire coat hanger to yield a piece of fairly straight wire. Poke half of a small or medium orange or apple onto the wire and slide it to the center. Twist the wire into a figure 8, with the fruit at the bottom of the lower loop of the 8. Twist the ends of the wire closed, like you would a bread tie. Hang the figure 8 on a shepherd's crook or other hook.

a photo opportunity, the fruit wouldn't be looking very good.

- It's easy to attract orioles with oranges because they've been accustomed to eating the fruit for centuries. Many Baltimore orioles winter in Florida, land of winter warmth—and orange groves. Put a taste of that "Florida sunshine" in your feeder, and orioles will follow.

A flicker may be your ally when ants invade your jelly feeder. This bird eagerly eats both ants and jelly!

### Uninvited Guests

Sticky-sweet things like fruit and jelly quickly attract insects, particularly ants, bees, and wasps. There's no way to keep flying insects away from a fruit feeder, but you can minimize their effects. Highly aggressive yellow jackets, the worst-tempered of the wasps, do not come out in force until fall migration of most fruit-eating birds, including orioles, has already begun.

Birds will continue to feed, unless the stinging insects became defensive. Red admirals and other butterflies are often attracted to fruit; they, too, will coexist with wasps and other insects.

- To minimize the number of yellow jackets you attract, remove the fruit feeder when orioles no longer visit daily—usually around late July. Remove any jelly feeders then, too. Clean and store them until next year.

- Defend against ants by attaching a moat to a hanging fruit or jelly feeder. Inexpensive moats—basically small, leak-proof cups that you fill with water—are available at bird-supply stores. The moat has a hollow center that slides down the hanger of your feeder to rest on top of it; one size fits most.

Remember to refill the moat as often as needed. You may need to refill the moat once a day in summer, because of evaporation.

These adorable "chickadees" are young British great tits, of the same family our familiar friends belong to.

## THE YOUNGER SET

When young chickadees, nuthatches, and titmice leave the nest, their parents often herd the family to the feeder. The young ones are used to their parents feeding them, and they expect the same treatment after they're out of the nest. They have to learn to find their own food.

Feeders are great places for parents to teach their youngsters to take care of their own needs. Better yet—you get a front-row seat for the lesson!

The lesson in independence begins as soon as the family arrives, which they will do as a group. Unlike some songbirds, these families stick together after the babies fledge.

### Begging for Favors

Baby birds have begging down to a fine art. Who could resist that gaping beak, those pitiful cries, those drooped, fluttering wings?

When baby birds are still in the nest, the one who begs the best tends to receive the most food. The open beak and other behavior elicit an automatic stuff-it-down-the-throat-quick response from the attending parent.

But once nestlings become fledglings and leave their happy home, parent birds aren't nearly so susceptible to the begging routine. Don't feel sorry for the youngsters—it's all for their own good. By ignoring the begging behavior, the parent birds teach their youngsters to find food on their own, instead of being dependent.

Here's what you can expect to see.

1. With one or both parents in attendance, the young birds will line up closely on a branch near the feeder.

2. The parents will fly to the feeder. The young will beg loudly until a parent returns and feeds them a bite of feeder food. That may continue for an hour or more.

3. Eventually the parents will stop feeding the fledglings. Instead, the adult will whack at the nut or other food beside the begging youngsters, then swallow it itself.

4. The parent will return to the feeder and repeat the routine, while the young continue futilely making begging gestures and calls.

5. Finally, one of the youngsters will follow a parent and make a shaky flight to the feeder.

6. Sometimes the parent will feed the fledgling at the feeder, but from what I've seen, usually the young bird

## No-Melt Suet

Melting suet can stain paving, wood decks, and tree trunks. Here's a recipe that resists melting in summer heat and appeals to all suet-eating birds. You'll need plastic margarine tubs; I get mine at the local recycling center.

*1 cup lard*
*1 cup peanut butter (I use crunchy)*
*2 cups quick-cooking (not instant) oatmeal*
*2 cups yellow cornmeal*
*1½ cups white flour*

1. Scoop the lard and peanut butter into a large saucepan over medium-low heat. Melt, stirring occasionally.
2. Meanwhile, mix the oatmeal, cornmeal, and 1 cup of the flour in a large heatproof mixing bowl.
3. Pour the melted lard and peanut butter mixture into the bowl, scraping the pan with a rubber spatula.
4. Mix well. If it is more runny than stiff, add the remaining ½ cup of flour and mix well.
5. Fill the margarine tubs halfway with this mixture.
6. Cover each tub with aluminum foil and place in the freezer.
7. When frozen, remove the suet from the tubs. Serve in a suet feeder, slicing the frozen suet in half, if necessary, to fit into the feeder. Store extras individually in zipper-lock bags in the freezer, until needed.

**summer secret** Save your corncobs after that summer picnic. Set them aside to dry, then twist a wire around the cob securely, as a hanger, and smear the center section of the cob with peanut butter or lard. Leave the ends bare so birds have a place to perch. Hang the cob from a shepherd's crook for chickadees, wrens, and titmice to discover.

quickly gets the idea and grabs a bite itself.

7. Other fledglings follow quickly, until the whole brood has learned the lesson. Generally, there's a slow learner or two among the group, one who continues to follow the parents around for several more days, begging loudly. Eventually those laggards, too, learn the lesson.

Families with fledglings may crack some seeds, but at first they go for the softer, higher-fat offerings that are ready to eat. At my feeders, they head for:

- Suet
- Peanut butter treats, such as peanut butter mixed with cornmeal
- Insect foods, like mealworms or suet with bugs
- Shelled nuts, such as peanuts

After a few days of those foods, the young birds quickly add sunflower seeds and other usual fare to their everyday diets.

Experimenting with unusual feeder foods helps us understand why the natural summer diet is so tempting. A cup of grape jelly may coax an oriole into paying some attention to our feeders, but as soon as real fruit begins to ripen, that grape jelly will have a hard time competing with fresh cherries or mulberries. In the next chapter, you'll learn how to add natural foods to your yard, so that you can see for yourself how irresistible summer's bounty is to birds.

# CHAPTER 7

# NATURAL FOODS AND NESTING PLANTS FOR SUMMER

SUMMERTIME, and the living is easy. The days are warm and long, the garden is growing a mile a minute, fruits and berries are ripening, and insects are everywhere.

## INSECT INVESTIGATIONS

Summer residents arrived in our backyards at the end of the spring season, just as insect life was rarin' into action. All of those bugs are still going strong in summer, with later-hatching species of insects adding to the menu.

By the summer nesting season, countless caterpillars of spring and early summer have matured into moths and butterflies; meanwhile, other caterpillars, having just hatched from eggs, are seeing the world for the first time in summer. Many grubs have transformed from underground larvae into brilliantly colored June beetles, Japanese beetles, or other species.

In summer, lots of insects are on to a new stage of their own cycle, with those that survived the onslaught of spring birds now reaching maturity. It's breeding season for them, too, so you'll see the flashing lights of signaling fireflies and hear the relentless drone of cicadas advertising for mates.

Birds appreciate insects at any stage of their life cycle, so they stay busy scarfing up

A casual flowerbed provides just the kind of habitat a catbird likes—plenty of cover with plenty of insects.

this natural food. Keep avoiding those pesticides, and your yard will do its share to fill bird bellies.

# SUMMER FRUIT

After months of eating tough, flavorless supermarket strawberries that were shipped in from across the country, I yearn for the first blush of red from the homegrown variety. Mmm, tender! Mmm, juicy! Mmm, a real strawberry!

That's if I can beat the birds to them. They keep an even closer eye on the garden than I do—and they get up way earlier. By the time I spy the really red strawberry that was hiding under a leaf, there's almost always a sizable slice taken out of it by a bird beak.

The only thing to do is plant more, so there's plenty to share. Or keep part of the patch just for you by covering a row or a bush with floating row covers or netting to keep birds from gobbling the fruit.

Small fruits are so popular with birds that I squeeze in a plant or shrub (or two, or ten) wherever I can find a bit of empty space. Most are inexpensive and fast growing, so they're fun to experiment with. If you start with container plants from a local nursery or garden center, you'll usually get a sampling of fruit the very first year you plant them—in fact, you can even buy plants that

Peak season for caterpillars neatly coincides with summer nesting season, when birds need lots of food for their families. Fat tomato hornworms go a long way toward filling the beaks of young brown thrashers and other summer nestlings.

are already in flower or dangling with berries! Bare-root plants are cheaper, but they generally take a couple of years to bear a crop.

When I needed a fast-growing hedge, for instance, I chose red raspberries. Fall foliage? Blueberries and serviceberries glow red in fall—and attract summer birds with sweet bite-size berries. Strawberries are one of my favorite groundcovers in sunny strips.

**summer secret** A deep layer of mulch around trees, shrubs, and other plants reduces the need for watering, plus the mulch improves the soil as it decomposes. It's also manna for birds seeking earthworms, ground beetles, and other insects in and under that mulch.

## Handy Half-Dozen

These easy, fast-growing plants will give you at least a taste the year you plant them, and a generous yield in the years that follow.

Fruit plants are often incredibly cheap—a bundle of 10 bare-root strawberry plants or a Happy Meal? Easy choice for bird lovers!

*Blackberries.* Go thornless, if you mainly want fruit. Stick with prickles for better protective cover and nest sites. Blackberries make an excellent casual hedge to deter cats from entering your yard.

*Blueberries.* Got thriving azaleas? Plant blueberries among them; they flourish in the same acid conditions. Or plant a group of them in your yard or along your fence, for cover and stunning red fall foliage, as well as irresistible fruit.

*Elderberries.* So you don't make wine or jelly. You can still add elderberries for the birds, who will eagerly seek them out when the branches are bending under the weight of those heavy clusters of tiny berries.

*Grapes.* No need to bother learning the ins and outs of pruning when you're growing for birds. In late winter, just whack back the vine, hard, when it overwhelms the arbor (and pile some of the clippings for nesting birds to investigate). 'Concord' is an old reliable, but try any kind that tickles your fancy.

*Raspberries.* Red, gold, or black, your choice, but do pick an ever-bearing variety (sometimes called fall-bearing) such as 'Heritage' or 'Carolina Red'. Raspberries are quick to fill out into a good-size patch—which will add cover and double as a possible nest site for catbirds and thrashers.

*Strawberries.* Choose varieties that mature at different times—and don't forget to include an ever-bearing type that may surprise you with a taste of summer in September. Step carefully in your strawberry patch; ground-nesting birds such as song sparrows may make a home there.

Elderberries bear a big crop the first year you plant them, attracting thrashers, catbirds, and other friends.

**summer secret** All brambles are easy to grow; it's keeping them in check that can be the problem, because of rambling roots and straying canes. Plant yours in a sunny strip between a building and a sidewalk or drive, and you'll have an instant barricade.

## Trees for Summer Fruit

Shrubs give you a lot of bang for the buck: fast protective cover, easy corridor plantings, possible nesting places, insect possibilities, and a feast of fruit. But summer-fruiting trees have their own niche as nest sites, while supplying natural food galore.

For summer bird appeal, consider:

- **Juneberries or shadblow** (*Amelanchier arborea* and hybrid cultivars such as 'Princess Diana'). Shadblow can grow in either tree or bush form. Tree types (*Amelanchier arborea* and its hybrids) give the best yield of these delicious, blueberrylike fruits. You may have to shoulder aside robins and cedar waxwings to get your share.

- **Sour cherries.** Get set for "cherry birds"—cedar waxwings, that is. And orioles, great crested flycatchers, and a host of others. Sour or pie cherries, such as 'Montmorency', have great appeal. The trees are susceptible to disease but are generally so fast-growing that they outrun problems by sending up new growth.

- **Sweet cherries.** It's hard to share a harvest of 'Black Tartarian', 'Royal Ann', or other delicious sweet cherries with the birds—they're so good, we want them all to ourselves. Sweet cherries need a pollinator cultivar, though, so you'll need to plant at least two trees;

three is even better. Choose dwarf trees to save space.

- **Wild cherries.** Nearly every region of the country has its own wild cherries; browse a catalog from a native plant nursery to take your pick of bird cherry (*Prunus padus*), pin cherry (*Prunus pensylvanica*), chokecherry (*Prunus virginiana*), and others. Birds heartily approve of all of them.

- **White mulberry** (*Morus alba*). Mulberries fell out of favor because of the staining purple fruit—and the droppings of birds that consume it. Try

Cedar waxwings rely so heavily on fruit that their nesting season is timed to coincide with peak season.

## Seasonal Habit

Bird diets are heaviest on insects in spring and summer. As seeds and fruit begin to ripen in late summer, many songbirds shift their everyday menu to add these items. Red-winged blackbirds and bobolinks, for example, depend heavily on insects in spring and summer; as seeds come into season later, their diet shifts.

Not all birds with insects in their bills are eating those bugs themselves. Adult cardinals and American goldfinches collect insects to feed their nestlings—but in between trips, they're likely to chow down on sunflower seeds at your feeder or in your garden.

Sunflower plants do double duty as bird food—they attract insects, and they serve up lots of tasty seeds.

the white-fruited species to avoid the problem and provide a feast for summer birds—plus handfuls for you.

# NESTING PLANTS

Lots of us are list lovers. We love to clip or copy lists of hummingbird plants, butterfly plants, berry bushes—and, yes, nesting plants—and carry them along when we cruise the local nursery. Lists of nesting plants can get unwieldy, because most birds use a wide variety of trees or shrubs. And

their choices often vary geographically—the plants that birds select as a home site in Massachusetts may not be the same as the ones they choose in Colorado, even though many of our backyard birds are the same species. So instead of depending on a list, consider the characteristics that birds look for when they choose a place to build their home.

## Height and Habitat

Bird species do have some distinct preferences when it comes to picking a height and

**summer secret** Most plants can adapt to much less watering than you might think they need. To "train" trees and shrubs, gradually expand the time between waterings for as long as the plants are looking healthy and not showing signs of distress (such as withered, yellowed, or dropping leaves). Many plants can actually become accustomed to and thrive on a less-frequent watering schedule: They'll develop efficient roots and, as scientists are discovering, depend on complex inter-relationships, such as their association with rhizobacteria, to acquire enough soil moisture to thrive.

habitat for the home site: Sparrows don't nest high in trees, jays don't nest on the ground; meadowlarks go for open fields, wood thrushes choose a forest. As long as your yard supplies trees, jays may nest there; if you have a field, you might look for meadowlarks.

The type of nest plant itself also matters to some species, especially those that live in a more specialized niche. Blackburnian warblers, which are birds of the northern woods, choose a conifer. Blue jays seem to single out deciduous trees.

That may be simply a matter of ingrained habit or the niche that bird occupies in the greater pecking order of the natural world. I suspect that it's also because the structure of that plant is perfectly suited to the type of nest built by that bird species.

## Choosing Nest Plants

Most backyard birds are adaptable. They eat a variety of foods, they thrive in a variety of climates, and, at nesting time, they adopt whatever plant suits their needs.

Instead of going to the nursery with a plant list, you can simply choose what suits you best. (In case you're unsure, you'll also find lists of suggested plants in this chapter.)

As you're making your choices, aim for a variety of plant habits. Backyard birds are flexible, but they appreciate nest plants that offer appropriate support. Here are some things to look for when choosing plants for birds to use.

- **Strong, supportive branches.** Look for shrubs with branches that are stout enough to support the weight of a nest.

Unafraid of humans, the chipping sparrow may make its nest in the shrubs right beside your front door.

## Which Came First?

American birds and American plants grew up together, so to speak, so it's no wonder that native shrubs and trees get high marks as nesting sites. For centuries, that's all the birds had available, and they're accustomed to working with them.

As civilization spread across the country, exotic plants became commonplace—and birds adapted. I find it amusing how often lilacs show up on lists of favored nest-site plants for the robin. Considering that no lilacs existed here just a few centuries ago, that backyard bird certainly adapted quickly.

House finches offer an even more dramatic example: The 1950s fad for a blue spruce in the front yard actually helped the finches expand across the Great Plains, as they spread outward from one backyard to another one down the block.

The graceful waterfall of a bridal wreath spirea bush (*Spiraea × vanhouttei*), for example, is too flimsy to hold up a robin's nest heavy with mud—or even a sparrow's nest, for that matter. But a lilac has heavier, stiffer, more upright stems—and it's a preferred nest plant for robins, cardinals, and other backyard birds.

- **Dense branches.** No bird wants its home exposed to full view, so shrubs with lots of branches are preferred. Burning bush (*Euonymus alatus*), forsythia (*Forsythia × intermedia*), flowering quince (*Chaenomeles speciosa*), and privet (*Ligustrum* species) all provide camouflage within.

- **Dense growth.** White pines are spindly, gangly things when they're young, with lots of bare stem between the needled branches. Spruces (*Picea* species) and firs (*Abies* species), on the other hand, are dense even when young. Which would you choose, if you were a bird that preferred conifers? Well, so would they.

- **Horizontal branches.** Why do we see so many robin nests in maple trees? Maybe it's because those nearly horizontal, forking branches provide a sturdy platform on which to anchor a mud nest.

- **Forking branches.** Vireos, waxwings, goldfinches, and other birds that build deep nests attached by material wrapped around nearby branches appreciate trees (and shrubs) that allow space for that building technique. Most backyard trees and shrubs, from blackberries and roses to Siberian elms and cottonwoods, share that habit, which is why the list of possible nesting plants for these birds is an almost endless one.

- **Armed guard.** Prickles and thorns help keep the growing family safe from climbing predators. Roses and bramble fruits, among others, offer prized protection.

# A Thorny Subject

As a kid, I quickly learned to treat wild blackberry bushes with plenty of respect. I'd been snagged more than once by a thorny cane—which ripped right through my jeans!—so I steered a wide berth around the patches.

Until the berries ripened, that is. All that free-for-the-taking fruit was too tempting to pass up, so I'd gingerly step close enough to reach the fruit and stretch out my hand toward a cluster of gleaming berries.

More than once, I jerked my arm back fast when a rapid scolding noise burst from the bush. After my heart slowed back down, I'd peer inside the thorny canes to find the catbird that had just put me in my place. Yep, there she was, glaring at me as she sat tight on her nest.

Thorny branches, whether blackberries, raspberries, barberries, or any other shrub armed with stout prickles, make it just as difficult for predators to approach as they do berry-pickers.

Robins often adopt a wreath as a nesting spot, especially if it's on a wall or door that's not in use.

The catbird that gave me such a fright joins with thrashers, cardinals, mocking-birds, and white-eyed vireos, among others, in seeking out the safety of thorny shrubs for extra protection at nesting time.

## Oldies but Goodies

Easy-growing shrubs from Grandma's day (or maybe it's Great-Grandma's day, to you) are popular sites for bird nests, thanks to their dense branches and supportive stems—as well as their availability in many backyards. They're often the cheapest plants in the nursery, because they grow fast and are easy to propagate. Look for these bird-approved shrubs at bargain prices.

- Barberry (*Berberis* species)
- Flowering quince (*Chaenomeles speciosa*)
- Forsythia (*Forsythia* × *intermedia*)
- Privet (*Ligustrum* species)
- Mock orange (*Philadelphus* species)
- Lilac (*Syringa* species)
- Viburnums (*Viburnum* species)

# Popular Nest Plants

A good supply of nest materials isn't enough to encourage birds to adopt your yard as their home. They need suitable plants, too, where they can build a safe sanctuary for their brood. Most backyard birds nest in natural places, not in birdhouses. They're looking for home sites in trees, shrubs, vines, and sometimes on the ground.

As you've seen, the "right" nest plant for most backyard birds is more a matter of structural suitability than it is of it being a particular plant. Still, recommendations can help narrow down the choice when we're faced with hundreds of possibilities at a well-stocked nursery. Try these on for size, but don't be afraid to experiment with others.

| PLANT THIS | FOR THESE POSSIBLE NESTING BIRDS |
| --- | --- |
| Barberry hedge | Catbird, chipping sparrow, song sparrow |
| Climbing rose or large shrub rose | Cardinal, mockingbird |
| Decorative door wreath or hanging basket | Mourning dove, house finch, robin |
| Dense conifers | House finch, purple finch, blue jays, robin, chipping sparrow |
| Hawthorn | Catbird, black-billed and yellow-billed cuckoos, mourning dove, brown thrasher |
| Lilac bush | Cardinal, catbird, robin |
| Mixed hedge or border of common shrubs, such as forsythia, viburnums, lilacs, privet, spirea, and barberry | Cardinal, catbird, robin, chipping sparrow, song sparrow, yellow warbler |
| Old-fashioned pear or apple trees | Bluebirds, eastern kingbird |
| Raspberry or blackberry patch | Catbird, brown thrasher |
| Spruce or fir tree | House finch, grackle, mockingbird, chipping sparrow |
| Weedy corner | Indigo bunting, native sparrows, common yellowthroat |
| Willow thicket (pussy willows work great) | Yellow warbler |

# Increase the Insulation

What's the first shrub that draws your eye in someone's yard? Not the hedge along the fence or the foundation plantings, unless they're in full bloom—it's the specimen shrub, all by its lonesome in the middle of the lawn, that draws our attention.

Some predators may react the same way. That lone shrub is an inviting target, so it may be the first place a prowling cat goes to check for birds on the nest or vulnerable fledglings.

Quantity wins out over quality when it comes to nesting plants: A yard with lots of protective cover is always more likely to attract nesting birds than a yard with only

Insects, fruit, nesting material, or home site? A tangle of grapevines fills all those needs for a gray catbird.

the "right" shrub stuck in an island of lawn grass.

Groups of shrubs and hedges are favored by birds in all seasons because they increase the amount of protective cover. During nesting season, it's a rare bird who will choose a specimen shrub as its home; most of them prefer the safety found in larger plantings, or in shrubs tucked against a building.

# FLOWER FIESTA

A flower garden is a threefold feast for birds. That high bird appeal is why I tuck flowers into any place I can find a bit of spare room. I plant flowers beneath and along my hedges. I snuggle them into the vegetable garden. I fill window boxes and containers. I hoe up a strip of soil along the garage to drop sunflower seeds into. Not only do flowers in every niche look pretty and make me happy, they also add to the bird appeal of my yard. That attraction begins with the insects that flowers attract—as you've heard me say before, bugs are a major incentive for birds. Here are some of the ways our favorite backyard birds make use of flowers.

- Hummingbirds seek nectar and tiny insects at flowers.

- All kinds of birds explore the flower garden for insect prey—including those beautiful butterflies you're so proud of.

Hummingbirds and orioles visit red-hot poker for nectar; cedar waxwings eat the flowers themselves.

Butterflies or hummingbirds? Plant a patch of red or orange-red zinnias, and you'll have plenty of both.

- Small seed-eating birds, including native sparrows and finches, glean seeds as they ripen from purple coneflowers (*Echinacea purpurea*), cosmos, zinnias, and other flowers. See "Seed-Producing Flowers for Birds" on page 134 for more suggestions.

Zinnias and cosmos are my workhorses, when it comes to annuals. They're easy to grow from inexpensive seed; they bloom about 10 weeks after sowing; and they attract butterflies and birds. But dozens of other pretty flowers will attract birds, too.

# THE WONDER OF WATER

My friend Laura and I take a lot of pride in our "make-do" approach. She and her husband, Kevin, and toddler, Scout, just moved from a modest house to one of the showplaces in town—but a showplace that has seen better days. Between plumbing, painting, window work, and other necessities, she doesn't have a lot left for furniture or decorating. Every time I visit, we share the glee of the finds she's managed to come up with, like the mid-century modern dining table, with chairs that the seller threw in for free.

I'm not big on home decorating, but I am an obsessed gardener. And I'm just as much a penny-pincher as Laura. When an acquaintance told me the astronomical amount she'd spent on plants, I went home and gloated over my patch of zinnias grown from 10-cent seed packets.

# Hummingbird Flowers

Filling your garden with orange-red and red flowers will guarantee that your place attracts hummingbirds. The color red (and red-orange, or orange-red) is an "advertising" device that some flowers developed to show off their suitability to hummingbirds. Most native flowers of this color are designed to be pollinated by humming-birds. That's why they have tubular blossoms with a wealth of nectar at the base of the blossom, and no interfering foliage or branches—the perfect arrangement for a hummingbird's long bill and hovering body.

Many other flowers, of all colors, also attract hummers. You can carry along a cheat sheet, like the one below, but lists like this one aren't complete, so you'll miss out on lots of other interesting plants. Instead, look for blossoms that are easy for hummers to access and which have a tubular shape that prevents nectar from being lapped up by other pollinators. And, when in doubt, choose a red flower: Even if it's not one that hummingbirds can use, the color will draw them to your garden, where they can then investigate other plants.

For a sure-fire hummingbird magnet that thrives in nearly all zones, try the garden annual known as scarlet sage or red salvia (*Salvia splendens*, many cultivars; 'Lighthouse' reaches 2½ feet tall; 'Red Hot Sally' stays at about 12 inches tall). You can buy a six-pack of plants in bud or in bloom for just a few dollars; they'll just get bigger and better right through to frost.

## Red flowers

Wild eastern and western columbines (*Aquilegia canadensis* and *Aquilegia formosa*)

Trumpet creeper (*Campsis radicans*)

Standing cypress (*Ipomopsis rubra*)

Red-hot poker (*Kniphofia* species)

Scarlet honeysuckle (*Lonicera sempervirens*)

Maltese cross (*Lychnis chalcedonica*)

Firecracker penstemon (*Penstemon eatonii*)

Cape fuchsia (*Phygelius capensis*)

Fire pink (*Silene virginica*)

## Flowers of other colors

Basil

Columbine (*Aquilegia* species)

Delphinium (*Delphinium* species)

Purple coneflower (*Echinacea purpurea*)

Fuchsia (*Fuchsia magellanica* and others)

Sunflowers (*Helinathus annuus*)

Spotted touch-me-not (*Impatiens capensis*)

Honeysuckle (*Lonicera* species)

Night-blooming flowering tobacco (*Nicotiana sylvestris*)

Penstemons (*Penstemon* species and hybrids)

Garden phlox (*Phlox paniculata*)

Mexican sunflower (*Tithonia rotundifolia*)

## Shrubs and trees

Red-flowering horse chestnut (*Aesculus* × *carnea*)

Red-flowering buckeye (*Aesculus pavia*)

Mimosa (*Albizia julibrissin*)

Red-flowering currant (*Ribes sanguineum*)

Azaleas (*Rhododendron* species)

# Seed-Producing Flowers for Birds

Try a mixed "cottage garden" of these easy-to-grow flowers. Just sprinkle packets of seeds onto prepared soil and keep it moist until they sprout. Some of these seeds are so desirable that birds will begin visiting the moment the seeds swell and ripen, to hang on the plants and pluck them off; others will be used by birds for months, from late summer into winter, and many of these will be picked up off the ground by native sparrows, juncos, towhees, doves, and other seed eaters.

Amaranth (*Amarathus* species)

Love-lies-bleeding (*Amaranthus caudatus*)

Cockscomb (*Celosia* species)

Calliopsis (*Coreopsis tinctoria*)

Cosmos, Sensation-type (*Cosmos bipinnatus*)

Purple coneflowers (*Echinacea species*)

Buckwheat (*Fagopyrum esculentum*)

Blanketflower (*Gaillardia* species)

Sunflowers, any variety (*Helianthus annuus*)

Sweet alyssum (*Lobularia maritima*)

Mexican hat (*Ratabida columnaris*)

Black-eyed Susan (*Rudbeckia hirta*)

Marigolds (*Tagetes* species)

Zinnias (*Zinnia* species)

Sure, I drool over the gorgeous bird feeders in the catalogs that come my way, and the pretty pottery birdbaths, waterfalls, and recycling fountains. But, like Laura, I've earmarked my financial resources, such as they are, for higher-priority things—a new furnace, for one, and travel, for another. Besides, I actually like to make do. It's a matter of pride to come up with something cheap or free that looks good and serves its purpose just as well as the luxury items do.

Take my "water feature," for example. (I detest that clinical-sounding phrase for something as soulful as water, but since I haven't yet managed to come up with a better one, I guess it will have to do.) No, I don't have that three-tier cascading waterfall of faux or real stone, nor any space for it, nor any inclination to do the maintenance that I know would be required. Neither do I have that graceful pedestal plastic-resin birdbath with the solar fountain making its tinkling music.

All I have is a 12-inch-wide clay saucer, borrowed from a houseplant that's spending its summer outdoors, and a foot-high section of cylindrical clay drainage pipe that I found in the cellar.

And water.

Aha. That's the magic word. Sure, birds will be eager to make use of fancier water features than mine. But in summer, when

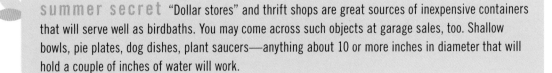

summer secret "Dollar stores" and thrift shops are great sources of inexpensive containers that will serve well as birdbaths. You may come across such objects at garage sales, too. Shallow bowls, pie plates, dog dishes, plant saucers—anything about 10 or more inches in diameter that will hold a couple of inches of water will work.

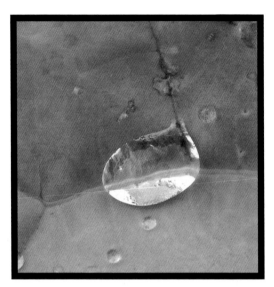

Kinglets, hummingbirds, and other small species often sip or bathe in rain or dewdrops that collect on leaves.

natural puddles are nonexistent, my simple saucer is all it takes to draw in every bird on the block.

# WATER IS BASIC

Food, shelter, water: Water is one of the Big Three basics that will attract birds to your yard. A reliable supply of water is as much of an attraction as your generous buffet of food and your yard full of protective cover.

Many water sources that birds are used to visiting for their daily drink and bath dry up in summer. Yes, rivers still run, and lakes still shimmer. But lots of birds depend not on the biggies, which may not be in their neighborhood, but on the smallest sources of water—the puddles and the brooks.

A couple of weeks without rain, and those puddles get harder to find. A drought, and brooks go dry.

When small sources of natural water become harder to find, your backyard birdbath will hit its height of popularity.

Figuring out where to put your birdbath is a balancing act. You want it to be where you will have a good view. You must also avoid putting it too close to places that cats can hide, while still providing cover in case birds need to take shelter from hawks. I put my bath at least 10 feet from shrubs or other cat ambush sites, and I place it next to a small tree that birds can easily fly up into, if need be.

Algae grows faster in water that's in the sun, so if you can place your birdbath in shade, you may reduce cleaning chores. A shady site will also reduce evaporation caused by the sun.

# Birdbaths—A Sure Bet

Birdbaths have been a backyard fixture for centuries. My mother kept two concrete pedestal birdbaths filled to the brim, and she delighted in every bird that came to drink.

A female oriole appreciates a daily dip. Watch for her brightly colored mate to take his turn, too.

## Practical and Pretty

I admired a snazzy, cobalt blue birdbath for years in a catalog before I finally treated myself to the beautiful creature. It was an exciting day when the UPS truck pulled up with two big boxes. The birdbath was just as beautiful as it had looked in the catalog picture, so I was delighted.

But once it arrived, where to put it became a big question. My first consideration was practical: I needed a location where birds would use it. But I also wanted a spot where the birdbath would look good, because it was a pretty ornament that would draw the eye.

### Practical

**Where would birds feel safe to take a bath?** Whole-hearted splashing puts birds in a vulnerable position, because they aren't watching for danger. And wet feathers make a fast takeoff pretty tricky. Providing protective branches overhead to guard against a stray hawk and no hiding places nearby for a cat to spring from were vital considerations.

**Was there a perching place?** I needed a nearby shrub or small tree with low branches where birds could pause before entering the water, look around for danger, and fluff and preen after the bath.

**How close was the hose?** I needed a spot near the faucet or hose, so that it would take just a minute to swish out and refill the bath, instead of requiring a complicated operation.

**How forgiving were nearby plants?** I needed a spot where nearby plants would enjoy the extra water from frequent cleaning of the basin and where flowers weren't so fragile or branches so brittle that they'd be damaged by a hose being dragged across them.

My grandma did the same. My great-grandma lived in Czechoslovakia, so I can't say what her yard looked like—but I'd wager there was a birdbath in there somewhere.

Old-fashioned birdbaths need no improvement because their design is ideal for many birds.

- **Height.** A pedestal birdbath, about 3 feet high, suits both birds of the trees and birds of the bush.

- **Stability.** The flaring base is sturdy and stable, and resists tipping.

- **Water depth.** The basin is just the right depth for most birds—about $2\frac{1}{2}$ inches at its deepest.

- **Perching space.** The rim of the basin offers birds a secure place to perch when they arrive, as well as to bend for a drink or make the short hop into the water.

 **summer secret** Go ahead, make that wish: A few pennies in a fountain will help inhibit the growth of algae. Older pennies are best, because they contain more copper than those of recent mintage.

### Pretty

**Where could I see it best?** Watching birds sip and splash is one of the delights of having a birdbath. I didn't want to place it where the action would be far away or out of view.

**What colors would it go with?** Blue is not a neutral, so my birdbath would have to be worked into the garden as if it were a flower of that color. Near the pinks? With the whites? Luckily, cobalt makes a good accent for just about any color, so I had lots of choices.

**Where would it catch the eyes of passersby?** I was proud of my birdbath, so I wanted to show it off to anyone who might be passing by. That meant the front yard, not back behind the house.

**Where would it look the best?** A 3-foot-tall birdbath on a sturdy pedestal base makes quite a focal point. I tried it out at the inside curve of a flower bed, at a fork in the path, in the center of an herb garden, and beneath a tree, among other spots.

Juggling all of those needs and wants, I spent a couple of days trying out the birdbath in different places in the yard. I'd lug it into place (carefully!), settle the basin on the pedestal, then stand back and squint. If it looked okay from that angle, I'd move to another part of the yard and look again.

Eventually, I found the perfect home: Beside a young red buckeye tree (*Aesculus pavia*), with clumps of Virginia bluebells (*Mertensia virginica*) at its feet. It was just a few feet from the comfy bench on my front porch and near enough to the sidewalk so that passersby could enjoy it, too.

- **Nonslip safety.** The interior of the bath is rough and gritty, so birds don't slip while they're splashing.

Our backyard birdbaths have to suit our own sensibilities, too, which is why new styles and colors seem to be popping up everywhere. Choose a bath that suits your wallet and your sense of aesthetics—but make sure it suits your birds, too. And be sure to select a birdbath that's easy to clean, because you'll be doing a quick scrub every few days. Any bath that offers the same sensible characteristics of the old-fashioned concrete classic will be a sure bet.

## FOUNTAINS AND WATERFALLS

Okay, I admit it: I want a babbling brook. A splashing fountain. A cascading waterfall. In fact, I'll take all three, thanks. And can you throw in a garden pool and a large pond, too? Thanks!

Now there's a real bird-attracting backyard. Running water, still water, muddy shores, and enough water to breed gazillions of insects. It'd be heaven to everything from the hummingbirds flying through the spray to the herons stalking the shallows.

# One Hour to a Bubbling Spring

Got an hour? A dishpan? Some rocks? You can make this DIY creation with hardly any money and very little time. The biggest cost is for the small recirculating pump: I used to use an electric model (about $20), but I've switched to solar, which costs more initially but is easier to install (no extension cords) and pays for itself (no electric bills).

This idea is one of my favorites, so I recommend it every chance I get. It satisfies my frugal soul, it looks like the natural springs I love (maidenhair ferns, anyone?), and it attracts towhees, thrushes, robins, and lots of other birds, as well as dragonflies and butterflies in summer.

You'll need a small recirculating pump; a recycled plastic or enameled metal dishpan, bucket, or kitty litter pan; a piece of ½-inch hardware cloth (wire screen with a ½-inch grid, available at hardware stores) that is 12 inches longer and wider than the opening of your container; leather work gloves (those screen edges are sharp); and a bunch of rocks about the size of your fist, plus smaller stones for filler.

1. Dig a hole deep enough to accommodate all but the top inch of your container, and settle it into place.
2. Test the pump to make sure it works. Set the pump into the container, following the instructions on the package. If you are using a bucket, you may need to stack a few bricks in the bottom to set the pump on, so that the outlet tube reaches the surface.

Most of us have to settle for something less, of course. We make do with whatever we like best, whatever we can afford either in money or do-it-yourself time, and whatever will fit into our own backyards.

Whenever I eventually make my water dreams come true, I'll keep these considerations in mind.

- The bigger the bathing space, the more bathers it attracts.
- Baths of different depths will attract more customers—small birds to the shallower basins, large birds to the deeper ones.
- The sound of water lures birds that may be passing through the neighborhood, either overhead or through the trees. During spring and fall migration, a dripper or fountain can tempt all kinds of out-of-the-ordinary birds to your yard.
- Water features require maintenance. Choose one that lends itself to your flexibility: A ground level setup makes the occasional scrubbing less difficult.

summer secret More types of solar pumps and fountains are becoming available these days, and prices are becoming more reasonable. Take advantage of the newer technology, and reduce your electric bill.

3. Run the electrical or solar cord out of the container to whichever side you need in order to connect it to the power outlet or solar battery.

4. Wearing heavy-duty work gloves, lay the hardware cloth over the container so that it extends at least 6 inches past all four sides of your container. Push the center down with your hands to make a slightly concave surface.

5. Lay a single layer of the larger rocks over the hardware cloth. Cover the edges of the screen first, to hold it in place. Then lay the rocks over the surface of the screen above the container, leaving the outlet of the pump exposed. Arrange the rocks until you like the way they look.

6. Place the smaller stones among the larger rocks, for a more natural look.

7. Fill the container to the brim with water. Connect the pump to its power source.

8. Add a few plants around the edges (ferns and grasses are always good with water) and beyond the wire, and plant a shrub nearby for perching.

Congratulations! You've just made a natural-looking, bird-attracting spring. Check the water level occasionally; you'll need to refill your spring as the water evaporates. And feel free to pass the idea along.

# MISTERS, WIGGLERS, AND DRIPPERS

Any device that creates the sound of moving water or a spray of water will help attract birds to your yard. Check store shelves and catalogs to see what's new on the scene, or try one of these reliable methods.

- **Misters.** Extra-tiny holes in a spray head that you attach to a hose create a fine spray that hummingbirds love to fly through and other birds like to bathe under. You can attach a mister to a water feature, including a birdbath, or hang it over a tree branch as a freestanding device.

Orioles are reliable visitors at birdbaths—once they find them. This bathing beauty is a Baltimore oriole.

Attach a drip tube to your garden hose and birdbath, and goldfinches are likely to arrive within minutes.

Native jewelweed *(Impatiens capensis)* thrives on the extra water near a birdbath and entices hummingbirds.

- **Wigglers.** Inexpensive spidery-legged plastic wigglers stir up the water in a birdbath or other shallow basin, increasing the charm. They're battery operated, so there are no cords or hoses to deal with.

Install a mister on a timer, and hummingbirds will quickly learn the schedule for their fly-through bath.

- **Drippers.** Drip. Drip. Drip. Install a drip tube on any basin of water to alert passing birds that liquid refreshment awaits.
- **Sprinklers.** Classic lawn sprinklers are highly attractive to birds, which will fluff their feathers while the water rains down. Robins appreciate the ease of finding worms under that "rain," too.

# CLEAN WATER

Birdbaths can get dirty fast, if they're doing their job and attracting birds. Feathers will accumulate, birds may track in seed, droppings may foul the water or the edge, dirt will cloud the water, and algae will grow. If you ignore it long enough—as little as 3 or 4 days—your birdbath may even turn into a mosquito-breeding pond.

To reduce disease possibilities, as well as keep your birdbath appealing, make it part of your routine to refresh the basin every other day, or even every morning, if the bath gets a lot of use.

Set aside a scrub brush or plastic scrubbing puff just for your birdbath; a long-handled scouring pad device works great because it keeps your hands out of the yucky water. You can make do with a scouring pad sold for doing dishes in the kitchen, or you can find cleaning brushes made just for birdbaths at wild bird supply stores and in catalogs. Soap isn't necessary; a little elbow grease and a rinse with plain water from the garden hose will get it clean.

If your dripper tube or fountain spout stops working, refer to your instruction manual. Usually the problem is easily solved by clearing mineral buildup from the opening, either by carefully poking the opening with a pin or by soaking the head in white vinegar or another recommended solution to dissolve the buildup.

# CHAPTER 8

# SPECIAL BIRDS OF SUMMER

I'M A FIRM BELIEVER in making time to do . . . nothing. Just strolling around my own backyard, looking at my flowers and listening to the birds is the quickest way I know to recharge my batteries. An afternoon of free time is great. But even as little as 10 minutes can do the trick. I do nothing special—and that's exactly what makes these bits of time so precious.

When I was a kid, summer meant long, lazy days stretching away to an endless horizon. I'd play outside all day, coming in only to grab a peanut butter and jelly sandwich or a drink. I spent hours playing in the woods, the creek, a puddle, or just lying on my belly watching ants.

I still spend some summer days doing exactly that, right down to the PB&J. It's just as much fun as it used to be, even if I have taken to using a chaise lounge for comfort.

Your own backyard may not seem like a very exotic destination for a summer vacation, but it sure is satisfying for a quick getaway. And the more time you spend in your yard, the better you'll get to know your summer bird friends.

In this chapter, you'll meet three groups of birds that bring life and music to summer days across the country. In the air, it's swallows and martins; in the treetops, incredible orioles; and in the bushes, clever "mimic thrushes"—better known as mockingbird, catbird, and thrashers.

These interesting birds are summer friends who head south in winter, so now's the time to get to know them. They will all be busy raising their families, probably in your neighborhood, and maybe even right in your own backyard. Read on to learn about their habits and how you can make them feel at home.

## THE SWALLOWS AND MARTINS

Summer brings swarms of insects to the skies, and that suits swallows to a T. From dawn to dusk, these superb aerialists spend most of their time swooping and looping after gnats, midges, flies, mosquitoes, and lots of other insects—an entire flying feast.

Because of that high-flying habit, it's not very easy to coax swallows and martins into visiting our backyards.

The trick to winning the favor of these graceful summer birds is to appeal to their family values. Housing and nest materials are the big attractions. Most members of this family get an early start on nesting—as soon as they arrive back on home grounds after spring migration. And many of them raise more than one brood a season, so you can continue trying to tempt them, even into midsummer.

But before we bring swallows down to earth, let's take a closer look at just which birds we're aiming our efforts toward.

## Built for Flight

One of my favorite songs—okay, I tend to think of it as my theme song—is an old Taj Mahal blues number whose chorus goes, "I'm built for comfort, I ain't built for speed."

Reverse that idea, and you have the swallows, a family that's aerodynamic in the extreme. Their small, flattened heads tuck tightly against their long, slim bodies. But it's those fabulous wings that say "speed" as clearly as the rocket ship fins on a 1959 Cadillac.

Swallow and martin wings are long and tapering. The birds look like miniature versions of an equally famous flier, the falcon. But not even a peregrine can keep up with the agile twists and turns of a swallow.

These birds are mesmerizing to watch in flight—and you can see them just about any day in summer. All you have to do is look up, where they tirelessly patrol the sky in their constant search for flying insects.

Best place to watch swallows? Try a

Aerodynamic swallows are built for speed and agility, so they can quickly outmaneuver flying insects.

chaise lounge or blanket in your backyard, and just look up. Swallows range through skies across much of America during summer. They're especially plentiful near rivers and lakes because that's where bugs are thickest. Lots of insects live their early stages of life in water, then hatch into the air in huge clouds.

## Range of the Swallow Family

Five of the nine species in this family—the northern rough-winged, bank, tree, cliff, and barn swallows—completely cover the skies of the Lower 48 states. In much of that huge range, swallows live throughout the entire summer season. In some areas, the birds are present only when they move through during migration. But the bottom

## Snowflake in a Storm

As a group, swallows are mesmerizing to watch; as a single bird, a swallow is a marvel of skilled motion.

The trick to appreciating swallow flight is to single out just one bird from the flock. Let your eyes settle on an individual bird, and try not to get distracted by all the other winged bodies darting through your field of view.

I use the same trick to appreciate the intricacies of a single gnat's dance, when the swarm of swirling bugs is backlit by sunlight, or to follow the motions of one snowflake falling through the glow of a streetlight.

line is, you'll see swallows in the air no matter where you live.

The purple martin comes close to country-wide coverage but is absent in a swath of the West. The violet-green swallow picks up the slack there, blanketing the western half of the country. In parts of Texas, the cave swallow adds to the mix, and in the very southern tip of Florida, the Bahama swallow adds some local color.

## Going, Going, Gone

Swallows mainly eat flying insects, and dinner-on-the-wing disappears when the air grows chilly. Swallows play it safe by leaving early when it's time for fall migration; that way, they're not stranded without food if an early cold snap sneaks in. They depart from our skies beginning in late summer. They return in spring, when temperatures are favorable for flying insects.

Tree swallows do stick around in some areas in winter, mostly because they can

adapt to eating berries. They hang out along the Atlantic and Gulf Coasts and linger in parts of the Southwest, including southern California.

## Birds of a Feather Flock Together

The marshes along the Atlantic coast, in New Jersey and Delaware, are some of my favorite places to watch birds. I've seen all kinds of wonderful birds and behavior there, but the one that sticks with me most vividly had to do with swallows.

In late summer, swallows begin gathering into groups for the flight to winter headquarters. You'll see them perched on utility wires in ever-growing numbers as smaller groups connect and form bigger congregations that can reach massive proportions.

One year, we were exploring the little-traveled roads of a wildlife refuge in coastal Delaware when we came upon a flock of thousands of tree swallows, sitting right on

**summer secret** Up close, you can see that swallows and martins have tiny beaks. Tiny when closed, that is. These birds have an extra-wide "gape" to their mouths, so they can open wide when they're in hot pursuit of a flying insect.

**summer secret** All swallows and martins hold forth with high, twittering notes, and a few species are surprisingly musical—not to mention loud. If you're selecting a site for a new martin house, consider the morning concert, when the birds greet the day with at least an hour of vocalizations that are so noisy they can wake you from sleep. My neighbor kept a martin house, and the morning wake-up routine was so loud in my bedroom—50 feet away, with windows closed—that it often had me reaching for a pillow to hold over my head when the birds sounded their 5 a.m. reveille.

the sandy road. The birds showed no sign of moving as our car drew up to them. We sat and waited for a while, then got out to see what was going on.

It was a heartbreaking scene. Apparently, a more impatient driver had actually driven right through the flock, leaving a handful of crushed birds in its wake. Swallows mate for life, and the surviving partners were absolutely grief-stricken. Each victim was attended by a mate, who touched it repeatedly with its bill and kept up a pitiful keening. The rest of the flock sat and murmured, like mourners at a funeral.

You won't see such a huge gathering in your backyard, but you may be visited by swallows and martins in number, especially if you live within a mile or so of water. I once tried to count the birds from my chaise lounge, and I reached more than 200 before I gave up trying to sort out the swarm.

## Housing, Not Food, Is the Key

The best way to attract swallows and martins to your yard is to supply nest boxes and mud—if you have the wide-open spaces they require for easy takeoffs and landings.

These birds nest in congenial colonies of their own kind, ranging from a few pairs to a huge swarm of hundreds of families.

Only half of the species in the swallow family have adapted to living around our houses. But any species may visit your yard to collect mud for nest-building, if the colony is nearby.

Here are the species most likely to turn up in your backyard. All of them are cavity nesters that will nest close to our own houses. Put up some birdhouses, and you

Be patient when you mount a purple martin house—the birds are finicky about starting a new colony.

## Drop-Ins Welcome

Four other swallow species generally don't nest around people. Unless you have a bridge, cliff, or cave in your backyard, you won't be hosting northern rough-winged or bank swallows (who like sandy banks, where they make nesting burrows), cliff swallows (nesting under cliffs and bridges), or cave swallows (it's obvious).

You may still be able to add them to your list of backyard birds, though. They may drop in to gather mud during nesting season, if you have an easily visible, easily accessible mud puddle.

may be privileged to host a nesting pair or a small colony. They can be finicky about giving their seal of approval, so try not to take it personally if they check out your real estate, then settle in elsewhere.

- **Purple martins.** Biggest and best known of the swallow family, these lovely birds become an obsession for some bird lovers. Some folks dedicate endless hours to maintaining the apartment houses that host their backyard colony; others fritter away time in frustration because they can't attract a colony.

- **Tree swallows.** Iridescent green-blue tops and snow-white bottoms make a snazzy outfit for these good-natured birds. You'll often see them living in bluebird boxes, even where a trail of birdhouses has been laid out; a bluebird box makes a good fit for a tree swallow, too. They also live in colonies in open woods, where knotholes offer inviting nest sites.

- **Violet-green swallows.** Similar to the tree swallow in looks and habits, this western species often nests in a "colony" of three or more backyard birdhouses that look out over open

areas, especially near water. A single pair expanding from a nearby colony may also adopt your birdhouse.

### In the Yard

- High-flying insects attract swallows to the open air, and you'll have plenty overhead in summer, wherever you live, from tiny gnats and midges to dragonflies, grasshoppers, bees, and wasps.

- A flower garden dancing with butterflies or a vegetable garden that attracts

Nonresident nest-building swallows may come for a visit if you offer soft white, curled feathers.

If you live west of the Rockies, put up a few single birdhouses for purple martins instead of a typical martin apartment house. Your martin is the Western subspecies, and these birds seem to have an aversion to living so close to their neighbors. In fact, they often nest as individual pairs rather than in a colony. They're more likely to be drawn to separate houses with several feet of elbow room in between than they are to a multicompartment dwelling.

cabbage white butterflies may entice swallows to fly in at a low level to grab a bite of butterfly. Herb gardens also attract a bevy of butterflies, and possibly swallows, too, as long as there's plenty of open space for them to maneuver in.

- A good-size meadow or prairie planting, especially one of about a quarter-acre or more, attracts a lot of insects—and they're likely to catch the eye of any swallows passing by.

- A large pond is prime territory for swallows, which often patrol low over water to catch aquatic insects, including mosquitoes, mayflies, and others that are rising from the surface for the first—and last—time. Sometimes the birds even swoop down to skim a drink of water in flight.

- Plant bayberries (*Myrica pensylvanica*, or, in the South, wax myrtle (*Myrica cerifera*) to lure tree swallows to your yard in fall.

- Soft, white, curled feathers are another possible attraction at any time during the long spring-into-summer nesting season of swallows and martins. Scatter them in an open area of your lawn, where the birds can easily swoop in and out.

- Swallows and martins are unlike the other birds you host in your backyard because their "habitat" is mostly the sky. They're called aerial birds because they spend so much time in flight. But when it's time to raise a family, these sleek fliers seek out more grounded home sites. If you have a large, open area of lawn, put a birdhouse on a post 4 to 6 feet high at one edge of it, facing the open area, for tree swallows or violet-green swallows who may come winging in.

- Ready for the Holy Grail of many a back-yard bird lover? Invest in a purple

**Put up a nest box in an open area for tree or violet-green swallows.**

## On the Waterfront

Swallows and martins are most plentiful near water because insects are enormously abundant there. Mayflies, mosquitoes, dragonflies, and other insects live as larvae in water and emerge en masse as winged adults, quickly taking to the air. That's when uncountable numbers of them get snapped up by swallows.

martin house, and keep your fingers crossed that yours will get the seal of approval from these notoriously persnickety birds.

# WHAT'S FOR DINNER?

Swallows and martins are nearly entirely insectivorous: That means bugs are the big thing. Tree swallows do depend on bayberries in winter, but otherwise, it's all insects, all the time. At the feeder, there are a couple of tricks worth trying, if you want to bring them down to earth.

### In the Yard

- Flying insects are everywhere, so there's no need to boost your mosquito population or nurture extra gnats; the birds will do just fine with the natural abundance overhead.

- Plants don't attract swallows in search of food, except for tree swallows drawn to bayberry in fall and winter. (See page 64 for more info on bayberries.) Large expanses of water are also attractive to these birds, because of the abundance of insects in the air over them.

### At the Feeder

- Flying insects are the bill of fare for the swallow family, and the birds nab nearly all of their food in flight. However, I wouldn't be surprised to see swallows or martins adapt to sampling mealworms at the feeder, especially during a late-spring cold snap when the birds are desperate for food.

- Even if swallows spurn your food, they may enjoy eggshells during nesting season, when extra calcium is wanted. Bake eggshells to kill salmonella and crumble the shells into a tray feeder or on the ground. (See "Crushed Calcium" below.)

## Crushed Calcium

Purple martins eagerly peck up crushed eggshells, and other swallows (as well as songbirds) may help themselves, too. The shells supply extra calcium in their diets. To kill any potentially harmful salmonella germs, rinse a few eggshells in cold water, then spread them out on a cookie sheet. Preheat your oven to 200°F, and bake the shells for 10 minutes. Let them cool, then use your hands to crumble them into 1/4-inch pieces. Scatter the eggshells on your lawn or driveway, or in an open feeder tray, so that martins can flutter down to eat them.

## Martha's Bayberry Nursery

No, not that Martha—we're talking about Martha's Vineyard (which, by the way, was Martin's Vineyard up until the late 1700s). This island off of Massachusetts is a prime wintering spot for tree swallows, which gather there in flocks so immense that they look like shifting clouds of smoke.

It's the bayberries that draw the swallows to this pricey chunk of real estate. The glossy bushes form thickets in many areas, thriving in the sand and salt air.

The bayberry thickets of the Atlantic coast have been a traditional tree swallow gathering place in fall and over winter since before Europeans arrived on these shores. During fall migration and in winter, tree swallows alight to eat bayberries.

When I explored the Vineyard a few years ago, casting a longing eye toward the shingled beach "cottages" bigger than any house I've ever lived in, I found several areas in the dunes that were covered with the weirdest stuff. It seemed to be a patchy layer of round, nubbly, blackish seeds, with bits of dirty gray stuff mixed in, and it stretched over many square feet.

It turned out to be the droppings of bayberry-eating tree swallows. The birds settle on the dunes to eat sand to aid in grinding their food. When I watched a flock lift off into the air, I noticed many of the birds, um, "lightened the load" as soon as they took wing. The indigestible parts of the bayberries were excreted, including the seeds. A little later, I came across the makings of a new thicket, an area of young bayberry bushes that had apparently sprung up from just such a "nursery" deposited a few years before.

# THE MIMIC THRUSHES

The mimic thrushes are great confidence boosters for us bird-watchers. They're big birds, so they're easy to spot when they're out and about. They sing a lot, so they're easy to hear. Most have extra-long bills. And they don't look much like any other birds, so identification is usually a cinch.

So, what's a mimic thrush, you ask? You'll recognize this family in an instant by familiar backyard members.

- The most famous representative? The mockingbird, a common backyard "friend" that can drive us to distraction with its nighttime singing and greedy ways at the feeder.

- Thrashers, including the well-known brown thrasher as well as several species of the drier West, share the mocker's big, slim body shape and long tail. Thrashers do include mimicry in their vocal routines, but they're not as good at it as the mockingbird.

- The catbird usually sticks to imitating an oddly mewing kitty but may also imitate other birds. It may sing its own pretty song at night, too—but only in snatches, not for an hour or more like the mockingbird.

The so-called northern mockingbird, which once lived mainly in the South, often vocalizes for hours at night.

You might guess from the name of this family that they're all a bunch of copycats. That's true mainly for the mockingbird, who holds forth, much like an unstoppable karaoke singer, with phrases borrowed from other birds' songs. The other mimics mostly sing their own musical songs, made up of run-on phrases, often repeated in pairs. That repetition of phrases is one of the easiest ways to peg a mimic thrush, long before you get a glimpse of the bird.

## Send in the Clowns

You may host a mimic thrush in your backyard in just about any area of the country, except for the Pacific Northwest.

By far the most common is the officially named Northern mockingbird, which isn't "northern" at all. It covers the country from coast to coast—except for the northern tier of states and a swath of the California mountains. In most areas of their wide

## Silly Songs

Translating birdsong into English makes for some funny results, but it's a great way to remember who's who when you can hear a bird but not see it. Even Thoreau was impressed by the lines used by farmers in his neck of the woods to describe the brown thrasher's song.

*Drop it, drop it,*
*Cover it up, cover it up,*
*Pull it up, pull it up . . .*

The verse goes on and on, as does the thrasher's song, but it's easy to get the rhythm from this bit. The same phrase repeated two or three times, in a song that goes on for miles: Call it a mimic thrush, and you're likely to be right on the money.

range, mockingbirds are easy to spot year-round. They nest and winter over the same wide area. But the mocker you see in summer may not be the same one you see in winter; individual birds may take short jumps to spend the seasons in different areas. If the one that's been singing on your roof is gone for several weeks, then shows up at your winter feeding station, it might not be the same bird.

The brown thrasher ranges over the eastern two-thirds of the country and often strays outside its official range to delight residents of western states. In winter, it retreats to the South and Southeast, although an occasional hardy soul may stay put in northerly regions. Some experts think that could be because of our feeding stations, which can sustain a brown thrasher even in a cold, snowy winter. It's the same for catbirds, which seem to be even a bit more cold-hardy than brown thrashers.

The other thrashers, including the California, are strictly birds of the West, and most can be spotted year-round. The sage thrasher, a bird that looks more like a thrush than a thrasher, ranges over all of the western states; the others generally stick to the dry Southwest.

## Name That Tune, Mockingbird-Style

The mockingbird wins the prize when it comes to imitation. I've listened to these birds run through phrases copied from more than 30 other species, in performances that can last an hour or more. Mockingbirds are even more fun for bird-listeners who travel, because their song list changes with the local species around them.

Rarely does the order of the repertoire stay the same. That's what makes them such

One of the biggest backyard birds, the brown thrasher is also one of the most secretive.

Bizarre bill? Nope, built just right! The California thrasher uses it to thresh the leaf litter under shrubs.

a delight to listen to—it's a "name that tune" game with endless variations. Of course, if the mockingbird is perched on your rooftop and holding forth at 3 a.m., you may be more inclined to wish for a slingshot than another go-round. That's another trait of many mimic thrushes: They sometimes sing at night.

The catbird and brown thrasher also borrow other birds' songs, as well as singing their own original tunes. Other family members stick to the song of their own species.

Mimic thrushes are even adept at imitating some mechanical or human sounds—like the whistle you use to call your dog.

# KEEPING SAFE

Mimic thrushes are natural-born skulkers. They spend much of their time hiding in thickets or brambles—except when they move to an exposed perch to sing, a habit that seems a little at odds with their predilection for staying out of sight. The birds themselves rarely fall victim to animal predators, because they're big and feisty; however, hawks and falcons may occasionally nab an unwary individual.

But their nests, which are often placed relatively low, often fall prey to snakes that climb the branches to reach them. In the East, Southeast, and Midwest, black snakes are a common threat to the brown thrasher:

They eat the eggs, the nestlings, and any parent that sticks around long enough for the snake to wrap it in its coils. (Black snakes are constrictors.) Although the thrasher and other mimic thrushes will mount a loud and determined attack against snakes, the slithery predators may pay a return call even if the birds managed to drive them off the first time.

I tried one last-ditch effort to protect a mockingbird nest after the parent birds had driven off a snake that discovered it: I piled a thick layer of thorny clippings from a locust tree all around the base of the eastern red cedar where the birds had their home. The spines were so long and vicious I said ouch many times myself while making the 6-foot-wide circle—but apparently it did the trick. The mockers managed to fledge three noisy youngsters from the nest.

# Shrimp Fork? Demitasse Spoon?

I haven't been to a 10-course dinner party in a long time—okay, ever—but I still remember the table-setting lessons my home economics teacher drilled into us when I was a kid. Each of the many kinds of spoons and forks had its own purpose, she insisted, and mixing them up was simply not done.

From the seriousness with which she treated the subject, I got the idea that fellow

## Tailored to Tastes

If you page through the thrasher section of a field guide, you'll see that there's quite a batch of these birds living in the desert Southwest. Each has a slightly different length or curve to its bill.

That variety of bill shapes and sizes allows the birds to coexist without competing with each other for the scanty natural foods of the dry desert. Those tools they carry enable each species to zero in on certain insects or fruits, reaching deep into crevices, between cactus spines, or among thorny branches.

dinner guests might simply drop dead if I used a salad fork for the spaghetti. But since I never seemed to encounter a demitasse cup in regular life, I soon forgot the finer points.

Nowadays, I'm lucky if there are a few clean forks in the drawer when company comes. My guests make do with an all-purpose implement, whether we're eating spaghetti or spinach salad.

Not so with birds—or at least not with those species that eat a specialized diet. An all-purpose beak may be good enough for jays and blackbirds, which dine on a variety of foods. But for birds who fill a more specialized niche, that lobster fork might be absolutely necessary.

Mimic thrushes are a great example of the variety of utensils birds carry. The mockingbird, which lives across the country and eats all kinds of things, has that all-purpose fork out front. But its cousins, the

thrashers, carry specialized bills that are adapted to each species' niche menu (see "Tailored to Tastes," above).

These big beaks mean business. It's mostly a half-and-half menu for mimic thrushes: Half insects, half fruits and berries.

Mimic thrushes use their bills in many ways, depending on the food they're seeking and sometimes on the habits of the species. Most use their bills as hoes, to search through leaf litter on the ground; as shovels, to dig deep for earthworms and other delicacies; as hackers, to whack foods into smaller pieces; as snatchers, to make a quick grab for a scurrying beetle or a lightning-fast lizard; as tweezers, to grasp leaves or litter and flick it aside; and even sometimes as hammers, to split and pry apart the occasional acorn. Those serious-business beaks of some western species are also perfect for finagling in between spines to pluck cactus fruit.

## Bad-Tempered Bully

Mimic thrushes are generally well behaved at the feeding station. They usually visit singly, perhaps as a pair, and they dine calmly among other birds.

Well, make that most mimic thrushes—because there's one glaring exception. Who's the bully? The mockingbird, which will commandeer a feeder as its own and viciously chase away any other bird that dares to try to use it.

*(continued on page 156)*

# Plants to Attract Mimic Thrushes

Just about any kind of fruit or berry will eventually be investigated by mimic thrushes. Here are some easy-to-grow suggestions.

| PLANT | TYPE OF PLANT | DESCRIPTION | HARDINESS ZONES |
|---|---|---|---|
| Red raspberries (*Rubus idaeus* 'Heritage' and other cultivars) | Deciduous shrub | Multistemmed, sprouts suckers. Long, arching branches with thorns; clusters of delicious red fruit in early summer, and again in fall on everbearing varieties. | 3–8 |
| Shrub roses (*Rosa* species) | Shrub | Large, mounding or arching shrubs, usually deciduous, although the leaves may be held into winter. Colorful, fragrant flowers. Thorny stems. | 2–9; most, 5–9 |
| Currants (*Ribes* species and cultivars) | Shrub | Small to medium-size, extremely thorny deciduous shrubs with dangling clusters of flowers in yellow, white, or pink to red shades, followed by chains of beautiful, translucent berries. | 2–10 |
| Mulberry (*Morus* species and cultivars) | Deciduous tree | Produces a myriad of small, juicy fruits that look sort of like skinny blackberries. Fast-growing; can reach 80' or more, but smaller cultivars are available. | 4–9 |
| Bayberry (*Myrica* species) | Evergreen shrub or small tree | Large shrub to small tree, with aromatic foliage and upright, multistemmed habit. Sprouts suckers from roots to form a larger clump. | Bayberry (*Myrica pensylvanica*), 3–6; California wax myrtle (*M. californica*), 7–9; wax myrtle (*M. cerifera*), 6–9 |
| Barberry (*Berberis* species and cultivars) | Deciduous or evergreen shrub | Small to medium-size, with ultrathorny stems; small, neat leaves; and dangling red, oval berries decorating the stems in fall and winter. | 3–9 |

| USE | COMMENTS | OTHER BIRDS ATTRACTED |
|---|---|---|
| Cover, nest site, food from insects or rose hips | Plant away from human traffic, and let it go wild. Let the interior grow dense and thorny. | Thrushes, woodpeckers |
| Cover, nest site, or food from insects on flowers or rose hips | Yellow 'Father Hugo' and pink 'Dr. Van Fleet' are easy to grow without resorting to a chemical arsenal. Rugosa roses (*Rosa rugosa* cultivars) are more upright in growth, but they, too, have lots of thorny suckering stems. | Crows, jays, thrushes, warblers, wrens, and vireos |
| Food from fruit and insects on foliage and flowers; cover | Currants native to your area are prized by your local mimic thrushes and make attractive garden plants. The native golden currant (*Ribes aureum*), a western native, and buffalo currant (*Ribes odoratum*), from the Midwest, adapt well to other areas, too. | Thrushes, woodpeckers |
| Food from fruit and from insects on foliage and at flowers | Because of the bountiful crop, the trees are often scorned as messy. Surround each with a bed of groundcover to disguise the dropped fruit and prevent it from staining pavement. | Cuckoos, flycatchers, orioles, tanagers, thrushes, and vireos |
| Food from fruit | Waxy white bayberries attract mimic thrushes winter through early spring, when most berry bushes have already been stripped of their bounty. You'll need a male and a female plant to get a good crop of fruit. | Small finches, tree swallows, thrushes, warblers, woodpeckers, and wrens |
| Cover, food from insects on foliage and flowers, food from fruit | Mimic thrushes don't care what color the foliage is, so try the cultivars with unusual chartreuse or moody, dark red leaves. These prickly shrubs help deter cats and kid traffic when you plant them as a hedge. | Thrushes, woodpeckers, and wrens |

summer secret Chinese chestnut trees, which bloom in June, have flowers that smell unpleasant to our nose but which attract hordes of insects—and hordes of insect-eating birds. If there's a chestnut in your neighborhood, watch for a flash of orange when it's in bloom.

## A Secret Life

The mockingbird may be a show-off, but catbirds, brown thrashers, and some of the other mimic thrushes are recluses at heart. You'll probably hear them way more often than you actually see them.

These are birds of the bush, and they have a habit of skulking or perching in dense shrubbery or other vegetation. Even when foraging on the ground, the catbird and brown thrasher stick close to cover, usually investigating areas beneath shrubs or hedges.

When nesting time arrives, mimic thrushes go into a total cloak-and-dagger routine, becoming even more sneaky. You'll rarely find a nest except by accident, because the parents are so secretive when building it and raising their young. These birds often nest in a welcoming backyard. If you happen to blunder too near a nest, you'll hear harsh alarm notes from the parents. And if the nest belongs to a pugnacious mockingbird, you're likely to be chased by a bird weighing less than 1/113th of what you do! Ignore that early warning, and mockers may follow through on their threat and dive-bomb your head. They attack cats and dogs, too, who don't understand why the birds are flying at them.

## Mulch for Mimics

Retire the rake, and you'll make mimic thrushes much happier in your yard. Leaf litter and other plant debris are rich with insects, snails, earthworms, and other critters. They'll eventually turn the stuff back into soil—if the birds don't get 'em first!

When I was a kid, I used to look under my mom's hedge of forsythia bushes for brown thrashers and catbirds scratching around. That's where many of the leaves that fell from our oak tree would settle into drifts, snuggling under the weeping branches of the bushes.

One day, I got curious and investigated to see what the birds were finding. When I scraped away some of the dead leaves, I discovered a whole cache of "curl-up bugs," or sow bugs—the odd, gray, segmented not-quite-insects that roll up into perfect balls when disturbed. Beetles, too, scurried away from the exposure, and earthworms quickly recoiled into their burrows. No wonder it was thrasher heaven.

From a bug-eyed perspective, the combination of darkness, moisture, and warmth from decomposition under a deep layer of dead leaves makes an ideal home. If you don't like the look of whole windblown leaves, chop them with your lawnmower and pile them under and around your shrubs. They're the absolute best mulch for mimic thrush needs.

# WHAT'S FOR DINNER?

Natural foods are the biggest draw for mimic thrushes, although the birds are quickly adapting to feeding stations, too, now that we're adding in the foods they like. Keep in mind that these birds stay low to find most of their insect food but that they will eagerly seek out fresh fruit at any level, from the strawberries in your patch to the juicy fruit at the top of a mulberry tree.

## In the Yard

- Don't forget the fruit. Mimic thrushes are extremely fond of many of the same fruits that we are. They eagerly gulp down grapes, strawberries, blueberries, raspberries, elderberries, Juneberries, figs, mulberries, and cherries. In the depths of winter, any apples still hanging on a tree are fair game.

- Let fallen leaves stay in place to make sure there are plenty of ground-dwelling bugs.

- Pile leafy clippings or dead flowers from other plants under shrubs. There, they can compost in place and invite insects, earthworms, and other critters—and mimic thrushes—to find them.

- Plant a hedge of shrubs, mixed with hawthorns (*Crataegus* species) and brambles for fruit as well as cover, and you may attract a pair of nesting catbirds, brown thrashers, or maybe a mockingbird.

- Include a patch of blackberries, raspberries, or other brambles for fruit, and it may be quickly claimed by a pair of nesting birds. Large, mounding shrub roses help make your yard prime real estate, too.

- Depend on native shrubs and small trees such as sagebrush (*Artemisia tridentata* and other species), mesquite (*Prosopsis* species), yucca (*Yucca* species), and cholla cactus (*Opuntia* species) to lure in the birds out West.

## At the Feeder

- Offer suet and other fat-based foods, such as peanut butter dough (peanut butter mixed with cornmeal to form a crumbly dough).

- Insect foods are a hit; try mealworms and insect-enriched suet.

- In winter, add millet and chopped nuts.

- Keep a birdbath freshly filled; these big birds love to splash.

**summer secret** Mimic thrushes have their own secret: Catbirds and other species sing a very quiet, for-your-ears-only "whisper song" in summer. It's a wonderfully romantic private performance, usually conducted from a hidden perch in dense shrubbery. When you hear a very quiet, very musical song as you're strolling your yard or sipping iced tea on the porch, try a discreet investigation to visually pinpoint the singer but not interrupt: You might find a mimic thrush singing for his lady love.

Hey, that's not a hummingbird! Orioles are quickly learning that a nectar feeder means food.

# The Orioles

Oh, wow! Did you see that flash of orange? Has to be an oriole!

One of the real delights of summer, orioles are our only big orange or bright yellow birds. In fact, there's only one other orange bird in America: the Blackburnian warbler, a tiny guy who isn't often seen.

These flamboyant birds have fabulous—am I running out of colorful adjectives yet?—orange or yellow feathers, contrasted with a dramatic black hood and back, and flashy black-and-white wings. Females are greenish, with hints of orange or yellow.

Orioles are outstanding in more ways than one.

Not only are they drop-dead gorgeous, but they also have the grace to frequently come out into the open, where we can admire them. They are true "standouts."

Orioles are strong fliers, so you'll often see them on the wing as they move from tree to tree. They're often way up in the tops of trees, moving among the leafy canopy.

Their musical songs are loud and sweet, and they last long enough that you can track down the singing bird with binoculars, if you like. The reddish brown orchard oriole isn't as vivid as its cousins, but it has the best voice of the bunch.

All in all, orioles offer quite a package.

## Imagine the Possibilities

Orioles are birds of the trees, but they're not birds of the woods. Most of them prefer open woods, suburbia, city parks, or backyards.

summer secret Orioles are part of the large blackbird, or troupial, family. The family resemblance becomes clearer when you take a look at a couple of other oriole relatives, the red-winged and yellow-headed blackbirds, during the summer breeding season. That's when these blackbirds desert our backyard feeders to move to marshy nesting grounds, where their colored wing or head markings will be on full display. The bright reds, oranges, and orange-reds that blackbirds show off are much smaller splashes for accenting their black bodies, but those patches are just as colorful as the full-body plumage of their cousins, the orioles.

# Fatal Attraction

Unfortunately, the personality of an oriole isn't as pretty as its plumage. The male can be absolutely vicious in driving away others of its kind from its selected territory.

This isn't always smart. I've noticed that one dead oriole on the road today will often be two dead orioles tomorrow. Those orange feathers, even when they're flattened, must trigger such a rage in the attacking bird that it is oblivious to oncoming traffic.

No backyard is bereft of the possibility of orioles in summer. These birds make sure every one of us has the possibility of oohing and aahing. Here's who you might see, depending on where you live.

**The closely related Baltimore and Bullock's orioles.** The Baltimore may show up anywhere in the eastern three-fifths or so of the country, ranging westward into the Plains, from Canada to the Gulf of Mexico. Bullock's, which has a black cap and throat instead of a full hood, overlaps with the Baltimore, picking up in the Plains and carrying onward to the Pacific, from Canada to Mexico.

**The orchard oriole** is at home from the Plains to the Atlantic and Gulf Coasts, and north into Canada.

The Southwest and the western states that lie along the east side of the Rockies, from Idaho down into Mexico, are home to the yellow-and-black **Scott's oriole.**

**The hooded oriole,** an orange bird, is limited to parts of the Southwest.

Orioles are migrants. When the time comes, they depart for wintering grounds, mostly in Mexico. This is a great time to watch them, because all along the route they'll be busy stocking up on the lingering berries of dogwoods and other fruits. In early summer, when other birds have already started nesting, orioles will be back, to pair off and start their families.

The male hooded oriole—shouldn't it be "bibbed"?—is yellow-orange in California, deep orange in Texas.

## Making a Switch

The beautiful American elm once graced the wild lands and lined the streets of small towns across nearly half of the continental United States. Then Dutch elm disease came along and changed the scene, as infected trees quickly succumbed.

That left Baltimore orioles in the lurch. American elms were their trees of choice for nesting, perhaps because the thin, flexible branches were difficult for predators to shinny along to reach an oriole nest at the tip. Many an elm once held a cradle of noisy nestlings swinging from the very end of a high branch.

Nesting orioles had no choice but to adjust. As the elms died off, the birds switched to other trees. In my small town, it's sycamores that now have the honor. I sometimes wonder if it's because they're so tall. Perhaps the climb discourages predators, just as the delicacy of elm branches once did.

One of the niftiest nests around, the hanging cradle of the Baltimore oriole is bird architecture at its best.

# KEEPING SAFE

In the treetop, often near the very tip of a branch, is where most orioles build their nests. These intricate constructions are soft, deep pouches woven out of plant fibers that the parent birds painstakingly tug free and work in with their bills. Inside is an even softer lining.

The weight of the nestlings and incubating parent works like a rock in a sock: It draws the nest downward and inward at the top, so that the family stays safe inside. And when the wind blows, the cradle does indeed rock—very gently. No need to worry about the babies sloshing around in a puddle: The mother's weight draws the pouch nearly closed at the top, and she spreads her wings to help keep the family dry.

Supplying fibers for nest-building orioles can be one of the thrills of summer. A pair in your neighborhood will be quick to spot any possibilities, from a fraying wash line to a forgotten string mop—or the lengths of white twine you temptingly drape over a bush. No need to separate the strands; if the birds decide the piece of twine is too thick, they will adeptly unravel it—another fun process to watch.

# WHAT'S FOR DINNER?

Insects and fruits, thanks, with a hearty helping of citrus and grape jelly, and maybe a long drink of sweet nectar: With orioles, you have lots of possible approaches to use when coaxing them to consider your yard. Oh, and don't forget the bathing facilities!

## In the Yard

- Plant fruit: mulberries, strawberries, cherries, apricots, raspberries, grapes, figs, peaches.
- If your climate is conducive to growing citrus, try oranges for orioles.
- Western and Southwestern orioles visit flowers for nectar. Try agave, aloe, and red-hot poker (*Kniphofia* species); red-flowered eucalyptuses are also popular sources of both nectar and insects.
- Plant a butterfly garden to gain oriole attention.

## At the Feeder

- Provide a nectar feeder with perches.
- Offer jelly in a feeder.
- Supply halved oranges in a fruit feeder.
- Try mealworms and insect-enriched suet.
- Keep a birdbath filled with fresh water.
- Offer white string and other nest materials.

In the Southwest, Scott's oriole often visits nectar feeders with large ports and perches built for orioles.

Orioles can peck every piece of pulp from an orange in just a few days, so keep some extras in the fridge.

## Plants to Attract Orioles

| PLANT | TYPE OF PLANT | DESCRIPTION | HARDINESS ZONES |
|---|---|---|---|
| Agaves (*Agave* species and cultivars) | Perennial succulents | A rosette of long, fleshy, usually spiny leaves is accented with stems of tubular blossoms—which in some species may top 20' tall! Most grow to about 6'. | 9–11 |
| Chokecherry (*Prunus virginiana*, including cultivars such as 'Schubert' or 'Canada Red') | Small deciduous tree | Dangling chains of fuzzy, creamy flowers mature to purplish fruits, bitterly astringent to our taste but manna to birds. Grow to about 20'. | 3–8 |
| Eucalyptus (*Eucalyptus* species and cultivars, especially red-flowered types such as red-flowering gum *Eucalyptus ficifolia*) | Evergreen trees and shrubs in a range of heights | Vary widely in habit, depending on species; clusters of fuzzy blossoms are typical | 8–10; most, 9–10 |
| Grapes (*Vitis* species and cultivars) | Deciduous vines | Fast-growing with large leaves and abundant clusters of fruit. Grow to about 20'. | 4–10 |
| White mulberry (*Morus alba*) | Large deciduous tree | Fast growing and quick to produce a prolific crop of white, soft berries—which don't stain like other mulberries! Grow to 50' or more. | 4–8 |
| Orange (*Citrus sinensis* cultivars, such as 'Washington') | Medium-size evergreen tree | Sublimely fragrant flowers are a hallmark of citrus; the white blossoms are followed by delectable orange fruit. Grow to 20–40'. | 9–10 |

| USE | COMMENTS | OTHER BIRDS ATTRACTED |
|---|---|---|
| Nectar | A terrific choice in desert areas of the Southwest and California. | Hummingbirds |
| Fruit, insects | Fast-growing and quick to bear fruit. Wild chokecherry trees are so abundant, the fruit (with plenty of sugar added!) was once popular for homemade jelly. | Flycatchers, tanagers, thrushes, mimic thrushes, vireos, warblers, wrens, and many other birds |
| Nectar, insects | Eucalyptus burns hot in western wildfires; do not plant near buildings. | Hummingbirds, tanagers, vireos, warblers, and other birds |
| Fruit, insects | Fast-growing cover and a crop of fruit the first year after planting. | Large finches, tanagers, thrushes, mimic thrushes, wrens, and many other birds. Peeling bark and dead stems used for nest materials by many birds. |
| Fruit, insects | Keep mulberries at a lower height, if you like, by pruning in late winter. Excellent in a mixed hedge. | Flycatchers, tanagers, vireos, warblers, and many other birds |
| Fruit, insects; cover | Orioles often winter in citrus groves, or in a backyard with an orange tree. | Some finches, vireos, warblers, and other birds |

# PART 3

# SECRETS FOR FALL

## FALL: GET READY FOR FLOCKS

Fall makes us feel alive. The clear skies and cooler days of fall are a welcome relief after a long, hot summer. Instead of languishing in the heat, barely able to gather enough energy to pour another glass of iced tea, we feel refreshed and energetic.

In the bird world, though, fall begins long before heat and humidity are swept from the skies. For birds, the new cycle begins almost as soon as the last babies are on their own.

What's the rush? It's time to get going. For birds, fall is all about moving on, from nesting grounds to fall and winter feeding territories. For most birds, that means it's travel time. Some species are long-distance migrants; others relocate by just a few hundred miles; and some shift by only a mile or two, or not at all.

Food and cover are the focus for fall birds, and in this season especially, the two are inseparable. Those flocks of sparrows, juncos, and other migrants are looking for a safe place when they land, and sheltering shrubs and garden beds are the keys to making them comfortable.

Along with all those birds in our gardens, feeder traffic picks back up again in fall, too. Cardinals, song sparrows, jays, and other year-round birds come in from the wild places around us, looking for a handout now that insects have dwindled. And migrants descend en masse at an inviting food source—like the sugar water in those hummingbird feeders, the berries on your dogwood, or the niger seed in your finch tube.

By late July, bird life is already beginning to shift to the new season. While we're still enjoying our August summer vacations, birds are in full fall mode. As autumn settles in and migration ends, the feeders are hopping with birds that will stick around right through winter.

In this section, you'll learn how to adjust your feeder offerings, add cover with bird-certified plants, and otherwise make your yard irresistible.

# CHAPTER 9

# MOVING ON

**H**AVE YOU EVER noticed how good your pets are at interpreting the signals you put out? Pick up the leash, and your dog is dancing by the door. Crank the can opener, and Kitty is tangling herself around your legs.

My dog, Duke, has become completely deaf in his old age. This makes him even more determined to figure out what I'm going to do next, because he doesn't want to get left out.

When I settle on the sofa with a book, he heaves a big sigh and stretches out beside me; he knows I'm not likely to be going anywhere for a while.

When I pull out the backpack and start loading it with clean clothes and toiletries, he looks at me hopefully, half wagging his tail. He's waiting for me to give the nod that says, "Yes, you're coming with me this time, not going to the kennel."

Of course, the communication with our pets works both ways. We learn to read their signals so that we know right away when they need to go out, or when they want to play, or when they're hungry.

Paying attention to backyard birds will tell you what their behavior means, too. Fall is a good time to practice, because the signals are so unmistakable that you'll be able to figure out bird behavior just as clearly as you interpret it with your pets.

## GETTING READY FOR THE JOURNEY

I tend to take birds for granted in summer. There's not much activity at the feeder. The fun of watching nest-building orioles help themselves to strings is over for another year. I haven't come across a baby bird in the yard for more than a month.

And besides, I've been busy trying to keep cool during the dog days, plus

In fall, flocks of robins gobble berries wherever they can find them, refueling along the migration flight.

167

A chokeberry full of dangling red fruit may be jealously guarded by a mockingbird until the astringent berries are ready to eat.

figuring out how to sneak the humungus zucchinis over to an unsuspecting neighbor.

While we're distracted with summer fun, big changes have been happening in bird land. The pressures of family life are finished, even for the late-nesting gold-finches and cedar waxwings. The sex hormones that have kept birds hopping since spring have simmered down. The season is shifting from a focus on the family to a time for travel.

## Singing Stops

The first sign of the times is that birds stop singing. You may not have even noticed that the dawn chorus was dwindling as singers dropped out over the course of summer. But by August, mornings sound way different than they did in May. Most birds have stopped making music. You'll still hear an occasional robin greeting the day, or an indigo bunting holding forth at high noon, but the rich symphony of birdsong is pretty much over and done with. Once nesting season comes to an end, there's no need anymore to win a mate or stake a claim against the competition.

## The Silent Type

I like to think I'm pretty good at noticing things, but every fall, my backyard birds remind me of how much I miss.

Take that September day when I was working right across the yard from a flock of, oh, about 40 fabulous birds, without ever noticing them.

I was clearing some space in the garden so I could squeeze in a maybe-it's-not-too-late planting of spinach when I heard an odd pattering noise. It sounded like a spattering of big fat raindrops hitting the ground, but the sky was clear blue with hardly a cloud in sight.

Then my eye caught a bit of motion in a nearby Bradford pear tree—a bird was shifting its position on a branch. That's when I realized that the bird wasn't alone: The tree was full of birds plucking the small reddish fruits.

Robins, tanagers, flickers, rose-breasted grosbeaks, a brown thrasher, and a mockingbird were all busy in the Bradford pear. If they hadn't been such messy eaters, I might never have noticed the feeding frenzy taking place just 50 feet away.

**fall secret** I make it a habit to quickly scan any trees and bushes that hold fruit in fall, such as dogwoods (*Cornus* species), Bradford or Callery pears (*Pyrus* cultivars), hackberries and sugar-berries (*Celtis* species), and others. You don't have to identify the plants: Just look at any tree or shrub that still holds some berries. If you scan the plants daily when you're strolling the yard, you just might catch a group of birds feasting on the fruit.

## Costume Changes

"I need some help," said a friend who was new to feeding birds, one fine fall day. "I have a whole lot of these little birds. Dozens, at least. Maybe a hundred, even. I looked in the book, and I think they may be pine siskins. But they don't look quite right. They aren't striped."

I had a good guess already, because I'd been fooled myself many years ago. "Check out the American goldfinch page in your field guide," I suggested. "Is there a picture of it in winter plumage?"

"That's it! They're goldfinches. They change color?"

Yep. They do.

In many cases, a bird's fall clothes look just like its spring outfit: cardinals look like cardinals; blue jays like blue jays. But in several species, the change can be confusing because the bird (usually male) changes its costume to one that differs from the "usual."

Watch how these species change their costumes in fall.

- American goldfinches are widespread and abundant, so you're likely to spot these color-changers first. Around October, adult males switch from bright yellow bodies with black wings and beret to dull greenish bodies with black

wings; they even lose the trademark black cap. In March, the male birds return to normal color.

- Another supercommon bird that's fun to watch change color with the seasons: my favorite starlings. (Yes, I have a soft spot for underdogs, and starlings don't get much respect.) In early fall, males and females change over from the glossy iridescence and bright yellow bill of breeding season to a coat that's spangled with little light spots, like a night sky full of stars. Their bills turn dark in fall, too.

American goldfinches start to look blotchy in fall, as their plumage shifts to the olive drab of winter.

## Junior? Is That You?

Juvenile birds—those that hatched during the just-past breeding season—often look more like the female than the male of their species, but with enough details to make us wonder if we're looking at a whole other species.

A juvenile red-winged blackbird, for instance, may show a dab of red feathers on its shoulders, yet its body is streaky brown, like the female. Juvenile orioles also look more like Mom than they do like Dad, as do not-quite-grown-up grosbeaks.

A comprehensive field guide, like *The Sibley Guide to Birds* (see Sources on page 320), which has pictures of youngsters, is invaluable for figuring out such fine points.

- Just as shocking a change as that of the American goldfinch is that of male scarlet tanagers, which turn green in the post-breeding molt of early fall. Western tanager males exchange their vivid red-orange hood for a green head. You'll see way fewer tanagers than you do other birds, so you might miss this shift altogether—unless you happen to have tanager-attracting berry bushes and trees in your yard.

- Male rosy finches take on drabber dress in fall, too—usually right about August. The adult males switch to plumage that looks like a cross between male and female coloration, with the body mostly a paler grayish brown instead of the rich, warm, rusty brown of spring and summer. Their winter coats also lack the beautiful flush of warm rosy red on belly and wings.

- Some blackbird species change costumes this season, too. Brewer's and rusty blackbird males lose their iridescent breeding plumage and acquire feathers with pale edges that give them a scaled appearance; the female rusty takes on a warmer chestnut tone. In fall, juvenile male blackbirds, grosbeaks, and tanagers can be confusing because they look more like females than like males.

- Male bobolinks look like an entirely different species in fall, when they adopt sparrowlike stripes instead of dashing black-and-white patches.

- Male golden-crowned sparrows lose their strong black eye stripe in the post-breeding molt, and if you look closely, you can see that their beak changes from bicolored to pale gray.

- Harris's sparrows and black-chinned

**fall secret** Beautiful western tanagers may become regular customers at suet or fruit feeders, especially during migration in fall and spring. Scarlet tanagers also seem to be adopting feeders, mostly in spring. Other tanager species may also turn to feeders, so keep an eye out for these beauties in your yard—whatever color feathers they're wearing.

sparrows, too, lose some of their strong black head markings in fall.

- The chipping sparrow's trademark chestnut cap fades to duller brown, and its jaunty white eye stripe becomes tan in fall.

- Male lazuli and indigo buntings become blotched with gray in fall, which gives their bright feathers a moth-eaten look.

- Bay-breasted and other wood warblers are notorious for plumage changes in fall: They've earned an entire section in some field guides, headlined "Confusing Fall Warblers."

## Flocking

Sometime in late summer, I'll be watching a dragonfly or admiring a flower, not even thinking about fall, when all of a sudden a bunch of birds enters my line of sight.

It might be a couple dozen grackles or red-winged blackbirds, or it might be a few hundred swallows. But it all means the same thing: The birds are flocking!

Why the excitement? Because flocking is the neon sign that announces that fall is on its way.

Once nesting season is over in late summer, birds no longer hang out two-by-two. Instead, most species gather in groups.

All over the world, swallows join together in huge flocks for migration. These British barn swallows will winter in Africa.

At first, it may be only the immediate family that sticks together. But soon, the group starts to grow.

Whether it's 4-and-20 blackbirds in a field or 100 tree swallows on a roadside wire, the banding together of birds is a signal that's impossible to misinterpret.

It means that the birds are on the move. Fall migration has begun.

The realization is tinged with melancholy for me because I realize that the natural year is on the downward slope. Spring and summer are the youth of the

**fall secret** Fall flocks can be all the same species, but more often they're birds of similar habits. Native sparrows of many species gather together in patches of seed-rich weeds—or in your gone-to-seed gardens. Barn swallows join up with rough-winged, violet-green, or other swallows. Fruit-seeking tanagers join orioles and thrushes wherever berries are abundant.

year; fall and winter . . . . well, let's just say that I'm on the same slope myself.

The melancholy never lasts long, though. Because once the birds are flocking, it's time for us bird lovers to get busy adjusting our yards for the new season.

## TIME TO TRAVEL

Fall is full of good-byes—but it's also time to say hello again to some old favorites. The exact timing depends on where you live, but in general, most songbirds are on the move from August through September.

## See You Next Year

Orioles, tanagers, house wrens, and some other species are fair-weather friends: They depend on fruits and insects to fill their bellies, so they get going while the going is good, before cold weather cuts off their food supply. Enjoy the pleasures of their company while they're passing through, and then bid them a fond fare-thee-well.

- Look up to catch the swallows, swifts, and martins swooping through the sky.
- Watch for flashes of bright oriole feathers in your shade trees.
- Get a last look at the long-tailed thrasher in your grape arbor or the catbird in your raspberry patch.
- Catch one more glimpse of the perfect posture of a flycatcher, perched and waiting for its dinner to fly by.
- Thank those active little house wrens for building in your birdhouse last summer.
- Feast your eyes on the black-headed or rose-breasted grosbeaks at your feeders, while they last.

## 'Roid Rage

In spring, male songbirds fight viciously with each other over the favors of a female. If you've ever watched one of these battles, you may find it hard to believe that the same birds would band together good-naturedly when fall migration rolls around. Just shows you how strong male hormones can be.

That springtime behavior is the birdie version of "'roid rage," the intense irritability that is supposedly fueled by the use of synthetic sex hormones. Birds don't use bodybuilding supplements, but they do have plenty of natural male hormones during the nesting season.

Those natural urges are what keep male birds on the alert, ready to chase off competitors and protect their families. More 'roid rage? Consider the poor cardinal who batters himself silly against a window or mirror. That hair-trigger temper kicks in because the bird brain can't decipher the image of a male bird as just a harmless reflection.

When nesting season ends, so does the extra dose of hormones, and with it the competition between males. Now they can be buddies instead of beating each other up.

## Cold Fronts

It takes less fuel to fly an airplane if there's a tailwind behind it. Birds take advantage of that push, so I take notice when the weather report says a cold front is coming in. Migrants will be just ahead of that system—and they may drop down in my yard, where my feeders will be freshly stocked.

- Delight in the hummingbird circus at your nectar feeder and among the flowers.
- Listen for the *chip*s of wood warblers busily working their way through the foliage.
- Remember the sweet voice of a vireo singing in your backyard, or the *witchety-witchety* call of a black-masked common yellowthroat in your meadow garden. They'll be back—next year.

## Vacation Planning

Colder weather in fall and winter puts an end to insects and fruit, and snow makes finding seeds difficult. That's a great reason for birds that depend on these foods to relocate in fall. Extreme cold can also be difficult for birds to survive, so they move south to escape it.

Moving to a winter home where it's easier to stay alive makes perfect sense. But birds have developed migration patterns over thousands of years, and sometimes the selection of a wintering spot doesn't seem to add up.

I've often wondered why some birds—especially the ones that nest in the South—migrate at all. Their lives seem pretty cushy already. Why flap your way for thousands of miles to, say, Brazil, when you could just loll about in Florida?

The answer: In many cases, we just don't know.

Some species seem to migrate because of long-standing habits, rather than because of current conditions. Take the blue grosbeak, for instance: It deserts its home in the hospitable, mild-wintered southern tier of the country to head for Mexico and Central

Hummingbirds are often feisty about their feeder, but during the fall migration rush, everybody shares.

Look for fall migrants at the "edge" between woods and grass, where varied foods and cover are abundant.

# Moving Out

I'm often out in the yard of my house, which is just a block from the city park and another block from the school, so I get to visit with a lot of folks when they pass by. Last summer, during the middle of a heat wave, several of us ended up having a conversation about where we were planning to travel to get some relief from the smothering humidity.

"Kentucky," said one fellow. "We have a place on the lake down there."

"Florida," said another. "If I'm going to be hot, I'd rather be on a beach."

"Minnesota," said a third. "We're taking the canoe up to the Boundary Waters."

"New York City," another chimed in. "Everyone will be in the Hamptons, so maybe we'll be able to get a good table and good tickets."

Over our heads, the branches were busy with songbirds: a family of Baltimore orioles, the warbling vireo that had been serenading me for months, the constant crowd of goldfinches waiting for a chance at the thistle feeder. Beside the garage, a tangle of greenbrier and honeysuckle concealed a Carolina wren, and the bushes along the fence held a catbird that mewed harshly at the neighborhood cats.

If the birds had been able to talk, their travel plans would've sounded just as varied as my neighbors'.

America. Hello? What's wrong with San Diego? New Orleans? Tampa?

Come to think of it, that was the same question I used to ask my sister, who lived in Pennsylvania but vacationed every year in Miami.

"Why not Myrtle Beach?" I'd ask. "It's not nearly as far to drive."

"I know," she'd answer. "But we're used to the drive. And we like it there."

I imagine a blue grosbeak might give me the same answer.

**fall secret** Many migrants are fond of insects, so serve mealworms in an open container—where the critters are visible—to catch the birds' attention when they're passing through.

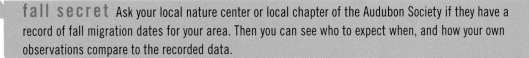

**fall secret** Ask your local nature center or local chapter of the Audubon Society if they have a record of fall migration dates for your area. Then you can see who to expect when, and how your own observations compare to the recorded data.

- Within weeks, the vireo would depart for Guatemala or El Salvador.

- The orioles might end up in Florida orange groves.

- The Carolina wren might travel a few hundred miles to Tennessee (or the Carolinas!), or he might stay right in my yard all winter.

- The goldfinches would probably relocate a short distance and be replaced by a flock that moved in from elsewhere.

- The catbird might be a vanguard of the species, which seems to be shifting its migration pattern to wintering in colder areas. But, most likely, the bird would take its leave and head for the Gulf or

The red-eyed vireo relies on insects, so it hightails it south before cold weather can cause a food shortage.

the Atlantic Coast, where winters are milder because of the ocean influence; it may travel even farther, to Mexico and southward.

As you can see, your own location determines which birds you're likely to see moving in—or moving out. (If you're not sure which particular birds spend this season in your area, check a comprehensive field guide, such as *The Sibley Guide to Birds* (see Sources on page 320). In some cases, only certain species of a particular group of birds migrate, while others stick around all year.

**Insect eaters.** First to go are the birds that eat almost nothing but insects. They begin their departure even before back-to-school time, and often while we're still donning swimsuits in what we call "late summer." To these birds, the season has already shifted, and by the bird calendar, it's fall: time to move along.

- Flycatchers
- Martins
- Swallows
- Swifts
- Vireos
- Wood warblers

**Nectar drinkers.** Orioles, downy woodpeckers, sapsuckers, and some other

**fall secret** The range maps in some field guides, such as my favorite, *The Sibley Guide to Birds*, may include a speckling of dots on the map that represent sightings outside a species' normal range. The dots don't seem very exciting until you remember that each one represents a real live rare bird that thrilled everyone who got to see it. Maybe one of them is yours. I still like to believe that one of the dots for the Harlan's hawk, a dark-colored version of the red-tailed hawk, is a bird I spotted and reported on an Audubon Christmas count several years ago—and which still hangs out in the same area, several years later.

birds sip nectar or sap. But hummingbirds are the bird family that depends most heavily on it. Hummers augment their diet with tiny insects, but flowers are a big deal to them. When the flowers are threatened by frost, hummingbirds, as you might guess, are already on their way south—unless you live in a mild-winter area, where you may host rufous, ruby-throats, or Anna's in the off season. In that case, keep an extra bag of sugar on hand to fill those feeders for hummingbirds. Otherwise, expect to see the nectar drinkers depart soon after the insect eaters.

**Fruit-and-insect eaters.** Wave good-bye next to the fruit-and-insect eaters—or stock up on dried fruit, citrus, suet, meal-worms, and other soft foods if you live where these species spend fall and winter.

- Bluebirds
- Catbird
- Orioles
- Tanagers
- Thrashers
- Thrushes
- Wrens (some species)

**Seed eaters.** Finally, say, "See ya next year" to the seed eaters—or add an extra feeder to take care of the crowd, since many of these species are fall and winter residents in large areas of the country.

- Blackbirds
- Buntings
- Finches
- Grackles
- Grosbeaks
- Juncos
- Sparrows

## Visitors from Afar

It took me quite a while to readjust to Indiana after living in Washington state for 5 years. Whew, the heat! The humidity! And where are the mountains?

So I can only imagine how a varied thrush might feel when it finds itself on a neatly trimmed lawn in small-town Indiana instead of its usual haunts of mossy green Northwest forests.

I spotted the thrush among a big flock of robins, on an early fall day. I was walking home after dropping my car off at the garage when I came across a hundred or so robins working over the yards on one of New Harmony's quiet side streets—obviously a migrating flock that had stopped to feed for a while before flying on.

It was a pleasure to stop for a while in the still-warm sun and watch robins. The birds didn't seem to mind my presence a bit. They were too busy sorting through the lawns and gardens for tasty morsels or taking turns in the three birdbaths on the block.

I was comparing the different shades of orange on the birds' breasts when I spotted a bird among the flock that wasn't a robin at all.

It was a varied thrush—a beautiful orange and gray bird with a bold, dark necklace. It lives in western forests.

I knew varied thrushes well, from when I'd lived in Washington and Oregon, where the birds are a treat to come across in the dim conifer forests. I sure never expected to see one in southern Indiana, hopping about on a neatly trimmed lawn in bright sunshine.

Still, robins are members of the thrush family, too, so this guy was with kin, of a sort.

The flock was gone by the time I came back with my camera, so I never got a picture of my oddball bird. But I did get

Not so great at reading a map, or just curious to see the world? The varied thrush may go astray in fall.

more evidence that, during migration, you just never know who might turn up.

Varied thrushes turn up far outside their usual range pretty frequently. So do other individual birds of many species.

Sometimes, an entire species eventually shifts its habits, as the rufous hummingbird appears to be doing these days. Our feeding stations, gardens, weeding habits, and other human activities can affect bird behavior. As our gardens grow and our bird feeding setups expand, birds may adjust their migration patterns to take advantage of the tempting conditions.

**fall secret** Climate change will have a huge influence on birds because it affects insects and plants—the basic bird foods—as well as weather. If you live in the southeastern quadrant of the country, keep your field guide handy in fall. Many western species seem to be adjusting their migration routes to include parts of the Southeast. Western tanagers, rufous hummingbirds, varied thrushes, and other western species are being spotted far outside of their usual ranges. Some of the birds are even wintering there, instead of continuing on to Central or South America.

# WELCOME BACK

I've always had difficulty putting together a summer wardrobe. The bright pinks, vivid greens, and knock-your-eye-out oranges that fill the racks are lively and eye-catching, but they just don't suit my style. I prefer to blend in with my surroundings rather than be visible from a quarter-mile away.

That's why, when fall clothes arrive on the scene, I'm happy to say good-bye to summer and shift my wardrobe back to the colors I feel at home in: shades of brown, tan, gray, rust—colors that are all around in the natural world. Bright summer colors may be fun for a change of pace, but when it's time to pack away summer clothes and deck myself out in my earthier fall wardrobe, I feel like myself again.

A seasonal transformation of color takes

An eye ring gives the field sparrow a wide-eyed look—or maybe he's surprised by all the seeds in your yard.

## LBBS and LGBs

The best thing about fall bird feeding is the big increase in birds: Instead of feeding only a handful of half-interested diners, we're hosting a constant crowd.

Most of those fall and winter friends are little brown birds (LBBs) or little gray birds (LGBs, to stretch a point). They may not be as breathtaking as orioles or buntings, but they sure add life to the outside scene. How many of them are you hosting?

### LBBs

Native sparrows (many species, including field, fox, golden-crowned, song, tree, white-crowned, white-throated, and others)

### LGBs

Chickadees (several species)

Juncos (several species and races, including dark-eyed, Oregon, pink-sided, slate-colored, and others)

Nuthatches (red-breasted, white-breasted, and other species)

Titmice (several species)

**fall secret** Jeweled hummingbirds are amazing when seen close up, so attach a suction-cup nectar feeder to a window that you—or your kids—often look out of.

place among our backyard birds, too. In summer, the trees are filled with birds of bright hues: orange orioles, red tanagers, bright blue buntings. But in fall, many of the vividly colored species of summer depart, and the quieter-colored birds of fall filter in.

It's all part of fall migration. And, like switching our wardrobe for the new season, it's a gradual process, not an overnight affair.

Most fall arrivals are dressed in those "natural" colors I love—the tans, browns, grays, and other neutrals that make them blend in with the background.

## The Quiet Type

Fall migrants behave differently than birds on the move in spring.

No need to stick to classic yellow: Sunflowers come in gorgeous colors, and all boast seeds that birds adore.

Spring migrants are full of themselves. Their hormones are already in gear, so they're feisty and active. Sure, they're interested in finding food—but they're just as involved in finding breeding territories or practicing their show-off moves or being belligerent with other males.

Fall migrants have a different agenda. Nesting season is over, so hormones have simmered down. Males aren't flashing their wings, chasing each other, or practicing their postures. Eating is the top priority; it's a long journey, and birds are focused on filling their fuel tanks.

Moving on is vital because the threat of cold weather can cut off the food supply.

## Hummingbird Mania

"Where'd all the hummingbirds go?" is the big question in early summer, when the stream of tiny birds zipping in to the feeder suddenly dries up. They're taking care of families, that's where.

By the time August rolls around, hummingbirds are back—big-time. Fall is peak season for hummingbirds. The traffic at the nectar feeder reaches fever pitch as families jockey for position and early migrants stop by. You'll find tips for feeding fall hummers in Chapter 10 (see page 197). For ideas on fall-blooming hummingbird flowers, see "Fall Flowers for Hummingbirds" on page 218.

# THE FEEDER SCENE
# IN FALL

**F**ALL BRINGS BIRDS back to our feeders. The summer boom of insects is over, and seeds, suet, and other feeder treats are what's for dinner these days.

Stock your feeding station with their favorite fall foods, and you can enjoy the attentions of just about every species that's passing through.

Fall is a great time to start a feeding station, or to freshen up an existing one with a new feeder or new foods. Winter residents and year-round friends will be checking in daily to see what's on the menu. And when the weather turns colder, the action will really heat up.

## CHOOSING A FEEDER

I love shopping, especially when I can do it without leaving home. So it's always a treat to find the latest catalog from a bird supply company in my mailbox. For days, the catalog sits on my kitchen table, where I can page through it over and over, figuring out my perfect feeder setup.

Should I indulge in that pretty suet feeder with the bird-on-a-bough design? Would my fox squirrels enjoy the challenge of that clever lift-the-lid peanut feeder? Is this the year to invest in a waterfall that looks and sounds almost like the real thing?

And just look at all those foods! Wouldn't my birds love a big bag of already shelled sunflower seeds? Oh, but that's nothing—check out this mix of fancy seeds and nuts *and* dried blueberries! Hey, that sounds even better than my own bowl of breakfast cereal.

And then there are those mealworms, which I know work like a charm on bluebirds. And the nut- or insect-enhanced suet cakes. And the molded balls of suet and pecans, with a sturdy metal feeder custom-made to fit

This appealing feeder is simple and practical. The lid opens for easy refills, and there's room for suet, too.

## Money Talks

Bird feeders and food have come a long way since we threw our bread crusts onto the snow 50 years ago. And that's great news for us bird lovers. Many of these foods cost more than simple seeds, but they are effective at bringing in birds—and often at bringing in the birds we really crave, such as bluebirds.

With today's special foods—mealworms, bluebird dough made from peanut butter and cornmeal (homemade or commercially made), pelletized suet, dried fruits, and all kinds of nuts sold as bird food or available at grocery stores—we can tempt in any bird that's in the area.

Today's feeders are a major step forward, too. They're built of better materials—cedar instead of particle board, and sturdier plastic instead of flimsy stuff that cracks with moderate use.

Specialty foods enable you to tailor your menu and your feeder to exactly the birds you want to attract. There are nectar feeders for orioles with a large reservoir and heavier-duty perches than those on hummingbird feeders. You can also find chickadee feeders that are just the right size for a tiny mite and its favorite treats.

You can exclude birds you don't want. Tired of gangs of starlings gobbling up the suet? Use a feeder that holds the cake of suet where starlings can't get at it. You can examine feeders yourself to make a guess at whether or not heavy perching birds like starlings will be able to use it, or check the label or catalog description. Feeders that discourage starlings or other "pest birds" are often labeled that way. One anti-starling design consists of a cake of suet held horizontally beneath a covered roof. Since starlings aren't as agile as lightweight chickadees, they have a hard time clinging to the swaying upside-down cake.

You can even say "Sorry, no squirrels allowed," by choosing feeders that keep them out. Look for labels or catalog descriptions that indicate the feeder is "squirrel resistant." Some designs include a door that slides shut if a weighty squirrel lands on the perch or feeder; others use barricades of wire grids to keep out squirrels. Or, if you're amused by silly squirrel antics, you can buy a feeder just for them.

Why all these choices today? Because lots of us are feeding birds—and it's a hobby that gives us a huge return on a very small investment. Plus, we can enjoy it right at home, without having to fill the gas tank. Of course, if you're on a tighter budget, you can do it the old-fashioned way, by sticking to inexpensive seeds or kitchen crumbs. Feeding birds is something anyone can do!

them. Look—I can even sign up for home delivery so I don't have to lug home heavy bags from the feed mill!

Ah, yes, indulgence would be so easy.

And the photos are so seductive. Colorful goldfinches, cardinals, bluebirds, orioles, rose-breasted grosbeaks, and other beauties happily share a meal of the catalog's products, at the catalog's feeders. Yes! Yes! I want my yard to be filled with birds like that, too!

Bird catalogs are definitely tempting. But the best way to select a feeder is to use common sense. Read on for tips on choosing the best feeder for your birds.

## Practical Matters

After drooling over those beautiful photos of bluebirds and orioles for a while, reality starts to kick in.

Hmm. What's wrong with these pictures? Well, nothing, exactly: This catalog uses actual photos of actual birds, not stuffed fake birds or exotic foreign species, like I've seen in some ill-considered advertising efforts.

No, it's not what is *in* the photos that's the problem: It's what is *not* in them.

There are no starlings gobbling that fancy suet. No jays hogging the nuts. No hordes of grackles or red-winged blackbirds scarfing down the high-priced seed mix. No squirrels sitting in the middle of the tray. There's not even a single house sparrow.

Could these photos be meant to tempt me by showing me only the prettiest, most well-behaved birds?

Of course!

So I take a closer look at the feeders themselves, with a more realistic eye. Each one on my wish list—and that'd be just about all the models in the catalog—gets a careful examination while I ask myself these questions.

Nuthatches quickly take to a birdseed bell. At about $2, this "feeder" is fun for kids to hang and watch.

- **How is it constructed?** Will the material it's made from hold up to my less-than-careful handling, plus heavy use by birds? Will it break if I drop it? Can a 'coon carry it away, or a squirrel chew off a corner?

## The Per-Year Price

Another big question when choosing a feeder: Is it worth the price?

To answer that, I look at how many years I can reasonably expect to use the feeder, then divide that into the price.

Fifty dollars may seem like a lot of money to pay for a feeder, but if it serves me well for at least 5 years, that's only $10 a year. Not bad at all, for an attractive, well-made, easy-to-use feeder.

- **How will I mount it?** Will I need to install a post? A special bracket? A hanger? Will I need any tools or skills? Does the mounting hardware come with the feeder, or will I need to make a trip to the hardware store?

- **Will it stay fairly clean?** Will droppings fall to the ground, or will they end up in the food? Are there lots of nooks and crannies where bits of shells or wet seed might accumulate? How often will I need to take it down and thoroughly clean it?

- **Is it big enough?** Will it hold enough food to go a few days without a refill? Will it serve more than a few birds at a time, or will there be frequent squabbling over a seat?

- **How easy is it to refill?** Will I need to use a scoop, or can I refill directly from the bag? How easy will it be to open and refill it with one hand, while holding the food in the other hand? Are there metal parts that might stick to my fingers on a frosty morning?

If more than a few of these questions have answers I can't live with, that feeder gets scratched off my list and I move on to the next possibility.

## Clean and Simple

Pour seed directly on the ground, and you'll get plenty of birds. So why not take that route? You can. Ground feeding is the way to go when snow or ice storms send a multitude of birds to your backyard. And a flat rock makes a great everyday feeder for doves, native sparrows, juncos, towhees, and other birds that are accustomed to eating at ground level.

But feeders have their advantages.
- They keep the yard cleaner.
- They make it simple to serve messy foods, like suet, nut butters, mealworms, or fruit.
- They save money by reducing wasted seed and keeping animals from gobbling up your treats.
- They keep mice to a minimum by keeping seed off the ground.
- They can exclude squirrels and starlings.

*(continued on page 186)*

# The Bird Table

Long before artistic bird feeders filled the shops, bird lovers were building their own setups out of old boards. They may not have been works of art, but they served their purpose better than many of the feeders on the market today.

The most basic was the bird shelf, or bird table. At its simplest, it was nothing more than a wide, rough board attached to a windowsill or nailed across a pair of posts. A generous helping of seed could be poured onto the board, and birds had instant access and plenty of room to gather.

If you decide to go this route, you can enclose the board with low edges (making it more of a simple tray than a table), to reduce the amount of seed that gets lost over the edge. You can also drill holes so there's drainage when it rains. Or you can make a fast-draining version by using stiff screen and wood braces for the bottom. (I stick to a plain old board, rather than a wire bottom, which I've found too flimsy for heavy use.)

I still haven't found a reasonably priced commercial feeder that beats this oldie but goodie.

## Sturdy Bird Table

This easy project is nothing more than a simple open tray. It's my favorite all-purpose feeder design, and it attracts birds like crazy because it's highly visible and totally accessible. You can adjust the dimensions of your bird table to suit the space you have available or the boards you happen to have lying around.

Don't worry if your results are a little crude; birds will be checking out the seeds, not your carpentry skills. Besides, any gaps between the bottom boards or between the boards and the sides will serve as drainage holes when it rains.

If you don't have any old boards lying around, ask a woodworking friend for a piece of scrap 2 × 10 or 2 × 12 (or a couple of 2 × 6 pieces, which you can join with a crosspiece underneath). Use a circular saw to trim the board or boards to your desired length. Since I don't own a circular saw for cutting lumber, I have my boards cut to length at the home supply store when I buy them. It takes just minutes and costs very little. *Variation:* If you don't have the brawn to set posts into place, or if you want to add a second tray feeder to serve additional birds, skip the posts and nail four short legs, cut from 2 × 4s, at the corners. You can use this table as a low-level feeder for juncos, native sparrows, towhees, doves, cardinals, and other birds that typically feed on the ground.

You can scale this feeder to whatever size best suits your space, from 1½ feet to 3 or even 4 feet long. Keep in mind that a larger bird tray feeder of about 3 feet long will which accommodate as many birds as half a dozen small feeders so it will keep your yard from looking cluttered. It also makes feeding the birds a snap, especially in bad weather, and is inviting to all species.

Many nature centers use a feeder like this as the main attraction of their bird observation windows in their visitor centers. Stop by a center near you, so you can see how you like the look of it and how successful it is at drawing a crowd. You can also get ideas for placement and height by seeing a similar feeder in action.

**Two 4" × 4" wooden posts of equal length, 4' to 5' long**
**Pine boards: Two pieces, 2" × 6" × 36"; one piece, 2" × 6" × 12"**
**Nails: Twelve 4-penny nails; six to eight 6-penny nails; four 8-penny nails**
**Lath strips: Two 36" pieces, two 12" pieces**

1. On each post, mark a line about 1 foot from one end. (Make sure the line is the same distance from the end on both posts.)

2. Dig two 1-foot-deep holes, 2 feet apart. Set in the posts to the same depth, making sure their sides are aligned in the same direction for a tidy look. Check the lines you drew in step 1, to make sure the posts are set to the correct depth. You can also use a carpenter's level to be sure that the posts are set vertically in the holes.

3. Lay the two 36" boards side by side, ends aligned, to make a 12" x 36" rectangle. Lay the 12" board across them near the middle. Nail the smaller board to the larger boards with two 6-penny nails at each end and a few in the center, to hold them in place and give the feeder more stability. (This will be the bottom of the feeder.)

4. Turn the "table" over so the crosspiece is on the bottom. Nail the 36" lath strips to the long edges and the 12" lath strips to the short edges, using 4-penny nails.

5. Set the feeder on top of the two posts. Position it so it's centered on the posts and it extends the same length beyond each post. Nail it into place using two 8-penny nails.

6. Pour some sunflower seed and millet into the tray, and maybe some special treats, like nuts or sunflower chips. Don't fill this feeder to the brim; a thin layer is easier for birds to sort through.

Refill as needed. Remove accumulated shells with a wide plastic spatula. If seed gets wet in rain or snow, remove some of it, scattering it on the ground beneath the feeder; spread the rest out across the surface so it can dry.

Keep your nectar feeder up until Thanksgiving to nourish any stragglers that may show up.

The feeder of choice in England is a plain and simple "bird table" that seats many diners at once.

# Begin with the Basics

If you've never had a feeding station before, fall is a terrific time to set one up. You'll have happy customers within days, and there will be plenty of activity to entertain you. If you already have feeders, fall is a great time to expand your collection or find the types that work best.

If you want to keep your setup simple, start with four basic feeders that can serve any bird that may turn up in your yard.

- **A tray feeder** for sunflower and millet, and for special treats like peanut butter dough or a cup of mealworms

- **A tube feeder** for niger seed, for two reasons: First, to dole out the seeds one at a time so that birds don't have to sort through shells, and second, to prevent the tiny, lightweight seeds from blowing away in the first strong breeze

- **A suet feeder** to hold inexpensive blocks of suet or lard or freebie fat scraps from the butcher

- **A nectar feeder** with perches, so that both hummingbirds and orioles can use it

**fall secret** The English language is different in England: "chips" instead of French fries; "crisps" instead of potato chips. And birdfeeders aren't called feeders: They're called "bird tables." Like our American suppliers, British feeder makers are now offering a variety of styles. But many bird lovers in Britain still use a simple open tray for their bird table. By the way, British watchers are even more passionate than we are about their pastime—it's almost achieved the level of a national sport.

## Special Feeders for Special Foods

After you have the basics, you'll want to add a specialty feeder—or two or four—for specialty foods. Feeder makers have come up with some innovative designs that make it easier to serve out-of-the-ordinary foods to your birds. You can also fashion homemade versions, if you're handy with wire cutters and other tools.

Shop for the designs you like best in feeders that serve these foods, and you'll have all the bases covered. Here are some general ideas of what the feeder types look like, but designs are frequently updated.

- Nut feeder: Usually a tube of wire mesh
- Fruit feeder: A platform with spikes to hold fruit
- Mealworm feeder: A small, steep-sided cup, often part of another feeder
- Log feeder: A section of log with holes drilled in it to hold suet, peanut butter dough, or nut butters.
- Stationary (not swinging) suet feeder, for large woodpeckers: A wire cage mounted to a backing board that is nailed into place
- Nectar feeder for orioles: A larger version of a hummingbird feeder, with a reservoir for sugar water and perches for the birds

**The big, bold red-bellied woodpecker quickly becomes a daily visitor at a suet or nut feeder.**

## Sky's the Limit

Once you have feeders for basic foods, you can sit back and watch the birds. Not for long, though! Because if you're like me, as soon as you see how many customers your basic setup draws, you're going to want to add more, more, more.

Bird supply stores know how obsessive we can get, so they make all kinds of spe-cialty feeders and arty designs. It's fun to pick up some pretty things to add to your feeding station, so go ahead—snap up whichever tempting feeder is calling your name.

Just keep in mind, though, that the feeder should be practical as well as pretty. If it's a hassle to fill, or not designed with birds in mind, it may turn out to be too much trouble for you—or the birds!—to bother with.

# SQUIRREL SUGGESTIONS

Believe it or not, there was a time in my life when I was thrilled to see a squirrel at my feeder. I only had one feeder then, an open wooden tray atop a post, but it served anybody and everybody that came along. One night, I had surprised an opossum in it. And then, one day, I looked out and saw the squirrel. He was a gray squirrel, with a dense, fluffy tail, a snowy belly, and delicate little paws.

I immediately went to the kitchen to find him some treats, even though he seemed to be liking the sunflower seeds just fine. (By the way, this was so long ago that the seeds

Plotting his next move—how to empty your fancy nut feeder—a gray squirrel waits until the coast is clear.

in my tray were big, plump, gray-and-white striped sunflower seeds, not the black oil type—which weren't on the market yet!) Searching the cupboards, I collected a can of salted peanuts, a bag of walnuts, and some mixed nuts still in their shells.

"Watch out, Casey," I said to our big shaggy dog, sidling past him to reach the door without dropping my squirrel treats.

As soon as I opened the door, Casey shoved past my legs and made a mad dash for the squirrel. What a commotion! In a flash, the squirrel leaped to the nearby larch tree and scooted high up, where he clung to a fat branch, chirring and scolding a mile a minute, his tail flailing with what sure looked like distress signals.

I put the nuts into the feeder for the squirrel to enjoy later and called Casey, who was playing deaf as he made his regular rounds of our big fenced backyard. "Okay, well, be good," I feebly admonished the dog, and went back inside.

I watched for a while, but the squirrel didn't come down. Eventually Casey came to the door, and I let him in. Not long afterward, I spotted the squirrel running for the fence like his life depended on it. Come to think of it, I guess it did.

Inadvertently, I had stumbled across the only surefire way to keep squirrels from vacuuming up the birdseed: A squirrel-chasing dog!

One important reason to shoo away squirrels is because they prey on bird nests. Bird eggs and nestlings are two favorite foods of squirrels in spring and summer, and these furry tree-climbers can reach the home of just about any tree-nesting birds. That's

**fall secret** Can't beat 'em? Try the Squirrel Decoy Feeder: Dedicate a tray feeder to your bushytailed pals, and set it up far from your birdfeeding station. Keep it stocked with ears and kernels of corn, peanuts, and other squirrel goodies, and they may—may—leave your other feeders alone.

why you'll often see a pair of robins driving away a squirrel in summer: The bushy-tailed predator ventured too close to the bird family's home. Squirrel predation is a natural part of nature's checks and balances, but nurturing a booming population of bushy-tails can tilt the equation in favor of squirrels. On the other hand, a bunch of fat-bellied squirrels is practically an open invitation to a hunting hawk, so it may all even out!

## Anti-Squirrel Measures

Squirrels eat way more than birds do, and most of us can't afford to serve them a fill-your-belly smorgasbord. We all have our favorite tricks for discouraging squirrels—or for making them tolerable. Here are a few that might work for you.

- Squirrels are reluctant to cross open spaces. Set up a feeder in the middle of a large area of open lawn, with a few nearby bushes for quick bird cover.

- When you're planning where to put your feeders, look up to gauge possible paths a squirrel might take to go from tree to tree to feeder, or utility wire to tree to feeder. Set up your feeding station as far from tree trunks and overhanging branches as you can manage.

- Many types of "squirrel-proof" feeders are available at bird-supply stores and in

catalogs. Some are truly squirrel-proof; others just slow down the critters a bit. You'll find some suggestions in Sources on page 320. Or try an online search, and read others' reviews of the products before you buy.

- If you're lucky enough to have an old-fashioned clothesline in your yard, you can suspend a feeder from the center of it to put it off-limits to squirrels. Squirrels may be acrobats, but they find it practically impossible to negotiate a skinny length of plastic-coated clothesline.

- Dogs are excellent anti-squirrel protection because they like to chase squirrels. They usually don't bother birds, at least those at feeders. If a squirrel has to cross any part of your yard on foot to get to your feeders, a dog is a definite deterrent. But if the squirrel can leap from tree to tree to get to the seeds, the canine threat goes way down.

- A motion-sensor device that hooks up to your garden hose and emits a sudden blast of water can help, but getting it aimed just right is tricky. You want the water to startle the squirrel, not soak the seed. (See Sources on page 320 for more info.)

- Squirrel baffles will work—until the squirrels figure out how to work around them. Don't doubt it; they will!

# DESIGNING A FEEDING STATION

No matter how much care we put into choosing pretty flowers for our yards, it's the manmade objects in the yard that get our attention first. Just why does that birdbath or iron bench—or the scrap of plastic that blew onto the grass—instantly draw the eye? Because they're so obviously not part of nature.

That kind of attention is exactly the effect you want when you're positioning that gorgeous new gazing ball or your quirky frog statue.

But do you really want passersby to stop in their tracks when their eye falls upon your thistle sock? Or that not-so-clean Lucite chickadee dome? Didn't think so! So spend a little time figuring out how to arrange your birdfeeders, and you'll create "curb appeal" as well as bird appeal.

## Depend on Design

Oooh, design—now there's a scary word! The idea seems daunting, not to mention mysterious. After all, any night of the week we can turn on the TV or pick up a magazine that intimidates us into believing that we need professionals to help us come up with a look that works, whether it's for our kitchens, our houses, or our gardens.

After a lifetime of living on a shoestring budget, I've learned that design isn't as daunting as it seems. All of us, I firmly believe, have the ability to know when something looks right. We also recognize when it looks wrong. Our eyes and brains have an instinctive knack for picking out a satisfying pattern, and that's all design is: An arrangement of objects in relation to each other.

The design steps that will get you to a good-looking feeding station aren't hard at all. You're probably already familiar with them from reading about gardens. In fact, you may find it easier to think about designing a feeding station if you think of it as a garden. The only difference is that you are putting together feeders and posts instead of plants.

**Decide on an area.** Choose a part of your yard where you will have enough open space to install feeders in an oval 10

## Dealing with Deer

Deer in residential areas have become real pests in some parts of the country, including the Northeast. As housing development spreads to what once was rural land, deer learn to forage on ornamental plants and find many a meal at birdfeeders. Some municipalities have passed laws requiring residents to take down their birdfeeders at certain times of the year, so as not to contribute to the problem.

If you have a problem with deer, concentrate on providing cover and natural foods for your birds. And count your blessings: In some areas, it's not Bambi that's raiding bird feeders—it's bears!

**fall secret** Try the Treat of the Day trick: Bolster your basic seeds with a small amount of treats every day—a scattering of chopped peanuts, say. Even though it's a limited amount, it puts your feeder offerings a notch higher in your customers' opinions.

to 12 feet long and 4 to 5 feet across. The area should be within about 12 feet or less of shrubs, hedges, or other cover, so that birds feel comfortable traveling back and forth from it. You can add cover corridor plants later, or select a spot where they are already in place.

**Start with a focal point.** Select a single post-mounted feeder with a lot of visual weight—one that's particularly eyecatching from a distance—to be the main element of your "feeder garden." It might be your biggest feeder, or the one that's painted white. Mount it atop a post of significant size (such as a 4 × 4, rather than a skinny metal pole), about 4 to 4½ feet high. Allow an open area of at least 3 feet on all sides, so that birds have a chance to spot sneaking cats.

**Go off-center.** Install your focal point feeder a few feet to the right or left of center, not in the very middle of your feeding area. Have a helper hold it in position so that you can see where it looks best in relation to nearby plants.

**Soothe the eye with similarity.** Paint the post the same color as the feeder. If the feeder is stained wood, stain the post to match. If your feeder is white, paint the post white, too. Pine-green metal feeder? Pine-green post.

Looks good already, doesn't it? Great! Let's add some more elements to the mix.

**Corral the clutter with a feeder tree.** Six frog statues dotted around the garden give it a herky-jerky, junky look. So do six miscellaneous feeders when they're hung here, there, and everywhere. Cut the clutter and combine your miscellaneous smaller feeders into one large element. How? Invest in or build a stand with multiple arms—sort of a coat tree for feeders. Place this "feeder tree" in a subordinate position to the focal-point feeder: Put it slightly back from and about 4 feet to the side of the main attention getter, so that the eye notices it second.

Your backyard will instantly look a lot tidier with a metal tree to hold that collection of hanging feeders.

**Add a second feeder tree,** if you need it. For the most pleasing effect, use a smaller version of the same style tree as the first one. Place it about 1 foot in front of and about 2 feet to the side of the first tree.

**Add a lower tray feeder.** Mount it on a short post of the same kind as your focal-point feeder, or choose a low feeder supported by short legs. Place it about 1 foot in front of the focal-element feeder and to one side, not quite midway to the feeder tree.

That's it. You now have a cohesive arrangement of enough feeders to satisfy a horde of hungry birds—and to delight the eye of anyone watching them.

# HIGH-OCTANE FUEL FOR MIGRANTS

I was savoring a piece of melt-in-your-mouth Belgian chocolate when it occurred to me that perhaps I should check the calorie count. Big mistake. No wonder Belgian chocolates are so delicious—that single small piece racked up 120 calories, mostly from fat.

Fats are fattening, all right. But that outrageous calorie count is exactly what makes them so vital to fall migrants.

Long-distance fliers, like the little brown birds that stop off at our feeders or forage the roadsides, need plenty of calories to fuel the exertion of migration.

No fat-free salads for these guys, please: When they stop by, they'll be wanting hearty meals to replenish the calories they've burned winging their way southward.

## The Basics and Beyond

Black oil sunflower seeds and white proso millet or a high-quality seed mix do a fine job as the basic "meat and potatoes" of seed-eating fall migrants, such as buntings, finches, juncos, and native sparrows.

But to keep the motors humming for even more species, you can add special high-calorie treats.

- Sunflower chips and finely chopped nuts are excellent high-calorie choices for small birds, including wrens and native sparrows.

Suet blocks are convenient to store and use. You can cut the cost a bit by buying them by the case.

- You can't go wrong with peanuts. They're one of the most popular bird foods around. Chop them and scatter them over sunflower seed, where they're highly visible and accessible.

- Mealworms are like potato chips to birds: They can't seem to get enough. Put them out in an open container, and be patient; it may take your birds a while to discover them.

- Offer a small amount of coarsely grated cheese, such as inexpensive American or Velveeta, on the ground beneath bushes or in a low feeder near a shrub. Catbirds, thrashers, thrushes, and robins may investigate it and quickly develop a taste for it.

- Wire suet cages can be tricky for less-agile birds to access. Chop packaged suet blocks into several pieces and serve in an open tray feeder for tanagers, wrens, juncos, native sparrows, and other nonacrobatic birds to enjoy.

- The pig fat known as lard is softer than commercial bird suet, which makes it ideal for warblers, orioles, tanagers, wrens, and other migrants, and it's free of fillers like cheap seed mix or cracked corn. Other suet-eating birds enjoy it, too. (See "Love That Lard" on page 194 for a nifty serving idea.)

- Make your own peanut butter dough or other high-fat dough by mixing peanut butter, peanut oil, or other nut butters and nut oils with cornmeal. Add currants or other dried fruit, if you wish. Use your hands to mix to a consistency

Slip some fat trimmings into a mesh onion bag and hang it up. You'll make your chickadees mighty happy.

## Love That Lard

True lard aficionados render their own by melting "leaf fat," the fat found around a pig's kidneys. But you can take the easy way out and buy lard at the grocery store in blocks, packaged like butter, or in plastic containers or pails. In fall, when melting isn't a problem, you can offer the food right in its container.

For an instant suet feeder that fall migrants will appreciate:

1. Poke two holes about 1 inch apart in the side of a plastic container of lard, insert a twist tie and form a loop, then insert a 2- to 3-foot piece of twine into the loop.

2. Remove the lid, and wedge the container into the crotch of a tree, open side facing outward. No tree? Go to Step 3.

3. Attach the container firmly to the tree or a post by wrapping with the twine; knot the twine on the outside of the branch or post and snip off any extra.

like cookie dough, then crumble into an open feeder.

- Spread sunflower seed butter, peanut butter, or other nut butters onto leftover muffins, bagels, or bread. Serve whole or break into pieces.

## FALL FEEDING FOR THE REGULARS

Remember those bird supply catalogs I was dreaming over earlier in this chapter? It's not only the feeders that I lust after: I want those fancy seed mixes, too. But thanks to a frugal streak that's been solidly in place my whole life, I look at those bird catalogs the same way I do the plant catalogs and clothes catalogs that come my way. I spend hours dreaming over them—and then I get real and pare down the wish list to a few essentials, plus a small indulgence or two.

Mostly, I examine the seed mixes to get ideas for making my own. After a lifetime of feeding birds, I have a pretty good feel for what birds like to eat—and plenty of ideas for keeping the cost minimal.

## Trimming Costs

I'd often wondered why a friend of mine didn't have a birdfeeder outside her window. She spent most of her time indoors, due to a health problem, whiling away many an hour sitting at her kitchen table, hungry for company. Her house was always neat as a

**fall secret** Lard is usually fairly inexpensive in supermarkets, where it sells for about $1.50 a pound. For an even lower price, check Mexican or Latino grocery stores, where lard is often labeled *manteca*.

pin, so I figured maybe it was the messiness factor that was keeping her from enjoying the pleasure of birdfeeding.

Finally, I asked her.

Her response was immediate. "Oh, I'd love to feed the birds!" she exclaimed. "But, Sally . . ." she lowered her voice, "I couldn't afford it."

I'd known my friend made do on a limited income, but I hadn't known things were that tight. "I guess $5 a week *is* a lot of money, just for birds," I sighed.

"Five dollars? Are you kidding? I thought I would have to spend hundreds!"

"Well, you sure could," I laughed. "But you don't have to feed birds lobster all the time! They're plenty happy with hamburger."

The next day, I put up a feeder for my friend and delivered a 50-pound sack of white proso millet, neatly contained in a galvanized trash pail, with an empty cottage-cheese cup for a scoop. Her husband promised to take on refilling duties. Total investment: Less than $25.

A few days later, I stopped by again. The couple had angled their chairs so they could watch the sparrows, juncos, and finches outside the window. They'd scattered cracker crumbs and bread crusts, which friends were saving for them now. I made a note to bring a second feeder and a sack of sunflower seeds, so they could enjoy the company of chickadees, nuthatches, and cardinals, too.

Soon after installing that second feeder, I went to visit another friend. She served me tea at her mahogany dining room table, where we could see the array of at least a dozen bird feeders outside the window—about $500 worth of feeders. I recognized many of them from my own wish lists.

While we enjoyed the comings and goings of the same birds I'd just seen on the other side of town, she told me about the new bird food mix she'd ordered. Expensive, yes—nearly $5 a pound, with shipping—but she loved finding special treats for the little friends that kept her company all day.

The moral of the story? We all feel good about feeding the birds, no matter how much or how little we spend doing it. Even on a very limited budget, you can enjoy a lot of company at your feeders.

## Birds Flock to Wealthy Neighborhoods

In February 2008 researchers from Sheffield University in England found that the number of birds is greater in affluent suburbs and in residential parts of the city where real estate is priciest, rather than in poorer areas. Why? Because there were more birdfeeders in those wealthier areas.

The study, published in the journal *Diversity and Distributions,* didn't address why poorer people put out fewer birdfeeders, but I think we can safely guess it's because they need their money for other things.

Further proof of the "birdfeeder effect," as it was dubbed, was that the birds that were found in increased numbers in those wealthier areas were the birds that commonly visit British feeders, such as great tits and coal tits (which look something like our chickadees).

A sturdy plastic trash can works great for birdseed—unless mice chew into it. Metal cans are mouse-proof.

Inexpensive proso millet is favored by song sparrows and other native sparrows that arrive in flocks in fall.

If you prefer to keep costs lower, here are some tricks I've learned.

**Sheer abundance is a huge attraction.** Even if the food isn't haute cuisine, plentiful food has high appeal. If you can't afford the high-priced stuff on a regular basis, go for "good enough."

**Investigate those mixes.** Many seed mixes are chockful of cheap fillers. Stick to plain old sunflower seed and millet, and you'll save way more money than you will buying bargain mixes full of wheat, cracked corn, and milo, which are less-desirable fillers. Read the label before you buy.

**Buy big bags.** Fifty-pound sacks are usually the cheapest way to buy seed. Sharing with a friend or neighbor will let you both save money, and you can take turns hauling it.

**Find a feed store.** Farmers and ranchers are frugal, and the places they shop often have lower prices than stores that sell to the general public.

**Watch for sales.** Some birdseed sellers offer sales at the beginning of the season, for customers to preorder, as well as sales throughout the year.

**Stock up on specials.** Nuts often

**fall secret** Letting other birds see the usual crowd gathered at your feeding station is a great way to attract new customers. Keep one of your feeders in an area where it's visible to birds flying overhead and the mere sight of your regulars, busy at the feeders, may entice flybys to drop down and join them.

go on sale around Thanksgiving and Christmas—when baking is at its peak. Stock up when you see specialty foods on sale.

**Buy by the case.** You'll save a few dollars by buying suet blocks by the case of 12 or 20. Shop online to find the best deals, or ask your local bird supply or discount store about getting a break.

**Keep an extra sack of seed on hand.** It's easy to blow the budget when you run out of seed and have to replenish the supply without waiting for a sale. Use metal trash cans to store an extra sack of sunflower seeds and an extra sack of millet.

# HUMMINGBIRDS HOME IN

Okay, hummingbird lovers—and who isn't one?—here's your chance to fill your yard and garden with so many of these tiny birds that they create an audible hum.

Are you ready?

The secret is to use a combination of feeders and flowers. As with other migrants,

## Hurricane Helpers

All kinds of relief efforts were mounted to help the victims of Hurricane Katrina. The need was massive. But even the victims who weighed less than a copper penny weren't forgotten.

Hummingbird migration coincides with hurricane season, and the birds have adapted over eons to deal with it. Still, Katrina was a real whammy. When the hurricane hit at the end of August, the Gulf Coast was buzzing with ruby-throated hummingbirds who were beginning to gather to cross the Gulf or to settle in for the season. A number of rufous hummingbirds, which have become more common outside their traditional western home, were in the area, too.

With the landscape obliterated and flowers underwater or ripped to shreds, the tiny birds were confused and desperate. Luckily, folks who weathered the storm didn't forget their hummingbird friends. Within days after the disaster, store shelves were bare of feeders, which had been snapped up by residents wanting to help the hummingbirds.

Everyone who put out a feeder reported the same story: Dozens of hummers hovering around the feeder, trying to get a taste of the sugar water.

Helping hummingbirds turned out to be a big lift to peoples' spirits. The heartbreak of losing a home, and the hard work of reclaiming what could be salvaged, seemed lighter when the little birds were around to focus on. Compassion makes us feel good, whether it's directed at humans or at hummingbirds.

Bird lovers from around the country pitched in, too. Audubon chapters, feeder makers, and bird supply stores, as well as lots of individuals, sent thousands of nectar feeders (and poles) to the Gulf Coast.

it's food, food, food that is the motivator in fall. So, by making sure you have plenty of natural nectar and sugar water on hand, you'll be perfectly positioned to catch the wave of early fall migrants.

## Nectar Feeders

Selecting a nectar feeder begins with the same considerations as choosing other birdfeeders: by thinking about (1) how easy it will be to fill, and (2) how easy it will be to clean.

The other big concern—how easy will it be for birds to use?—is one that may take some trial and error. I've noticed that subtle differences in the way perches are attached, or in the angle at which feeding ports are set, can determine how much birds favor, or avoid, a certain feeder.

One of the easiest-to-use feeders is Dr. JB's 16-ounce Clean Feeder, which is easy to

## X Marks the Spot

If you've ever had a hummingbird investigate your red eyeglasses or your red lipstick, you may have noticed a confused look on its face as it tried to find the right place to insert its beak. The color red is such a strong attractant to hummers that they'll check it out, just in case it's a source of nectar.

A little guidance is a good thing, and in nature, many flowers accomplish that by adding a dab of color or streaks leading to the center.

It was my son who first noticed that hummers were having a hard time getting situated at one of our feeders.

Two of the yellow plastic flowers that marked the feeding ports had fallen off. Though the openings in the red plastic were still visible to our eyes, apparently they weren't so noticeable to the hummers. The birds moved around and around the feeder, fighting over the ports that still had yellow flowers and seeming not to realize that they could use the others, too.

"Let's try an experiment, Mom," said David. He went inside briefly, then returned with a pad of yellow sticky notes and a pair of scissors. Snip, snip, jab—there was a crude "flower" with a hole in the center.

He pasted it over the port. Almost instantly, a hummingbird zeroed in on it, inserted its bill, and began to feed.

Remove the sticky note, and the bird was lost. Press it back in place, and it was feeding time again.

We tortured the birds in the name of science for a few more minutes, adding and subtracting yellow "flowers" to various places on the feeder. The results were clear, at least to us: Our birds needed a little guidance to know where to get a drink. And it took them a long time to recognize when a flower had no hole to drink from.

By the way, our makeshift solution lasted for weeks. That 3M miracle adhesive stayed stuck throughout the remainder of hummingbird season.

# Peak Season

Hummingbird traffic dwindles during nesting season but begins to pick up in July, when family groups leave their nesting grounds and get ready to move.

The number of visitors at feeders and flowers increases throughout August, as migrants move in, with the boom lasting well into September. Depending on where you live, you may still be hosting a few migrating hummers in early October.

disassemble and run through the dishwasher (www.drjbs.com/product.html). It fits together so securely that you can even mix the sugar and water right in the feeder, using it like a cocktail shaker.

I've tried a lot of different models of nectar feeders, and I fill all of the ones that are still in working order. But the one I keep coming back to is the one I started with, many years ago: The original Perky Pet glass bottle type with four flowers and perches, which you can find at bird supply shops or discount stores. It works for me and for the hummingbirds. I've noticed that when hummers have a choice, they prefer it to the other nectar feeders hanging in my yard.

Take a close look at fall hummers and you might see a rufous or other species that's expanding its range.

# CHAPTER 11

# NATURAL FOODS
# AND COVER FOR FALL

**W**ITH ALL THOSE BIRDS from far and wide funneling through your yard in fall, plus a whole new batch of winter residents arriving on their heels, it's easy to see that abundant cover and food to feed a multitude are tops on the agenda.

Good thing you can satisfy both needs at the same time, by choosing plants that do double duty. Many fall migrants, including thrushes, tanagers, and grosbeaks, have a real fondness for fruit, so trees and shrubs that deliver a late summer/early fall crop will be just the ticket—and they'll provide plenty of protected perching places and travel corridors.

In autumn, your vegetable garden becomes a mecca for native sparrows and other seed-seeking birds.

All of the shrubs and trees mentioned in this chapter will provide both cover and food.

A little later in the season, your flowerbeds, veggie garden, and meadow or prairie plantings will be a big draw for the flocks of native sparrows, juncos, and other fall residents that are looking for a likely spot to call home. The grasses and stems will shield these ground-dwelling birds from predatory eyes, and the plants will produce a shower of seeds to fill those hungry bellies.

## PERFECT TIMING

The effect of a single sour gum, or tupelo (*Nyssa sylvatica*), is incredible in fall, when the tree turns a show-stopping red. But it's even better when a half-dozen trees stand shoulder to shoulder, as they did in a yard I visited years ago in Georgia. It was early autumn, and the graceful, drooping branches of the trees were in full fall glory.

"Come under," the gardener beckoned me. From underneath, the brilliant red leaves, backlit by the sun, were as luminous as stained glass. It was magical—until the spell was broken when we were pelted with something from above.

The tupelos were full of thrushes gorging on the small blue berries and knocking an occasional fruit onto our heads. I spotted hermit thrushes flicking their tails and caught a flash of a veery's rusty back. Robins and a few bluebirds were dining on the tupelo berries, too.

Tupelos are just one of our native trees and shrubs that provide nourishment timed perfectly with fall migration—and tailored to the tastes of the birds that will be moving through. Your best bet for picking a native plant for your yard is to watch birds in the wild, and plant the same shrubs and trees you see them in there. You'll find hundreds of beautiful plants in any native-plant nursery or catalog, and every one of them will be used in some way by birds, whether it's for insects at the flowers or on the foliage, fruit or berries, nest materials, home sites, or other practical purposes. Natives are the plants that birds know, so they're instantly appealing to your local birds. Choose your favorites according to what you like: The possibilities are endless. One person's list might include wild azaleas, such as the lovely pink whippoorwill azalea (*Rhododendron periclymenoides*), for spring hummingbirds; spicebush (*Lindera benzoin*) and arrowwood viburnum (*Viburnum*

Fall berries draw quiet brown thrushes, including the hermit thrush with its nervously twitching tail.

*dentatum*), for fall berries; and staghorn sumac (*Rhus typhina*), for winter comfort food. Another person's choices might lean toward eastern red cedar (*Juniperus virginiana*), for excellent cover and winter berries; bayberry (*Myrica pensylvanica*), for evergreen cover and another batch of berries; pines or spruces, for bad-weather protection and a crop of cones and myriad insects; and a glade of cinnamon ferns, whose stems supply the soft fluff that chickadees are fond of using in their nests.

As you can see, there are loads of choices when it comes to choosing natives to benefit you and your birds. Take a look around your local wild places, then seek your favorites from a specialist nursery or plant sale. You'll find a sampling of mail-order native plant nurseries in Sources on page 320.

*(continued on page 204)*

# Hedge Fund

Every time I see a green wall of arborvitae bordering a yard, I think, ah, if those people only knew what they were missing! They could be helping birds—and having fun watching them—if only they'd planted something different. A hedge of mixed shrubs, some bearing fruit, some with flowers for nectar and insects, some of more open growth, will make your yard much more inviting to birds than a solid hedge of densely branched arborvitae or similar evergreen shrubs. Just look around you at wild places: Nature mixes it up with a variety of plants. That means there will also be a variety of insects, because different kinds of plants attract different kinds of insects. And those bugs are a big attraction to birds, which will search the plants to see what they can find to gobble up.

An occasional arborvitae does have value to birds as a roosting place at night or in bad weather. But a whole hedge? The dividends that hedge pays, in terms of birds, are a really poor return on the investment.

A mixed hedge, on the other hand, is an ideal investment in the bird quotient of your backyard. Instead of a wall of arborvitae or boxwood, or other single-plant hedges, try a mix of shrubs, berry bushes, and roses, for fruit *and* four-season cover. The plants supply bird food—berries, insects, and flowers. They serve as nesting spots. And—unlike arborvitae, with its congested branches—they add excellent corridors of cover through which birds can move easily.

The plants in a mixed hedge will quickly knit together into a casual hedge, or hedgerow, like the kind that springs up naturally between plowed fields or along roadsides—and that's the kind of hedge that birds like best. This casual style requires next to no maintenance: You can retire the hedge clippers and let the shrubs grow in their natural form. Of course, if you'd rather have a neatly clipped, solid green, formal boundary hedge, you can still enjoy that style, and add shrubs for birds elsewhere in your yard.

But a mixed hedge adds lots of valuable places for birds to hang out, without breaking up the living space in your yard. Before you buy, read the tags on the plants you've chosen, to find out how big and how fast they'll grow.

Here are some general guidelines to help you get started with your own bird-approved mixed hedge.

- Pick three kinds of shrubs for your basic mix. There's no need to make every plant different in your hedge; just repeat the three plants you've chosen. If your hedge is a long one, you can tuck in other kinds of shrubs here and there along its length, to add variety.

- Choose plants that will mature to roughly the same size to avoid a higgledy-piggledy effect. For highest bird appeal, aim for shrubs that fall within the "medium size" range of 4 to 8 feet tall and 4 to 6 feet wide: Think forsythia, weigela, lilac, and shrub roses.

- Nearly all shrubs are reasonably fast-growing. A young shrub rose, raspberry bush, blueberry bush, or red-twigged dogwood bush (in a 1-gallon pot or a bare-root shrub), can easily reach 3 to 4 feet across in a year or two. Some plants, such as boxwood, are slower growing; in general, evergreen shrubs grow at a slower rate than deciduous types. Read the label or ask the nursery staff to find out how fast yours will grow.

- Shrubs vary in their ultimate size, but keep the spacing about the same from plant to plant in your mixed hedge; this will avoid an odd effect in winter, when the spacing will be visible. Because of size differences, some of your plants may weave their branches among their neighbors; to birds, that's just another benefit of a mixed hedge: It allows them to travel freely under protection of covering foliage.

- If you've chosen plants that reach 4 to 6 feet wide at maturity, space them 3 to 4 feet apart, to create a mixed hedge that knits together quickly. To cover 60 feet, you'd need at least 15 plants. Some shrubs, including shining sumac (*Rhus copallina*), lilac (*Syringa vulgaris*), and others, will produce suckers to form an expanding clump; these, too, may work their way in among their neighbors.

- Take another tip from Mother Nature and mix up your shrubs when you plant them: Instead of repeating arrowwood viburnum (*Viburnum dentatum*), Cornelian cherry (*Cornus mas*), and winterberry (*Ilex verticillata*) down the length of the hedge, arrange the plants so they aren't in such a rigid order. Two Cornelian cherries, then a winterberry, then a trio of arrowwoods, then another winterberry, and so on, will be more pleasing to the eye than a tightly controlled order.

- Shrubs vary widely in price, from just a few dollars apiece to collectors' conifers that cost hundreds. To save money, use common, inexpensive shrubs—the pussywillow, weigela, lilacs, privet, peegee hydrangeas (*Hydrangea paniculata* 'Grandiflora'), and other reliable workhorses that graced our grandmothers' yards—for at least half of the hedge, and save the pricier ones for occasional accents.

## Share the Wealth

Include some "people food" when you choose berry bushes for your yard or for a hedge. Late-season blueberries, huckleberries, and fall-bearing raspberries are tops with birds—and mighty tasty, if you can grab a few berries before the birds clean them all off.

## Native Shrubs for Fall

Most American native shrubs and small trees get short shrift in nurseries and gardens, yet they're tops for birds because their berries ripen when birds are at their peak in fall. Our native plants, our native insects, our native birds, and every other thread of the vast, interconnected fabric of natural life evolved together so that they are in sync with each other. Plants simultaneously attract pollinators and deter pests, and they have also evolved strategies for getting their

Plant a trio of blueberries to tempt early fall migrants to your yard. 'Chandler' has an extra long season.

seeds spread around. Fall berries are one of those clever ways of ensuring a new generation: Birds (and other wildlife) eat the berries and pass the seeds through their digestive tracts, distributing future generations of the plant.

Nonnative plants also attract birds because birds, like us, are opportunistic: If a branch of yummy berries beckons, birds won't turn it down. So there's no need to rip out those Chinese hollies or other nonnative shrubs in your yard. But why not add some natives to the mix? They're guaranteed to attract birds. And in some places, they've become harder to find in the wild because of habitat destruction due to development or because introduced shrubs have run wild. The notorious Japanese honeysuckle (*Lonicera japonica* 'Halliana'), autumn olive (*Elaeagnus angustifolia*), and multiflora rose (*Rosa multiflora*) have all run rampant because birds ate their berries and spread the seeds.

Native fall fruits are drier and higher in fat than summer fruits, such as mulberries and strawberries, which are soft, juicy, and higher in sugar. Fall berries don't pass through a bird's digestive system as fast as summer fruits, so they allow migrants to build fat reserves to fuel their flight.

Natives are enjoying a surge of popularity as we learn to appreciate our own

**fall secret** Let the wind blow fall leaves under the hedge, where they will serve as mulch to block weeds and eventually decompose into humus. That layer of leaves will be an inviting home for beetles, worms, snails, and other living bird foods. Look for robins, thrashers, thrushes, towhees, and sparrows foraging there.

national treasures. More native plants are showing up in garden centers and mail-order catalogs. Ask for them at your local nursery, or investigate native plant nurseries like those listed in Sources on page 320.

Each region of the country has its own native shrubs, so investigate those from your own area. Here's a small sampling of fast-growing, reliable native shrubs that bear fruit in fall, a trait that makes them sought

## Super Spicebush

Why spicebush *(Lindera benzoin)* isn't in every nursery is a mystery to me. The bare branches of this multi-stemmed all-American shrub are as graceful as any fancy nursery plant. Every bit of the plant smells wonderful when you rub it between your fingers; it's as sharply aromatic as wintergreen. Spicebush is also graceful in an almost Oriental way, with smooth bark and an open, horizontal branching habit that's lovely in wintertime. It's tough as nails, too.

The gleaming, bright red berries studding the stems are beautiful against the yellow foliage, and they smell like tangerine when you squash them. You won't get to admire them for very long, though, because thrushes clean them off as soon as they appear. Whenever I want a long, lingering look at the more elusive thrushes, such as the gray-cheeked or hermit, I sit and wait by a spicebush that's loaded with berries. I've never been disappointed.

Spicebush grows beneath the trees in eastern and midwestern forests, but it's surprisingly adaptable—which is turning out to be the case with many native plants. Although it may not occur in the wild in a particular region, the shrub often thrives in garden conditions. Its native haunts are in the shady humus of the forest understory, but it flourishes in partial sun as well as shade and will adapt to wet feet or dry soil. It tolerates clay, humidity, hard winters, and some drought. Like other natives, individual spicebush plants can vary in their response to conditions, depending on where the plant originated from. Plants from Texas, say, may have more built-in drought tolerance than plants from a rainier area in Michigan, so it's worth your while to see where the plant was shipped from before you make a purchase.

*(continued on page 208)*

# Autumn Native Shrubs

The berries of these easy-to-grow, medium size shrubs provide a feast in fall, when they ripen to tempt migrants and

| PLANT | TYPE OF PLANT | DESCRIPTION | HARDINESS ZONES |
|---|---|---|---|
| Gray dogwood (*Cornus racemosa*) | Deciduous shrub | Forms a thicket or large clump as new shoots emerge around the parent plant. White flowers followed by clusters of white berries on bright red stems. Red fall color. Grows to about 15'. | 4–8 |
| Silky dogwood (*Cornus amomum*) | Deciduous shrub | Forms a thicket or large clump as new shoots emerge around the parent plant. White flowers followed by clusters of metallic steel-gray berries. Red fall color. Grows to 8–10'. | 4–8 |
| Spicebush (*Lindera benzoin*) | Decuiduous shrub to small tree, often clump-forming | New shoots often sprout around parent to form a multistemmed clump; does not spread into a colony. Bundles of yellow flowers in early spring, before leaves emerge. Clear yellow fall color. Grows to about 10'. | 4–8 |
| Winterberry (*Ilex verticillata*, species form, not cultivars) | Deciduous shrub or small tree | Forms a clump or thicket as new shoots emerge around the parent plant. Small white flowers followed by brilliant red berries closely studding the stems. Yellow fall color. Grows to about 10'. | 5–8 |
| Oregon grape holly (*Mahonia* species) | Evergreen shrub | Forms a colony as suckers arise from roots. Glossy, hollylike leaves with fragrant yellow flowers, followed by blue-black berries. Depending on species, grows from 2–6'. | 5–8 |

resident birds. And their fall foliage will add a splash of color to your yard.

| USE | COMMENTS | BIRDS ATTRACTED |
|---|---|---|
| Berries, insects, cover | Perfect in a hedge or along a fence. Widely adaptable to moist or dry soils; native from Maine to North Dakota, south to Nebraska, Arkansas, Kentucky, and Virginia, and extending into South Carolina; also in Texas. | Wrens, native sparrows, and other finches. Orioles, vireos, warblers, and other birds visit flowers for insects. Excellent cover for many birds. |
| Berries, insects, cover | Great choice in a hedge or group. Native from Maine to Florida, and west to Illinois, Iowa, Missouri, Tennessee, and Georgia. | Wrens, native sparrows, and other finches. Vireos, orioles, warblers, and other birds visit flowers for insects. Cover for many birds. |
| Berries, insects, cover | Grows well in "dry shade," such as beneath maples and other shade trees. Native from Maine to Florida, west to Texas, Oklahoma, Nebraska, and Iowa. | Bluebirds, robins, and thrushes. Wood warblers comb the foliage in spring. Spicebush swallowtail butterfly uses as host plant. Inviting perch for all songbirds. |
| Berries, insects, cover | Recent cultivars seem to have lost bird appeal; berries remain on the branches uneaten. Stick to the species or the older and bird-approved cultivar 'Winter Red'. You'll need both male and female plants. Read plant labels or ask your nursery for male cultivars. Native to the eastern half of the country, from Maine to Florida, west to Minnesota and south to Louisiana; also in Texas. | Waxwings and other birds, but bluebirds are the prize with this bush. They're often first on the scene when the berries are ripe. |
| Berries, four-season cover | Many species, mostly native to the West; *Mahonia aquifolium*, a popular garden choice and the state flower of Oregon, is native in the Northwest, from Washington to Montana, south into California. | Thrushes, including the beautiful orange-and-steel-blue varied thrush, and many other birds, from small wood warblers to grouse. |

The arrival of wild turkeys at your feeder is a real occasion, because they often come in groups.

The magenta stems of pokeweed berries attract catbirds, bluebirds, and waxwings, but they're toxic to humans.

by fall migrants; they'll also be useful to other birds year-round. These shrubs are widely adaptable; you'll find others suited to demanding conditions, such as mountain or desert regions, in mail-order catalogs or at nurseries that specialize in native plants.

# OH, GROW UP!

For extra fruit and cover, I'm all in favor of growing vines. You can squeeze them in just about anywhere. I may not have room for many new trees or shrubs, but it seems like I can always tuck a few more trellises into the yard.

Grapes became my top candidate once I discovered that I don't need to be a pruning wizard to get a great crop. Here's how I do it.

- Simply transplant a volunteer grapevine seedling, or plant a bare-root vine of any variety that sounds interesting, beside a trellis. Tie it in place when it needs it, and stand back. Native muscadine grapes, native river and fox grapes, and classic 'Concord' are trouble free, but even fancy grape varieties from the nursery are easier than you might think. I've experimented with dozens, and birds like them all.

- In late winter, after the vine has served up fruit for thrushes, orioles, wrens, and other grape-lovers, I cut it back hard, using loppers and hand pruners, until it's just a few main stems 5 to 6 feet tall, with stubs of branches. It may not be the method recommended in how-to guides for growing fruit for humans, but it works just fine for bird grapes. No matter how drastically I hack back the vine, it still produces plenty of fruit the following season.

- By the way, don't toss those clippings: Pile them in an out-of-the-way corner and you can have the fun of watching

# Better Than 'Bradford'

Many towns plant pollution-tolerant, fast-growing Callery pear trees (*Pyrus calleryana*) along the streets, and in years past 'Bradford' was the cultivar of choice. (In some places, it still is.) The small, upright trees are beautiful, with fragrant, profuse white blossoms in spring, glossy leaves, and deep red fall color. The plentiful small fruits that ripen in autumn attract migrant thrushes and other birds.

Too bad 'Bradford' had a structural defect built into its genes: Because of its upright shape, with branches held at very narrow angles, the tree is not very sturdy when faced with strong winds. Even the weight of the maturing branches can cause the tree to suddenly split apart after 10 to 20 years of growth. Many cities are preemptively removing the trees from public property, to avoid damage to parked cars or passersby.

Callery pear makes a great small tree for a bird lover's backyard. But avoid the cultivar 'Bradford', which is still sold in garden centers, and try sturdier 'Aristocrat' or 'Red Spire', instead.

thrushes, cardinals, and other birds sorting though for nest materials next spring. You'll no doubt have clippings of many different lengths; just let the birds pick through them to find those that fit their needs the best. Thrushes and other birds may also tug strips of bark from the clippings to use in their nests—and some mockingbirds and cardinals I have known had a fondness for the curly tendrils!

## The Mockingbird Lesson

When I was a kid back in the late 1950s, I was lucky enough to have a serious bird-watcher as my teacher at Rosemont Elementary in Bethlehem, Pennsylvania. I think she may have been pleased to have me around, too, because we both loved to talk about the birds we'd been seeing.

No matter what bird I reported, my teacher knew all about it. She'd fill in details and tell me fun tidbits about whatever bird it was I'd seen.

I'll never forget the morning I saw my first mockingbird perched on the roof of a nearby ranch-style house. The ranch house was new to the neighborhood—it had been a

Multiflora roses were a big reason that mockingbirds expanded their range. The small hips are a big favorite.

**fall secret** Sumacs are famous for flaming fall color. The native species of these shrubs or small trees grow into small colonies that are stunningly beautiful in fall—and of great value to birds year-round. Three beauties to consider are shining sumac (*Rhus copallina*), smooth sumac (*Rhus glabra*), and staghorn sumac (*Rhus typhina*). They provide perching places, cover, insects on foliage and flowers, and fuzzy clusters of tiny red berries that feed birds all fall and winter. Look for blue-birds, robins, and flickers at the fruit, especially as winter deepens and other fall berries disappear.

field of great big purple violets the year before—and so was the mockingbird. I'd never seen anything like it.

Neither had my teacher. "Are you *sure*, Sally?" she kept asking. "White patches in the wings, you say? Are you sure it wasn't a catbird?"

I couldn't understand why my teacher was acting doubtful.

Turns out, mockingbirds were rare in Pennsylvania back then. Until the early 1900s, the mockingbird was a signature species of the South, associated with magnolias and moss-draped trees. The birds rarely ventured north.

Gradually, the species expanded its range above the Mason-Dixon line. But the big shift occurred because of the multiflora rose. When multiflora roses were introduced

by the USDA and distributed to farmers in the eastern part of the country for planting, mockingbirds suddenly had an abundant source of fall and winter food in the sprays of bite-size rose hips. That was just what the USDA had intended: The roses were part of an effort to provide food and cover for wildlife.

By the mid-1960s, about the time I saw my first Pennsylvania mockingbird, the big gray birds were common everywhere that multifloras grew—which was way north of their traditional haunts.

The multiflora rose turned out to be a troublemaker, because birds spread its seeds far and wide, and landowners began trying to eradicate them. This isn't an easy task, even with strong herbicides; the tenacious plants quickly regrow from any bit of root

## How the Thrasher Got Its Name

"Thrasher" is another version of the word *thresher,* which describes how these interesting birds find their food. Watch the brown thrasher in your yard as it works through the leafy litter below your shrubs. It swings its long bill back and forth, like a farmer with a scythe. That action stirs and lifts the leaves, uncovering insects and other goodies. Thrashers (and towhees, and some sparrows) also stir up the leaves with their feet, causing insects to scurry for cover before the sharp-eyed birds can nab them.

It's yet another good reason not to be a neat freak about fall leaves! Let them settle into place below your shrubs and among your plantings, providing insulation—and thrasher food.

that survives. Nowadays, you won't see as many multifloras growing wild in pastures and along roadsides as you would have a few decades ago. And as for the mockingbirds, they declined right along with the roses until the birds reached a level that could be supported by the foods around them.

## Doubts about Dogwood?

Flowering dogwood (*Cornus florida*) is a traditional beauty that's sadly susceptible to a fatal blight. Although nursery growers tried to limit the spread of the disease, trees sold at garden centers and other outlets helped to spread it to many areas of the country. The blight causes the tree, or a major part of it, to suddenly wither and die.

So far, there is no cure. There's also no way of telling whether a young tree you're thinking of purchasing will become infected. Maybe it will. Maybe it won't.

Even with that dose of bad news, dogwoods have a lot to recommend them. Dogwood berries are an absolute magnet for birds in fall, when the clusters ripen to gleaming red. The bluebirds, tanagers, and rose-breasted grosbeaks that they draw in may be enough of a reason to risk planting the tree in your own yard. Maybe, by the time you read this, a resistant cultivar will be available.

Eastern flowering dogwood (*Cornus florida*) is the benchmark when it comes to bird appeal. And there's a bit of brighter news on the horizon for dogwood lovers:

The blight seems to be diminishing, and many dogwoods manage to shrug it off.

If you don't want to risk it, though, there are some alternatives.

- Kousa dogwood (*Cornus kousa*) resembles dogwood in flower, but not in fruit. Its soft, raspberrylike fruits are eaten by birds, too, but it's not nearly the magnet that its cousin is.

- Hybrids between flowering dogwood (*Cornus florida*) and Kousa dogwood have entered the scene. *Cornus ×*  *rutgersensis* cultivars, such as 'Constellation', 'Galaxy', 'Saturn', and 'Venus' are resistant to the disease.

- In the West, western dogwood (*Cornus nuttalli*), which flowers in fall as well as spring, is worth tracking down at native-plant specialists.

- Shrubby native dogwoods also tempt fall birds. Cornelian cherry (*Cornus mas*), gray dogwood (*Cornus racemosa*), and silky dogwood (*Cornus amomum*) eventually grow into thickets, offering excellent cover and ground foraging, besides their bounty of berries. Brown thrashers and catbirds, as well as bluebirds and thrushes, are particularly attracted to their fruits.

- And how about a dogwood that's just 6 inches tall? Meet bunchberry (*Cornus canadensis*), a beautiful wildflower of woodsy places. Bunchberry looks like somebody made a nosegay of a single dogwood flower: Each plant has one white blossom, surrounded by a collar of green leaves. The flower matures into a cluster of red berries, very similar to those on a dogwood tree. The plants will spread to form colonies about 2 feet across in shady parts of your garden.

## Tempting Trees

My yard often holds a few tree seedlings that sprouted from seeds that blew in on the wind or were deposited by birds. Nearly always, these baby trees are native species—and that means they will have some special use to native birds. In fall, before the leaves drop, I scout my yard for seedling trees. Often, the trees have sprung up in flowerbeds or in other spots that aren't ideal locations for a tree. So in fall, I move them to better homes. Seedling trees grow fast, and they recover easily from transplanting.

This is a great trick for adding to your stock of trees without spending a cent. Use a shovel to make deep slices in the soil all around the seedling, several inches from the trunk-to-be. Then lift out the tree. Be sure to dig deep, and stop if you meet resistance: Even young tree seedlings can have a taproot that goes down a foot or more! When you have freed the root, lift the seedling and replant it in its new home, placing it at the same depth.

If you've only planted nursery-grown trees before, you'll be surprised by how fast seedling trees can grow. Potted or balled-and-burlapped trees take a year or two to establish roots and begin putting on much growth. But seedling trees, transplanted in fall when they become dormant, can really zoom. Two to three feet of new growth a year is about par for the course for many species of native trees. A sugar maple (*Acer saccharum*), for instance, may reach 6 feet tall in just 3 years. A redbud (*Cercis canadensis*) may reach blooming size at 6 to 8 feet in 4 short years. A Douglas fir or white pine can zoom from a few inches tall to 2 feet in a single year, and to 4 feet tall the next.

Sugar maples, redbuds, Douglas firs, and white pines are all highly favored by birds, just like other native tree species. All of them supply superb bird food in the form of insects, as well as offering nest sites, cover, and other benefits. So check your yard in early fall and see if any tree seedlings have sneaked in. Who knows what you may find?

Tree seeds are another source of natural bird food, so don't forget to look up to see grosbeaks and others.

# THE SEASON OF SEEDS

Binoculars are a fixture around my neck in fall, when the woods and fields are alive with all kinds of interesting possibilities. I raise my binoculars every few minutes when I'm walking along, pausing to look at this or that, without even thinking about it.

A city friend and I were moseying along a country road one fine September afternoon when curiosity finally got the better of her.

"I've been watching you with those binoculars," she said. "You check out every patch of weeds—I mean, really check it out. What are you looking at? I can't see anything in there."

"Lots of cool sparrows in there," I said, handing over the binocs and showing her how to focus them.

"There's so many! And they move around so much, I can't even tell what I'm looking at," she said after a while.

Sparrows are a challenge even for folks who have been watching birds for years, and my friend was brand new at this. I pulled my field guide out of my pocket and flipped it open to the sparrows. "See this one? He's there. And this one? Him, too. And there's a whole bunch of these, and some of these, oh, and I saw one of these back there a ways . . . ."

"Why are they there?" she said, putting the binoculars to her eyes again.

"Listen," I said, grabbing a dead stalk of ragweed and giving it a shake so that thousands of tiny seeds went flying.

Field sparrows, tree sparrows, juncos, and other small birds glean seeds from goldenrod for months.

Goldfinches are so fond of the seeds of purple coneflower that even a single plant will attract them.

## Clean-Up Compromise

I'd much rather watch lively birds all fall and winter than win the prize for a tidy yard, but I do make some effort to meet neighborhood standards.

- After frost, I remove anything that has sagged into blackened mush, like impatiens or coleus.

- Stiff-stemmed annuals, such as zinnias and marigolds, remain until the birds pick them clean.

- I let most of the dead perennials remain until late-winter cleanup, to lend off-season architecture.

- Some perennials have a beautiful form even when dead, especially those with dramatic seedheads.

**Native sparrows are a great reason to hold off on cutting back your flower garden.**

Yarrow (*Achillea* species), goldenrod (*Solidago* species), and coneflowers (*Echinacea* and *Rudbeckia* species) are charming when capped with snow.

- Ornamental grasses are welcome to stay, until they begin to shatter and toss dead tan stems all over.

"Sparrows eat seeds . . . ," I began.

" . . . and the weeds are full of them," she finished.

That's it exactly. It's another neat piece of the natural cycle: Seed-eaters move in, right at the time when seeds become abundant.

## Garden Seeds

A flower garden full of frost-killed plants may not look very attractive to our eyes. But birds will find plenty to appreciate.

**Meadow in a can? Tempt birds instead with a casual mix of zinnias, coreopsis, and sunflowers.**

- The still-standing plants offer protective cover—another part of your yard where birds feel safe to forage or move about.
- Like wild plants, our garden flowers are burgeoning with seeds in fall. Goldfinches, pine siskins, tree sparrows, and many other birds will eagerly examine the seedheads of coneflowers, cosmos, sunflowers, zinnias, marigolds, and other plants.
- Mourning doves, juncos, towhees, cardinals, quail, and other birds that forage on the ground may patrol your garden patch, too, looking for any seeds that have fallen.

## A Good Word for Weeds

Think of the weeds you've been pulling all year. Dandelions, no doubt. Plantain? Probably. Certainly some chickweed and cranesbill. Maybe you've weeded out a big chicory plant that snuck into the tomato patch, or dug deep to get a stout root of sorrel out of the flowerbed.

We sure have plenty of weeds. And most of them didn't originate on this continent.

Weeds are sneaky. Most of our "favorites" came to America from other countries, hidden in the fleece of sheep, the tread of a boot, the track of a tire, or mixed with

## Weed Seeds to Go

All of our most abundant backyard weeds are beloved by the small birds that are so abundant in fall—goldfinches, tree sparrows, field sparrows, pine siskins, and many other finches and sparrows. Here's a sampling of their bill of fare.

| | |
|---|---|
| Burr marigold | Mustards |
| Chickweed | Pigweed |
| Crabgrass | Plantain |
| Cranesbill | Purslane |
| Dandelion | Ragweed |
| Filaree | Sorrel |
| Foxtail grass | Thistles |
| Lamb's-quarters | |

**Wild grasses are prime targets for small seed-eating birds. Arching foxtail grass is actually a kind of millet.**

Native tickseed sunflower, or *Bidens*, holds a plethora of seeds that keep birds coming back for months.

Before you start muttering bad thoughts about those birds, keep in mind that the birds digest way more weed seeds than they drop. Thanks to their appetite for weed seeds, birds help keep the pesky plants in check.

## Seeds with a Sunny Side

I often wondered what finches and sparrows ate before our imported weeds were so widespread. I learned part of the answer when I visited the Midwest for the first time many years ago and found wild sunflowers (*Helianthus annuus*) stretching in a golden river along every roadside.

These are the wild species form, not the cultivated variety. Instead of a single towering stem topped by a massive head, our native sunflowers are beautiful plants with lots of arching branches and a multitude of small sunflowers. They fill wild spaces across the Plains, growing all the way west to the foot of the Rockies.

desirable seed. Their foreign origin is part of the reason they grow so well here—we don't have the insects or the climate and soil conditions that keep them in better balance in their homelands.

We do have lots of weed-seed-eating birds, though, like our many native sparrows and finches. And that's another reason why weeds are so widespread. Birds eat seeds, birds make droppings, undigested weed seeds spread weeds.

Finches, sparrows, and other seed-eaters also nibble the seeds of native asters (including New York aster, *Aster novi-belgii*; New England aster, *Aster novae-angliae*; and other species), goldenrods (*Solidago* species),

**fall secret** If your weeding talents are anything like mine, there are bound to be plenty of weeds hiding here and there around the yard. If anyone looks askance at the lamb's-quarters in your flowerbed, just tell them you're saving it for the finches. Saves face—and it's true! Of course, you'll probably want to hoe off some of the extra seedlings that sprout the following year, or smother them with mulch, so that your weed crop stays at a reasonable size. Just a few plants are enough to feed a lot of birds, because they produce seeds so prolifically.

# Purple Plenty

Pokeweed (*Phytolacca americana*) is an all-American weed that zooms from a seedling to the size of a shrub in just a single year. Old-timers knew the plant as a boiled spring green (it's full of toxins, so proper preparation is essential), but nowadays it's the bright magenta stems that attract the most attention.

By early fall, when migrants are on the move, pokeweed is a stunning sight, with fantastic fuchsia stems laden with long clusters of blue-black berries that attract bluebirds, veeries, and other migrating thrushes. The berries, which are toxic to humans but not to birds, are full of purple juice (as are the droppings of pokeweed-eating birds).

In Costa Rica, where the veery and other thrushes winter, the similar berries of jaboncilla (*Phytolacca rivinoides*) are visited by thrushes on winter vacation.

In fall, our thrushes are often joined at the pokeweed feast by waxwings, tanagers, thrashers, catbirds, and mockingbirds. In Costa Rica, those same migrant thrushes keep company with toucans, manakins, and honeycreepers instead, while they dine on the exotic "pokeweed" berries.

If you have young children, use caution with pokeweed: Those pretty magenta stems and intriguing berries may be just too tempting, even if you warn the kids that they're poison. You may want to wait until they're older to add pokeweed to your yard.

**A young northern mockingbird visits a "bush" of pokeweed to fill its belly.**

vetches (*Vicia* species), lupines (*Lupinus* species), smartweeds (*Polygonum* species), and a whole field guide's worth of other native wildflowers. Field flowers make beautiful and bird-friendly additions to casual flower gardens; many of them bloom into fall, adding late-season color and more butterflies and insects—which means more birds. If your gardens aren't suited to the wild look, why not dedicate part of your yard to a meadow garden, so you can enjoy the birds that will come to seek seeds in fall and winter?

The onward push of civilization—including the spread of imported weeds and nonnative grasses—has made many of these plants scarcer than they once were. So it's a good thing that sparrows and finches adjusted to more exotic fare.

You won't want to fill your garden with a bumper crop of ragweed, no matter how much birds enjoy it. But a patch of native sunflowers and other seed-rich wildflowers sure paints a prettier picture.

## Cover Considerations

Plan your yard so that fall migrants can move from one patch of plants to another, instead of having to cross large areas of open space. Hawks are on the move in fall, too, and small birds are favorite targets.

A lush lawn may look lovely, and the earthworms, ants, and beetle larvae beneath the grass will attract robins, flickers, and grackles in spring and summer. But in fall and winter, an expanse of lawn is just wasted space as far as birds are concerned.

If you have a large lawn, break it up with beds. Group a few shrubs together, or try a prairie or meadow planting. Set aside some space for beds of seed-bearing annuals, such as sunflowers, marigolds, cosmos, and other bird favorites. (See "Seed-Producing Flowers for Birds" on page 134 for suggestions.)

If you already have trees in your yard, you're ahead of the game, because the bark and branches will supply sleeping insects to birds all fall and winter. But don't rest on your laurels—add shrubs and other plants, too. Many fall migrants are birds that live on or near the ground, including the multitude

Most birds are reluctant to cross wide-open spaces, so break up your estate with travel corridors of plants.

of native sparrows and juncos that will be heading your way. Keep them safe and well fed by staggering plantings around your yard to break up open spaces. In fall, those beds will be hopping with native sparrows and other small birds.

## Fall Flowers for Hummingbirds

Dotting feeders around your yard is one way to get a lot of customers during the fall hummingbird migration. A yard full of flowers is a huge attraction, too.

**fall secret** I'm all in favor of keeping things simple, which is why I like to recommend salvias for fall hummingbirds. You'll find dozens of cultivars at garden centers and nurseries, and every one will tickle your hummers' tongues. Just find the salvia counter and pick your favorite.

Red or red-orange blossoms are the magnets, but once the hummingbirds are in your yard, they'll linger at any other color of flower, too, as long as it holds nectar. Look for a tubular shaped flower as a clue to hummingbird appeal: Think lilies, petunias, and, on a much tinier scale, mints.

Here's a sampling of late-blooming hummingbird favorites that will nourish fall migrants with plenty of nectar.

- Cardinal climber (*Ipomoea × multifida*)

- Cypress vine (*Ipomoea quamoclit*)

- Hibiscus (*Hibiscus* species and hybrids)

- Hollyhocks (*Alcea rosea*)

- Lobelias, especially fall-blooming cardinal flower (*Lobelia cardinalis*) and great blue lobelia (*Lobelia siphilitica*)

- Salvias, including annual scarlet sage (*Salvia splendens*) as well as perennial salvias of many species; *Salvia greggii* is a tough, adaptable late bloomer

- Standing cypress (*Ipomopsis rubra*)

- Starflower (*Pentas* cultivars)

What a finale! Native cardinal flower fires up in late summer and keeps going well into fall.

# CHAPTER 12

# SPECIAL BIRDS OF FALL

**F**ALL IS A BUSY TIME of the year for backyard birds. Long-distance migrants are moving on through, and old bird friends are returning to our feeders. In this chapter, we'll turn the spotlight on three groups of birds that deserve a closer look in fall: thrushes, native sparrows, and small finches. Some species from each group are likely to turn up in your backyard during this season, no matter where you live. You'll notice the sparrows and finches first, because they'll seek out the seeds at your feeder. But many of the thrushes aren't accustomed to visiting feeders; to best appreciate these interesting birds, it helps to have a handle on their habits.

In this chapter, you'll learn the secrets to encouraging lovely thrushes to alight in your yard while they're en route to far-away wintering grounds, as well as how to tempt one of our most beloved thrushes, the bluebird, to your yard. You'll also get a behind-the-scenes look at the lives of some of our most reliable fall feeder birds, the native sparrows that return in force this season, and the cheery, active small finches. Fall brings both groups of birds back to the buffet of seeds in our gardens and at our feeding stations.

By following some of the secrets in the preceding fall chapters, you've made your yard extra appealing to these birds. So let's get better acquainted with these special friends of fall.

## THRUSHES

Thrushes are birds of the forests, but in fall they often show up in backyards during their long migration to Central or South America. The best-known thrush doesn't go by that name: it's our pal, the robin. Almost as famous is the bluebird, another thrush that doesn't carry the name. Even if you've never

Not all thrushes bear the name, but the spotted breasts of young bluebirds reveal the family ties.

## Super Singers

Birders like to argue over which of the thrushes is the best singer.

- Three species are most often singled out for top honors, and each has its defenders: Some give the prize to the wood thrush, others nominate the hermit thrush, and a third fan club roots for the veery.
- Townsend's solitaire earns support in the West, where its clear, glorious song rings out.
- Bluebirds are the most beautiful thrushes, but their songs aren't like the others': Their music-making is just a short, simple whistled phrase.
- The robin is so common that most of us don't give it a second thought. But its song is beautiful, and it's one of the main components of the dawn chorus in spring. Robins sing the day to sleep, too, right before dusk.

seen a bluebird in your backyard, this beloved bird has such great appeal that it's used to sell everything from calendars to sweatshirts.

The other members of the Thrush family aren't as well known these days as they were 100 years ago, when most people lived in the country. The other thrushes are birds that prefer wooded areas, with plenty of solitude. In summer, they raise their families in the shady understories of forests; in fall, they often stop over in parks and backyards with plenty of shrubbery, to take a break and fill their bellies. Most of these thrushes are brown on top, with whitish breasts and bellies speckled with brown. Townsend's solitaire is an exception—it's gray.

Thrushes are specialists: They depend on a particular habitat and they're picky about foods. And these birds travel long distances, so disruptions of their homes on either breeding grounds in North America or wintering grounds in Central and South America can have major consequences. They're particularly vulnerable to habitat destruction, which has contributed to the unfortunate decline of many thrush species. By making your yard a welcoming rest stop, you can help these birds migrate successfully. Meanwhile, enjoy them while you can. Our forests simply wouldn't be the same without these sweet singers.

The voice of a thrush "steals upon the sense of an appreciative listener like the

The sweet-voiced veery needs a helping hand—it's much rarer than it was just a few decades ago.

quiet beauty of a sunset," noted Montague Chamberlain, a founding member of the American Ornithologists' Union, in the AOU's publication, *The Auk,* in 1882. But you'll have to wait until spring to appreciate these fabled songsters. By fall, the birds are no longer singing.

## Seasonal Habits

Flocks in fall, pairs in summer: That's the general rule for thrushes.

Once the babies leave the nest, thrushes often pal around in small family groups. In fall, the families gather together into a larger group, forming loose flocks for winter.

Bluebirds, especially, are seldom seen all by their lonesome: Usually you'll see a small bunch of the birds together, even after the youngsters are full-grown. Seems like the kids just like to stay close to Mom and Dad.

"You want to see robins in winter?" an old-timer in eastern Pennsylvania once asked me. "Just go up on the mountain and kick 'em out of the bushes."

I was young and dumb then, and I thought he was pulling my leg. It took me a few years to take his advice and see for myself. Turned out, country wisdom was right again.

And "kick 'em out of the bushes" was pretty close to the truth. I didn't see any robins until I parked along the narrow, graveled mountain road and explored the brushy edges. Sure enough, I flushed out a whole bunch of robins.

But they weren't acting like the spring-time robins that boldly hopped about on my lawn.

They were skulking in the bushes and foraging for food on the ground, well beneath the branches. They were behaving like . . . thrushes.

## Range of the Thrush Family

During nesting season, the robin, hermit thrush, and Swainson's thrush show up across the entire country. Townsend's solitaire, mountain and western bluebirds, and the varied thrush are limited to the West; the eastern bluebird, wood thrush, veery, and Bicknell's thrush appear in the East, with the veery sneaking into some western states, too. If you're in the Southwest or southern Texas, you may spot a rufous-backed or clay-colored robin.

**A backyard with abundant cover may draw the attention of thrushes in a nearby woods.**

## Under Cover

Cover is vital to most thrushes. Any area with shrubs, brush, or scattered trees, including fields and woods' edges, may host some of these birds.

All thrushes spend a large part of their time on the ground, usually near the cover of sheltering shrubs or other vegetation. But they also come out into full view to forage for their favorite foods.

- The brown thrushes—the veery and the birds whose names include the word "thrush"—are the most secretive members of this family. They skulk about in thickets, forests, and other areas with plenty of cover. Generally, they prefer large, unbroken areas of such habitat, where they can range about freely, although they also visit backyards, especially during migration.
- Townsend's solitaire and the varied thrush mostly stick to coniferous forests, while the other thrushes live in deciduous or mixed woods.
- Bluebirds aren't such skulkers. They often perch in the open, frequenting fields, pastures, cemeteries, and golf courses, as well as brushy places and woods' edges.
- You'll often see the robin out in the open on lawns in spring and summer. In fall and winter, this bird shows its more secretive side, and like other thrushes, retreats to shrubby thickets and brushy places.

All thrushes are migrants. Robins and bluebirds may relocate only regionally, or they may move a long distance. All but one species of the brown thrushes travel far, to Central and South America. The hermit thrush winters across a wide stretch of the country, along the Pacific, Atlantic, and Gulf Coasts and in a curving swath from New Mexico to Pennsylvania; it may occasionally show up elsewhere, too.

## Helping Thrushes Feel at Home

Your gardening habits can definitely affect how much your yard appeals to thrushes. Cover is the key word. Hedges, groups of shrubs, trees underplanted with shrubs, and

Dogwood berries attract thrushes way better than any feeder treat can.

**fall secret** Snails are a big part of the wood thrush diet, or at least they used to be. The scourge of acid rain has caused a decrease in snail numbers, because it softens or dissolves the material their shells are made of. Some experts theorize that the decline in wood thrush populations could be related, as this food source is becoming harder to find. Next time you see a snail sliding along, be grateful it's still around—to maybe become a thrush's dinner.

other areas that offer dense, low-level cover are what make them feel at home. Even the more outgoing robin and bluebirds appreciate the cover of leafy shrubs and small trees, although they will visit an open yard.

Since space is always at a premium in my yard, I concentrate on plants that supply berries and serve as cover, too.

## What's for Dinner?

The thin, pointed beak of a thrush isn't much good for cracking seeds, but it's ideal for eating insects, earthworms, and similar critters, and for gulping down berries or pecking at fruits.

Any insects or other small critters moving about on the ground are pretty much fair game for thrushes: beetles, grasshoppers, crickets, ants, sowbugs, spiders. Caterpillars are also prized food items, and bluebirds have perfected the art of snatching butterflies on the wing. Then the diet takes a turn toward the slimy. Slugs, snails, salamanders, and earthworms are favored by many members of this family.

Fruits are the other mainstay. All species of thrushes will eat huge quantities of fruits and berries when they find them. Those robins I "kicked out of the bushes" in winter were thriving on frost-shriveled wild

grapes, wild crabapples, mountain ash (*Sorbus americana*) berries, and wild rose hips, even when snow was deep on the ground.

### In the Yard

- Plant a hedge or group of berry bushes, to supply cover and food.

- Add native shrubs or small trees that bear fruit or berries in fall, when thrushes are migrating. (See "Autumn Native Shrubs" on page 206 for some suggestions.)

- Tolerate slugs and snails; avoid using chemicals to kill them.

You can tell that it's a hermit thrush eating fall berries on your bushes by its habit of flicking its wings and tail.

## "Planted" by Thrushes

Ever wonder how in the world poison ivy got planted along your fence? Ask a thrush!

Thrushes swallow the berries whole, later depositing the undigested seed where it may sprout into a new plant. Thanks to thrushes and other berry-eating birds, some of our least-favorite plants, including poison ivy, poison oak, deadly nightshade, and multiflora rose, are spread far and wide.

Sumacs (*Rhus* species), barberries (*Berberis* species), elderberries (*Sambucus* species), and wild cherries (*Prunus serotina* and other species) also get a big assist from fruit-eating, seed-spreading birds like thrushes.

- Let fall leaves nestle under shrubs and trees; they'll nurture thrush-favored insects and other foods.

- Choose double-duty plants that can supply food and cover, such as blueberries, dogwoods (*Cornus* species), serviceberry (*Amelanchier* species), and other berry bushes.

- Include a few elderberry bushes in a mixed hedge along your boundary line, to entice migrating thrushes.

- Tolerate a pokeweed plant or two, if you don't have small children who might be tempted by the toxic berries.

- Plant shrubs in groups of three and in travel corridors, so that thrushes have a larger area to search for food in without being exposed when crossing a large open area.

- Allow some lawn areas in which robins can search for worms.

- Start a compost pile and consider a brush pile for twigs and small branches. Both will soon harbor a healthy supply of sowbugs, snails, and other creatures that seek decomposing plant material, and which thrushes will seek out.

### At the Feeder

- This is the kind of news a feeder-keeper loves to hear: Of all the members of the thrush family, it's bluebirds that are easiest to bring in! Other thrushes may sample the treats, especially during migration, but it's bluebirds that often become feeder regulars.

- Start with mealworms or waxworms. Now that these delectable critters are

**fall secret** Much of the natural food for thrushes is found on the ground. To ensure a bounty of beetles, snails, and other tidbits, you'll want to put a layer of lawnmower-chopped leaf mulch around new plantings, and let fall leaves stay in place when they drop or blow around shrubs and trees. Decomposing leaves attract top-notch thrush food.

"Birdbaths" come in all sizes and shapes, including these tempting puddles in a natural stone formation.

Bring bluebirds and—maybe!—other thrushes right up to your window with a stick-on mealworm feeder.

widely available, it's easy to supply bluebirds and other thrushes with their five-star favorites.

- If bluebirds are in the vicinity, they'll come for "doughs" made from a mix of fat and cornmeal or other carbs. You can quickly mix up a batch yourself by blending peanut butter, suet, lard, or shortening into cornmeal until it has the texture of crumbly cookie dough.

- The varied thrush also visits feeders, usually in winter. At my feeders, they prefer millet to other foods.

- Robins appreciate a handout during snowstorms and ice storms, when they'll eagerly eat bread, chick scratch, apple halves, chopped suet, and other soft foods.

- In some areas, thrushes are becoming accustomed to visiting feeders for a snack of mealworms or suet. Hermit thrushes seem to be adapting most readily to feeders, and they may visit in fall or winter.

- Keep a clean birdbath ready and waiting; thrushes relish a good splashing bath.

## Moving Water

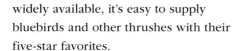

The sound of water is a great way to let migrating birds, including thrushes, know that they can satisfy their thirst or freshen their feathers in your yard.

Resident birds have plenty of time to discover a basin of still water on their own. A pedestal-type birdbath may signal to migrants that water is available, because many birds are accustomed to finding water at a birdbath. Or you can help alert migrants to the facilities by making your water trickle, gurgle, or splash. Install an electric or solar pump that powers a small fountain, or hook up a drip tube, which you secure to your birdbath and connect to your hose.

**fall secret** Most of us don't need any help attracting the house sparrow, also called the English sparrow. This common backyard bird isn't a native American species. House sparrows are noisy and can be aggressive, but they are loyal customers—a plus if you live in the city, where bird species can be scarce. And they can be fun to watch as they pal around in gregarious flocks and take dust baths together.

- Invest in a small fountain or drip tube for your birdbath, to catch the ear of passing migrants. The sound of water is an incredibly powerful attraction.

Native sparrows spend the bulk of their time right on the ground, foraging in leaves or fields, so that's the best place to look for them.

# NATIVE SPARROWS

See a little brown bird scratching about on the ground? Good chance it's a native sparrow, one of the biggest groups in the small finch collection. "Little brown birds" (LBBs, as many birdwatchers call them) all seem to look alike until you get to know them. But sparrows are a real pleasure in your backyard, because you'll have plenty of time to appreciate the fine points that set apart each of the 30-plus species. Don't worry, you won't see all of them at your place!

# Fall Favorite Sparrows

Nearly 50 species of sparrows show up here and there across North America, fitting into niches in every wild place, from deserts to grasslands to swamps to forests. This sampling includes some of the most familiar and widespread species of sparrows, all of them frequent visitors or residents in backyards. See how many of them stop at your place in fall!

**Song sparrow.** The most common backyard sparrow and a year-round friend who visits feeders in all four seasons, the

## Feathered Frustration

Tons of information and advice has been written about bluebird houses and house-tending. Most of it boils down to, How do you keep out house sparrows?

The quick answer is: You can't.

Until the day someone invents a house sparrow–proof birdhouse, you'll probably be a lot less frustrated if you stick to feeding bluebirds and planting berries for them, instead of housing them.

House sparrows only hang out around humans, and country bluebirds are spared the competition. So if you live in the country and can mount your bluebird boxes along the edge of a wood, far from human habitation, go right ahead. For the rest of us, it's mealworms and suet nuggets and peanut butter dough at the feeder.

streaky-breasted song sparrow is also an indefatigable singer. It's one of the first birds to start vocalizing in spring and one of the last to stop in late summer. You may have come across its tidy nest in your yard, on or near the ground, perhaps tucked among your perennials. Song sparrows vary from grayish to deep brown in various areas of the country, but all have a streaked breast with a dark "stickpin" in the center.

**Field sparrow.** A white eye-ring gives this plain, gray-breasted sparrow a surprised, wide-eyed look. It often shows up in flocks to quietly scratch for seeds beneath a feeder or to cling to seedheads in the garden or wild places. Like the tree sparrow, it often twitters companionably while feeding,

Field sparrows are declining throughout their range, but you may still host some at your fall feeder.

keeping up a steady patter of soft, sweet whistled notes.

**Tree sparrow.** Back in the days when it was more common to know the names of backyard birds, this small sparrow was called the "winter chippy" because it looks very much like the rusty-capped chipping sparrow, which is a summer bird except in the South. In fall, the tree sparrow moves south from the Arctic to spend the winter across much of the country, except for the southern tier of states. You'll often see these little guys with field sparrows, gleaning seeds from the flower seedheads or weeds in your garden.

**Fox sparrow.** One of the largest sparrows, the fox sparrow is about the same length as the white-throated or white-crowned, but it's a heavier bodied bird. Rusty or deep umber in color, this plump, active sparrow has a heavily streaked and splotched breast. Like other sparrows, it stays at or near ground level. You'll see it vigorously hopping forward, then kicking its feet back to uncover seeds in leaf litter or snow. It's a fall and winter friend for most of us, except in the West and Northwest, where it lives year-round.

**White-throated sparrow.** A firm favorite of feeder-tenders, this species is one of the birds that announces, "Fall is here." It often shows up at about the same time that juncos do. It nests only in New England and in some areas around the Great Lakes, but it can show up across much of the country during fall migration. Its winter range is a wide one, from Arizona to Vermont.

**White-crowned sparrow.** A fall and winter friend with an air of elegance, the white-crowned sparrow has an erect posture and often raises the head feathers that give it its name. This species may show up in mixed flocks with other kinds of sparrows, but its vivid white crown and black head stripes make it easy to pick out of the crowd. Young birds are trickier because their head markings are dull brown, and that flashy white crown is not yet apparent.

**Golden-crowned sparrow.** A common fall and winter friend in the West, in a wide strip along the Pacific Coast from Washington to southern California, the golden-crowned is an adaptable species that may show up in parking lot landscaping, backyards, or wild places. Its snazzy golden crown is not always visible, but a dab of yellow above the bill is usually present if you look through binoculars.

## Keeping Safe

Sparrows are prime prey for hawks and other predators, which may be why they have such a predilection for cover. You'll rarely see them out in the open, unless there's a sheltering tree, shrub, or tussock of grass to hop to in a hurry.

Cover is vital for putting sparrows at ease. Give them hedges, shrubs, meadow gardens, and flower or veggie beds for travel corridors and foraging.

These charming little birds are one of the best reasons not to be too quick to cut your gardens back in fall. If you let the dead stems of your perennials and annuals stand, or if you let your veggie garden collapse on its own instead of tidying it up after frost, you'll find that you have created the perfect habitat for the tribe of sparrow species that may come calling in fall.

## WHAT'S FOR DINNER?

Small seeds are the number one choice for native sparrows, which is probably why there are so many of these active little birds—because there are plenty of small seeds to be eaten! They also eat some insects, especially during summer. But when the fall crop of weed seeds, grass seeds, and flower seeds ripen, native sparrows are in their glory.

Watch for a tree sparrow perched at the tip of a weed, bending it to the ground as it plucks out the seeds.

We'll never be rid of weeds, but sparrows help keep them at a manageable level. These eager eaters devour zillions of weed seeds each year. Sparrows are like little vacuum cleaners. They forage busily on the ground below plants, picking up any seeds that dropped. And they travel together in small flocks, like a whole squadron of vacuum cleaners. It's a great system, and it cleans up a myriad of seeds that would otherwise sprout.

Sparrows usually feed on or very near the ground, scratching busily among weed stems, in brushy places, or beneath shrubs. If a stem of tempting seeds is hanging out of reach, a sparrow will cling to the tip, bending it down to where it can get a better grip. Sparrows will also spring upward from the ground to snatch a bite from seedheads that are a few inches out of reach.

Sparrows are gregarious birds that pal around together, with various species joining together in loose flocks at foraging places. They're also creatures of habit, and they'll return to a good eating place over and over, as long as they feel safe. So hold off on pruning back and cleaning up, and enjoy a fall and winter of sparrow watching, instead.

Native sparrows are adept at pulling down grass stems to pluck the seeds. A sudden shower? That's a bonus.

## In the Yard

- Tolerate a few weeds in your beds, and you'll give sparrows plenty to chew on come fall and winter. Lamb's-quarters blends in well in a casual flower garden, and it's a sparrow favorite.

- Weedy grasses are also a favorite, and goodness knows our yards have plenty to spare. I'm not talking about lawn grass, but the grass that sneaks into our garden beds. Cheatgrass, with its habit of burrowing its seeds into my socks and sneakers, is my nemesis, but I also have crabgrass, orchard grass, and lots of other seedy types I'd be happy to be rid of. I bet you do, too. In fall, sparrows do a great job of helping out with that.

- Cultivate a naturalistic meadow area or prairie planting, where grasses and flowering plants can mimic the wild places that sparrows frequent.

- Let fall leaves settle under shrubs, for more sparrow feeding possibilities.

- Plant annual flowers that produce a bounty of seeds; you'll find suggestions in the "fall secret," above.

## At the Feeder

- Millet is the top choice for native sparrows: The small seeds serve a huge crowd, and very little waste is created because the lightweight hulls scatter quickly.

- Sparrows also eat niger seed, if they can get to it. A tube feeder isn't their natural choice, because it's elevated and it requires eating out in the open. Scatter niger on the ground or on snow, though, close to a shrub or brush for cover, and sparrows will quickly make short work of it.

- Other small seeds, including finch mix, will also get their interest if served in a feeder that's near ground level.

- Sparrows find plenty to eat underneath feeders, where seeds drop as other birds feed at higher levels.

- Native sparrows appreciate a shallow birdbath, especially one near ground level. Try a clay plant saucer of fresh water set on a low rock; place it near a garden that offers a close-by escape to a quick cover.

**fall secret** Which goldfinch are you greeting? The American goldfinch is common across the country. In some areas, the lesser goldfinch and the Laurence's goldfinch may join their cousin at the feeder. When you see a goldfinch at your feeder who "doesn't look right," take another look—it may be one of the more unusual species. If you live in the West or Southwest, watch for the smaller, darker-backed, lesser goldfinch; in Arizona and southern California, you may spot Laurence's, which is gray with daubs of yellow on the wings and breast.

# SMALL FINCHES

These little birds are some of the best friends a backyard bird lover could ever dream of. It takes very little coaxing to bring them to your yard—in fact, many of them are probably already there.

We can depend on some small finches to delight us year-round, but fall is when we get a whole flurry of finches at our feeders.

## Plenty of Finches

Your visitors may include the house finch, purple finch, rosy finch, Cassin's finch, and goldfinch. The males are the standouts in these species, with rich strawberry red, raspberry red, or sunshine yellow feathers.

Females are streaky brown, except for the female goldfinch: She's olive green. In some species, the male changes to drabber feathers in fall; see page 169 for more details on that process.

Not all finches have the word "finch" in their name. Pine siskins are tiny finches that look like pale brown, streaky goldfinches. Siskins are similar in size and shape to goldfinches, and like goldfinches, they have a sharply forked tail. Buntings and redpolls are officially finches, too. So are juncos. The gray on top, white-below junco is one of our most reliable feeder friends, although it may look a little different depending on where you live—this species has several geographic subspecies, or races, such as the dark-hooded Oregon junco.

## The More the Merrier

Small finches aren't usually loners—where you see one pine siskin, you'll probably see a dozen . . . or 50. Purple finches seem to prefer to be in pairs or small groups. Juncos usually arrive in fall in a bunch. And part of the pleasure of a bird-friendly yard is watching goldfinches gather in ever-increasing numbers during migration.

Some winters, an "irruption" of small finches takes place as species of the Far North fly south when food is scarce. Then, even gardeners outside the usual range may see redpolls, rosy finches, pine siskins, or other northern species.

**fall secret** Small finches are a great reason to let some of your flowers stand in the garden, even after frost makes them drop their leaves and the plants get bleached and brittle. These birds can usually find something worth investigating, even in the depths of winter. And the thicket of plant stems will give them that all-important cover.

## Pleased to Meet You

Small finches are little sprightly birds of the trees. They move quickly, but not nearly at the hyperspeed of kinglets or warblers. Some members of this group, such as juncos, purple finches, and pine siskins, are at home in forests, but others, including the abundant American goldfinch and the lesser and Laurence's goldfinch, as well as redpolls, frequent more open areas with scattered trees and shrubs. And some, such as the lovely indigo bunting, live in fields where there's nary a bush in sight, or in areas of bare rocks or tundra, as rosy finches do. But all of the small finches may show up in backyards in fall or winter, when they move around looking for seeds. And usually they'll show up in a group, because these are birds that typically travel around in small flocks.

Most small finches have lovely, musical voices. During nesting season, they sing frequently. Even the females are known to break into song, sometimes when they're sitting on the nest.

## What's for Dinner?

Okay, gardeners, let's all join in a great big cheer for small finches. These little guys are huge consumers of weed seeds—and each one they eat means another dandelion-, ragweed-, pigweed-, or chickweed-to-be bites the dust. Not to mention all the hundreds or thousands of progeny that would've been produced by the plant that sprouted from that single seed.

Seed-cracking is the name of the game for small finches. Take a gander at that conical beak—for a bird this small, that tool promises quite a bit of strength. These

**Finches sure aren't loners. They drop in by the bunch, and the party goes on for hours as new guests arrive.**

*(continued on page 236)*

# Plants to Attract Native Sparrows and Small Finches

The same kinds of seeds appeal to both groups of these popular fall birds, and these plants supply seeds in plenty. Sow them among your flowerbeds or dedicate a stand-alone patch to these seed-eater favorites. Be sure to let the dead stems stand in winter to provide the cover that is necessary for making finches and sparrows feel safe.

| PLANT | TYPE OF PLANT | DESCRIPTION | HARDINESS ZONES |
|---|---|---|---|
| Annual sunflower (*Helianthus annuus*) | Annual flowers | Grow 4–8' or taller. Big, cheerful daisy flowers in yellow, orange, or russet tones. | Annual; all zones |
| Lettuce (*Lactuca* species and cultivars) | Annual plants | A rosette of green or red-tinged leaves from which arises a tall, leafy stem of small flowers that quickly mature to fluffy seeds. Grow to about 5'. | Annual; all zones |
| Mustards (*Brassica* species; especially rapeseed or canola, *Brassica napus*) | Annual plants | Mustards have four-petaled flowers shaped like a cross; they produce tons of small yellow blossoms that mature into pods filled with small round seeds. Grow to about 3'. | Annual; all zones |
| Purple coneflower (*Echinacea purpurea*) | Perennial flower | Purple daisies crowned with upstanding russet-orange "cones." Grow to about 3'. | 3–9 |
| Sensation Series cosmos (*Cosmos bipinnatus* Sensation Series) | Annual flowers | Feathery-leaved cosmos produce abundant pink to red or white flowers. Grow to about 3–4'. | Annual; all zones |
| Zinnia (*Zinnia elegans* cultivars) | Annual flower | Big, bright flowers in bold or pastel colors top these easy-to-grow plants. Grow to about 4'. | Annual; all zones |

Although the birds eat a similar menu, you'll soon notice that the finches prefer to glean the seeds from the standing plants, while the sparrows seek out dropped seeds at or near ground level.

| USE | COMMENTS | OTHER BIRDS ATTRACTED |
|---|---|---|
| Seeds | Classic sunflowers with a single large head are guaranteed to attract birds; other cultivars with multiple, smaller flower heads will also appeal. | Large finches, especially cardinals, plus chickadees, doves, jays, juncos, nuthatches, quail, titmice, and woodpeckers |
| Seeds | Stock up on bargain seeds. Any variety is a temptation to finches and sparrows once it goes to seed. Plant thickly, in a patch or row, where you'll have a good view of your visitors. | Small finches and house sparrows may nibble the green leaves. |
| Seeds | Wild mustards of many species grow across America; they're common garden weeds. If they turn up in your garden, let a few of these pretty plants stay. | Doves, blackbirds, and quail. Flycatchers, jays, orioles, thrushes, and other birds will eat the butterflies, caterpillars and other insects the plants house or attract. |
| Seeds | Purple coneflower came to America back in the 1970s. It became an instant favorite due to its easy care and abundant flowers. Large plants make good cover; let them stand in winter. | Blackbirds, doves, quail, and sparrows |
| Seeds | The seeds of this type of cosmos are much more appealing than those of the yellow and orange 'Klondyke'-type cosmos. | Blackbirds, doves, goldfinches, quail, and sparrows. Warblers may forage for insects during fall migration. |
| Seeds | Zinnia leaves may get straggly and mildewed in late summer, so plant them near the back of your bed, where other plants can hide their foliage. Large plants make good cover; let them stand in winter. | Blackbirds, doves, juncos, quail, and sparrows. Hummingbirds nectar at the flowers, especially red or orange cultivars. Large finches, flycatchers, jays, vireos, and other birds eat butterflies that gather. |

Cosmos and sunflowers are a perfect pairing, as far as finches are concerned. They'll clean off every seed.

lightweight birds are built for clinging to plant stems, even when they bow under their weight. Siskins, buntings, redpolls, and birds with the word "finches" in their names usually feed in this acrobatic style.

## In the Yard

- At the end of the season in the veggie garden, allow any plant in the mustard family to flower and go to seed. Small finches will appreciate the bonus of turnip seed, radish seed, and broccoli seed in fall and winter.

- Let lettuce, cress, arugula, and other salad green–plants go to seed in your vegetable garden, too; finches enjoy their seeds.

- Let dead stems of perennial and annual flowers stand all winter, instead of cutting them down to the ground in fall. Finches will appreciate the cover and the seedheads.

- Start a birdseed garden in summer by sowing finch seed mix, packaged for indoor or outdoor bird-feeding.

- Tolerate some of the weeds you find least annoying; small finches love 'em all.

- Plant a birch tree or alder; goldfinches, redpolls, and pine siskins eat the seeds.

## At the Feeder

- Feed niger seed, black sunflower seed, white proso millet, and finch mix.

- Use a tube feeder to prevent pricey finch seed and niger seed from falling to the ground or being blown away by the wind.

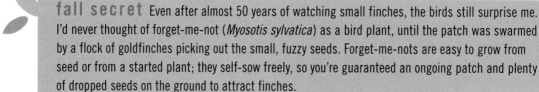

**fall secret** Even after almost 50 years of watching small finches, the birds still surprise me. I'd never thought of forget-me-not (*Myosotis sylvatica*) as a bird plant, until the patch was swarmed by a flock of goldfinches picking out the small, fuzzy seeds. Forget-me-nots are easy to grow from seed or from a started plant; they self-sow freely, so you're guaranteed an ongoing patch and plenty of dropped seeds on the ground to attract finches.

fall secret I like to scatter handfuls of finch seed mix in my flowerbeds in early summer, wherever I can find a scrap of open space. Those mixes usually include red and white proso millet, German millet, annual canary grass (not to be confused with invasive perennial canary reed grass, an unrelated species), and rapeseed (a mustard). The grasses and mustard add airiness to the bed— and a full-service buffet to small finches when their seeds ripen in fall.

- Look for a tube feeder with a tray at the bottom of the tube; it will catch dropped seed and provide more perching space for finches.
- Add reusable, store-bought "socks" of niger seed when finch traffic gets heavy in fall, to accommodate the extra guests. You'll find seed socks wherever bird-feeder supplies are sold.
- If squirrels are a problem in your yard, or if you want to prevent competition from larger birds, try a feeder with spring-loaded perches that close the feeding ports when heavier bodies land on them.
- Provide a clean, shallow birdbath. Small finches are enthusiastic fans of birdbaths and will visit daily.

# PART 4

# SECRETS FOR WINTER

## WINTER: GETTING DOWN TO BASICS

There's an ice storm raging here in the Midwest as I write this. "Raging" isn't exactly the word: What feels like a gentle rain is falling. From here inside my warm, cozy house, with a fire crackling in the living room, it merely looks wet outside. As soon as I step out the door, though, it's a different story. Whoops! Wow, is that slippery!

The temperature dropped hours ago, and the ground and plants are colder than the rain that's falling. So as soon as those raindrops land on a tree or the ground or any other surface, they freeze to a slick, solid coat of ice. The effects of the storm are fierce. Cars in ditches, meetings canceled, businesses closing, power outages, property damage, impossible travel. It's a mess out there.

With all of the disruption to our usual routines, it's easy to forget about the poor creatures that have to live outside in this kind of weather.

In a winter storm, birds are desperate.

This is when our efforts to provide food and shelter can really make a difference.

Luckily, I stocked up on birdseed before this storm. In 2 days, I poured out more than 150 pounds of cracked corn, sunflower seed, and millet, and 5 pounds of suet. I think I had every bird in town in my little yard—hundreds of goldfinches, red-winged blackbirds, cardinals, and others, all grateful to get a bite to eat.

In this section, you'll find plenty of suggestions for "survival foods" to stock your feeders with and for other sources of food for your yard. You'll also learn how to supply suitable shelter, where birds can hole up and wait out the worst or find a safe place to snuggle up during the long, cold nights. And you'll discover an unexpected attraction for the winter season: water. Finally, you'll get a closer look at some of the special birds of winter, and learn how to keep them happy in your own yard.

# CHAPTER 13

# WINTER SURVIVAL

**I**T WAS JUST after Christmas when I set foot in southern California for the very first time. Venice Beach was where I was staying, just south of Santa Monica and the celebrity-studded stretch of Malibu. Holiday decorations were still strung along the boulevards, and the family I was staying with was busy planning a New Year's Eve party.

I was already experiencing culture shock, just from seeing the Bentleys and Porsches clogging the streets and the Hollywood sign perched in the hills. (Yes, I'm a rube: My first comment, upon seeing those famous, blocky white letters, was, "Wow, so Hollywood is real!")

And now it was time to add climate shock to the experience.

I followed my hostess's lead as far as what to wear, even though it felt bizarre to pull on a gauzy skirt and a sleeveless top at Christmas. No woolens? No chunky sweaters? No long underwear? I kept my mouth shut and did as the Romans did.

A warm breeze gently played against my bare arms as we walked up the street. I could get used to this, I thought. It was a perfect early-summer day—in the middle of winter.

Then I heard the hummingbirds.

Just up the walkway from my friends' house was a tiny yard holding a single tree. The tree was some exotic species that looked like it came right out of a jungle, covered in brilliant red-orange flowers. Hummingbirds hovered all around it, as if the tree were a giant nectar feeder—which, of course, it was.

"Hummingbirds!" I called to my hosts, who looked at each other and laughed.

"Wait'll you see the butterflies," they said, as I tried to comprehend the difference between a Zone 10 winter and my usual Zone 6 snow and cold.

Not all birds, or all bird lovers, are lucky enough to live in a land of year-round summer, of course. This great big continent of ours has so many variations in climate that we've all had to learn how to cope with whatever our particular region offers.

**winter secret** You'd think that summer birds would stick around all year in regions that have enviably mild winters. After all, there's plenty of food, what with all those blooming flowers and buzzing insects. The answer? Old habits die hard. And we're talking *old*. Migration instincts were formed long, long ago, when the world was very different than it is today. So wood thrushes still wing away to southern Mexico or Panama, even though they could probably find plenty to eat in, say, Alabama.

In order to survive such drastic changes in climate, birds—and butterflies, and people, and all other living creatures—had to adapt. Bears hibernate. Butterflies and other insects go into a kind of suspended animation called diapause. People insulate their houses, or plan vacations. And birds either migrate or make the best of it.

That's where we come in. A helping hand can make all the difference to birds in winter.

# WEATHERING THE WINTER

Along about January, when even the diamond-dusted beauty of a fresh snow has begun to wear thin, I sometimes consider migrating, myself. For most of us, getting away from the weather is only a temporary option at best, so we learn to make the best of it. We dish up meals that stick to our ribs, add weather stripping around the drafty door, and pile on extra blankets at night.

Birds follow the same tactics for thriving in winter weather. Watch your backyard friends during this season, and you may notice some of these behaviors.

**Birds spend more time at the feeder.** Moving about in search of natural food requires more calories than staying in one place to fill the belly.

**Birds eat more suet and other high-fat foods.** Cold weather requires birds to burn more calories to keep warm, so they turn to high-fat foods for efficient fuel.

**Birds draw their feet up into their feathers.** Scaly bird feet aren't too susceptible to freezing, because there's not much meat on those bird feet bones. But cold tootsies are uncomfortable, so birds often draw up one foot into their feathers to keep it warm while they balance on the other leg. They may also lower their bodies to cover both of their feet and legs with puffed-out belly feathers.

**Birds leave the feeders earlier— or stay later.** Temperatures drop sharply when the sun goes down, and birds conserve heat by getting settled in roosting

**winter secret** Keeping the body warm is job number one in winter. In this season, when bird activities are all about survival, a snug place to roost overnight is just as important as a full belly. Eating enough to fuel the body is vital, of course, but so is conserving precious body heat. That's why birds seek out a protected place to sleep. Perching in a less sheltered area, exposed to cold and wind, quickly saps a bird's energy because it requires more calories to stay warm. On a very cold night, the right choice of sleeping place can spell survival. Titmice, chickadees, and bluebirds seek out holes in trees or recycle nest boxes as nighttime roosts to stay snug in winter, while other birds huddle deep within conifers or other protected spots. Carolina wrens and house sparrows may sneak into your garage or garden shed.

**winter secret** Black-capped chickadees can maintain their usual body temperature of 107.6°F (42°C) all night, researchers at Cornell University showed (in a study published by Susan Budd Chaplin in 1973), as long as they have adequate food during the day and the nighttime temp doesn't fall below freezing. But on nights when the temperature fell to 32°F (0°C) or lower, the chickadees lowered the thermostat: They dropped their body temp to about 86°F (30°C) and shivered constantly to survive the cold night.

spots long before dark. Most customers will depart well before dusk. If a winter storm is coming, however, birds will linger later than usual, stocking up for the lean times ahead.

**Birds seek sheltered nooks.**
Birdhouses, dense vines, roosting boxes, conifers, and other protected places that are small enough and enclosed enough to help birds retain some body heat are popular sleeping areas for a long winter's night. Often, birds roost in a group, sharing the warmth of their bodies.

## Surviving the Cold

Even my warmest winter coat is no match for winter cold on some mornings—and I live in southern Indiana, not the woods of Maine or the plains of Wyoming, where folks know what cold really is. But even here, in the lower Midwest, it still gets down near zero some mornings. On those days when the cold takes my breath away, I pull up my scarf, pull down my hat, and fill those feeders in a hurry!

So how do those chipper little chickadees and goldfinches keep from freezing to death?

That's the question that a relatively new branch of science is working to answer.

"Cold ecologists," such as Peter Marchand of the Mountain Research Station near Boulder, Colorado, are working to uncover real answers to the question many of us have wondered about for years: "How do things survive in brutal cold?" Turns out that animals and birds have all kinds of tricks up their sleeves.

So why don't chickadees freeze to death? Here are a few adaptations that birds have developed to stay alive.

- Feathers supply insulation, which birds can regulate by puffing those feathers out. Even better, goldfinches and redpolls grow additional feathers for winter, so that their down jackets are extra cozy.

- Duck legs and feet keep from freezing by constricting veins on their surface, sending the cool blood toward the center of the leg, where it is warmed by coming close to arteries full of warm blood. It's a heat exchanger that follows the same principle as the device some of us use to keep our houses warm. The official name for this network of blood vessels is *rete mirabile,* or "miraculous net."

- What do you do when you get cold? You shiver. That response helps to maintain body temperature, and it's one that birds

**winter secret** The word "calorie" has dastardly implications to us chocolate lovers, but in reality it's simply a measure of heat. It can be used to describe the fuel value of a food ("How many calories did you say are in that candy bar?"), or to measure how much fuel is burned by the body during an activity ("And I'll have to walk *how* far to make up for eating it? Uh, never mind."). Because cold air depletes the heat from a bird's body, the bird has to take in more calories to make up the difference. So in winter, birds eat more especially high-fat—and high-calorie!—foods and nuts.

use a lot. A research study revealed that goldfinches that are accustomed to cold regions can increase their body heat by more than five times just by shivering.

- Smaller birds, which are more susceptible to cold than big birds are, may shiver almost continuously in frigid weather to generate enough body heat to stay alive and flying. The black-capped chickadee can shiver all night long to stay warm, while sound asleep.

- On cold nights, chickadees can also enter a state of torpor in which respiration and other body processes are slowed down to conserve energy. Hummingbirds are known to do the same, and other small birds may share this survival trait, too.

## Shelter for Survival

Sometimes my penny-pinching streak makes even me laugh. It happened again last year, when I was shopping for a space blanket to add to the survival kit I keep in the car. Space blankets are a great invention: They're a lightweight plastic film with a silvery coating that reflects your body heat back to you. They come folded in small packets that

you can slip in a pocket, and they're simple to use: Just shake the blanket out and wrap up in it, to trap body heat so that you warm up fast. I'd decided it was wise to carry one with me, just in case I got lost on the logging roads in the mountains or fell through the ice. Not likely, I hoped, but you never know. Some people prefer bivouac (or bivy) sacks to climb inside, but I was looking for portability and a small investment.

Small investment. Right. There I am, standing in the camping gear aisle of the store, trying to decide between the $1.19 bare-bones space blanket and the bigger, sturdier $3.99 model, when I realized what I was doing and burst out laughing. I could just see myself, fingers turning blue, teeth chattering from the cold, wishing I'd spent the extra two bucks on the deluxe model. I now have not one, but *two* of the better space blankets, I'm happy to say. Still folded in their original wrappers, but ready if I need them.

Staying warm is vital for survival. Just ask the astronauts for whom space blankets were invented in 1964, or the outdoorsy types that have had to rely on them.

Birds don't have the luxury of space blankets or bivy sacks for survival. But they employ a similar principle to stay snug during a long, cold night: They choose an enclosed space to snuggle into, so that their precious body heat doesn't dissipate so quickly.

You can help birds stay warm by making sure there are plenty of nooks and crannies around your place where birds can seek shelter for an hour or overnight. You'll find more details on choosing specific plants, putting up roosting boxes, and other tactics in Chapter 15 (see page 274).

## "Survival of the Fittest"?

As a pretty wimpy physical specimen, I take comfort in knowing that "survival of the fittest" was once intended to refer to the species that is best adapted to its surroundings, not to how physically fit an individual within that species might be. Once I began working out at the gym some years ago, I quickly became addicted to it. But my knees are way too creaky, my back too unpredictable, and my triceps too flabby to ever give true gym rats a run for their money.

Biologists aren't fond of this familiar "survival" catchphrase because it can be misleading when it comes to the process of natural selection. As Darwin's work showed, how a species survives depends on how well that species is adapted to its surroundings and how quickly it can adapt when that environment changes. In other words, it's just as much about brains as it is about brawn. And those clever tricks and traits need to be able to be passed down from one generation to the next: They need to be "heritable," so that they can be shared by the entire species, not just one genius in the bunch.

When it comes to winter birds, survival is the name of the game. And for individual birds, as well as for entire species, it's the combination of physical fitness, smarts, and adaptability that determines which birds survive and which ones don't.

## The Helping Hand

Birds can get along just fine without us for most of the year. Insects are everywhere in spring, and wild fruits dangle along the roadsides in summer. In fall, a bounty of seed ripens in every field and on every weed.

But by the time winter rolls around, those easy pickings aren't so easy anymore. Passing flocks of migrating thrushes have

**winter secret** All of the species that walk, crawl, or fly over the earth have figured out ways to survive in the face of whatever Mother Nature throws at them—or else they're no longer among us. Sometimes individuals don't make it through the tough times, such as when bluebirds die off during a spell of severe cold. But individual losses are an accepted part of the survival of the species, as long as enough individuals manage to come through to keep the species going.

**winter secret** "Natural selection" is the way Nature weeds out individuals whose genes may not be quite up to snuff. The bluebirds that are first to die off during severe weather may merely be unlucky—but it could also be that they weren't quite as clever as their peers when it came to finding food or shelter. Or perhaps their feathers didn't have quite the insulating properties as those of the bluebirds that survived. Some people have ethical qualms about interfering with Nature's course. Not me. If the roosting box or peanut butter dough I provide can save a bluebird's life, I'm all in favor of it. And I think that bluebird might be, too!

plucked off all those beckoning berries. Scores of native sparrows have cleaned off the best seeds, leaving just shriveled stems behind. And as for insects, they're sleeping until the weather warms up again next spring.

Now, as wild foods become harder to find, our helping hand is eagerly accepted.

## THE WINTER REGULARS

You and I weren't around—and neither was Methuselah, for that matter—when birds developed their migration patterns. So we have no way of knowing why it is that some birds travel, while others stick around. We can make some good guesses, though: Swallows eat insects, so when bugs are gone, it's bye-bye, birdies. Same deal with birds that favor a combo of bugs and fruits, like tanagers and thrushes.

What's left in winter? Mostly seeds.

Which birds are still around in winter? Mostly seed eaters.

Unless you live in the South, that is. That's where many of the birds that prefer soft foods take their winter vacations.

You'll find lots of ideas for stocking your winter feeding station in Chapter 14 (see page 255).

## Survival Statistics

I'd love to tell you that scientific research proves that birds survive better with feeder help, but the question is still unresolved. It's not easy to keep track of individual birds, for one thing. And other issues, like predation and disease, complicate the findings. For whatever reasons, very little research on the question has been attempted.

A couple of studies on chickadees did show, however, that the birds quickly returned to foraging for natural foods when feeding was discontinued. Generally, feeders were found to provide roughly a quarter of a bird's daily needs—which is a whopping amount, relatively speaking.

We may not have much science yet to back us up, but feeding birds just feels right. Sharing and showing compassion for our fellow living creatures make us feel good, too.

**winter secret** In colder regions of the country, our feeders and bird-beckoning backyards can make a real difference to the birds of winter. Colder temperatures require more calories to keep a bird's body heated, so a ready source of belly-filling foods is really welcome. Seed eaters predominate, so stock up on sunflower seed, white proso millet, niger seed, and nuts.

# The Good Side of Gray

After a few days of gray and gloomy winter weather, my brain starts to feel befogged. It's hard to get moving in the morning without seeing the sun. In the Pacific Northwest, I depended on a powerful therapeutic light box to give me my daily dose of sunshine when what the locals called "suicide weather" set in.

Southern Indiana, where I live now, doesn't have nearly the amount of drizzly days as the state of Washington did, but we do have a lot of overcast days in winter. And that lack of sunshine can definitely affect my mood.

I don't need a light box in Indiana because the gloom isn't as sustained as it is in the Northwest. Besides, when I get the winter blues, I've got a quick pick-me-up that works like magic: Instead of focusing on the blues, I focus on the grays—the little gray birds whose activity makes me feel more cheerful, even on the dreariest day.

I'm sure you have the same antidote to the winter blahs right in your own yard. They're regular visitors to feeders. And they even hang out together in winter, traveling in loose-knit feeding flocks, like a group of friends gathering at Denny's after a long night out.

So say good-bye to the winter blues, and say hello to the winter grays.

**Chickadees.** How can you be gloomy when you're watching chickadees? With their bright black eyes and quick little bodies, these little birds just look happy. These gregarious little guys often visit feeders in small groups of a few to several birds. The

## Now Appearing, Nationwide!

Seed-eating birds are spread across the country in winter. Each region gets its special birds, but there's also a core group of birds that we all get to enjoy.

| | |
|---|---|
| Chickadees | Juncos |
| Doves | Nuthatches |
| Goldfinches | Native sparrows |
| House finch | Titmice |
| Jays | Woodpeckers |

black-capped chickadee is the classic icon of this group, and it ranges across all but the southern tier of states. Other species, including the Carolina, the mountain, the boreal, and the chestnut-backed, add to the chickadee commotion.

**Nuthatches.** The white-breasted nuthatch looks almost like a little gent all decked out in his tuxedo. Very dignified. Well, sort of. Poor nuthatches have the same problem as penguins—they start out looking serious and end up making us laugh. As soon as you add those stubby little legs and put him in his usual upside-down pose, a nuthatch's fancy duds look pretty funny. You can expect to see between one and a few nuthatches at your winter feeders. Besides the white-breasted, you may see a red-breasted nuthatch in most areas of the country, a pygmy nuthatch in the West and Southwest, or a brown-headed nuthatch in the South.

**Titmice.** A hat can make all the difference in your attitude—just ask the wearers of the fancy hats at the Kentucky Derby, or, for that matter, the Queen of England. Or a titmouse! Titmice sport a snappy little crest of feathers atop their heads, which makes them stand out from smooth-headed winter birds. Combine that jaunty headgear with active, acrobatic habits, and the titmice that visit your winter feeder

will quickly become favorites. You won't see them in small groups, like you will see chickadees, but even one or two titmice are enough to make a winter feeder scene feel alive.

You'll find more secrets about all of these winter bird favorites in Chapter 16, Special Birds of Winter (see page 294).

## Social or Solitary?

Are you a people watcher? Me too. Sometimes I like to admire the fashions—or feel nostalgic when I see which fads from my generation the young kids have brought back around. Sometimes I marvel at the electronic devices everyone seems permanently attached to these days. But mostly, I simply enjoy watching the behavior of our own species. No matter how civilized we like to think we are, a few minutes of observing *Homo sapiens* shows clearly how much we really are just like other animals.

Take levels of sociability, for instance. Some of us are the outgoing kind, preferring to be part of a lively group of friends. Others would rather stick to just their partner, and a few of us might admit we like our own company the best—at least on some days!

Dining out isn't a very good scientific indicator of that personality trait, because it's a special occasion. But you can still notice the sociability differences among people when you look around a restaurant. Some fill a big table with a gregarious group of friends or family, all talking a mile a minute. Others dine in pairs, enjoying quiet conversation. Sometimes a solitary sort will be enjoying a meal.

The same scene happens at your bird restaurant. Here's what you'll notice when you check out the regulars at your winter buffet.

**Table for 30, please!** Look for pine siskins, goldfinches, and evening grosbeaks to show up in big, noisy bunches at the

## Bright Spots

Not all birds of winter are dressed in quiet colors. You'll see occasional splashes of bright color around your yard, too. Keep an eye out for these colorful characters.

**Bluebirds.** Yes, you are very lucky to have bluebirds at your feeder, you who live near natural bluebird territory of wild open space and woods' edge. No, I don't have any myself—yet. (Although sometimes they tease me by flying over.) Eastern, western, or mountain bluebirds may visit feeders across a wide sweep of the country, generally the southern half and far west. If you have them, consider yourself blessed, and don't stint on the mealworms and peanut butter dough!

**Cardinal.** Officially called the northern cardinal, the familiar "redbird" is a beloved bird of winter in the eastern two-thirds of the country and in the deep Southwest, where it is joined by the similar but grayer pyrrhuloxia (peer-uh-LOX-ee-uh) from the Greek *pyrrhoulas*, "a red bird." Cardinals occur year-round, but snowy surroundings and winter drab landscapes are where they really stand out.

**Purple finch.** The standout of the purplish red finches, a group that also includes the ubiquitous house finch and Cassin's finch of the West, and the lovely rosy finches of the mountain states. This beautiful big finch is deeply stained with raspberry red in the male; the species shows up at feeders in winter across the eastern half of the country and along the Pacific states, and occasionally elsewhere, especially during years when the cone crop fails in the Far North.

**Evening grosbeak.** Yes, they go through sunflower seeds like a house afire, complete with sound effects like crackling flames, which is only the noise of many big beaks cracking seeds simultaneously. Look for an occasional roaming flock of these yellow, white, and black birds anywhere in the country, or enjoy their regular company in the upper West.

**Jays.** The other blue birds, jays are loud and active—just what we need to liven up the winter scene. Various species make sure that we all get to enjoy the antics of these big birds, wherever we put out our peanuts.

**winter secret** Back in the old days, Anna's hummingbirds were "the" winter species. Nowadays, they have lots of company. Hummingbird ranges are changing, and many species show up far afield from where they're "supposed" to be, possibly because of our sugar-water hospitality and tempting gardens. In recent years, more and more species are changing their winter vacation plans. Instead of heading for Central and South America, they're sticking around in the warmer parts of the good ol' US of A. So keep that nectar feeder handy, just in case you hear buzzing wings in your winter backyard.

winter feeder. Oh, and let's not forget starlings! English or house sparrows, too, may make a scene at your feeders. House finches used to be the biggest flock at my feeder, but since an eye disease decimated their ranks, they're only moderately abundant these days in most places.

**Baker's dozen.** Winter feeder-watching wouldn't be nearly as much fun without the constant presence of juncos and native sparrows. These birds don't move together in a tight-knit flock, but they do forage in the same places—wherever seeds are abundant. In our backyards, that's usually in the garden beds or under the feeders. If you live in an area where quail roam, you may spot a group of them enjoying a meal together, too.

**By the handful.** Look for just a few or possibly several individuals of some winter regulars, including cardinals, jays, purple finches, red-bellied woodpeckers, titmice, chickadees, and mourning doves.

**A treasured few.** What a treat to spot a sprinkling of not-so-abundant birds among the usual crowd! Keep an eye out for towhees and fox sparrows at the feeder, nuthatches and woodpeckers at the suet,

and maybe a sprinkling of kinglets cruising the trees.

**Solitary diners.** We may never be able to tell one white-throated sparrow from another, but we sure can recognize "our" fox sparrow among them. A single bird stands out as an individual, so we give it special attention. In winter, you might host other "table for one" birds, besides that fox sparrow. Keep an eye out for any of these singular diners: a robin, a catbird, a brown thrasher, a mockingbird, a yellow-rumped warbler, a brown creeper, a Carolina wren, or maybe even a house wren. Any other loners in your neighborhood?

# Winter Hummingbirds

If you have snow and ice outside that window, hey, give me a call and let's hop a plane for a quick trip to sunny California or sultry Louisiana. We'll loll about in our shorts, sipping exotic drinks with little umbrellas, and watch the hummingbirds zipping in and out of the flowers. Hummingbirds? In winter? Yep. For some of us.

If you live along the Pacific Coast, near the Gulf of Mexico, or even along the Atlantic coast, go ahead, puff up those feathers and preen with pride. While the rest of us are coping with snow shovels and bulky coats, you lucky ducks get to host hummingbirds in winter. Better stock up on those little paper umbrellas—a whole flock of us will soon be on your doorstep!

From Mexico to Canada, the brilliant pink head and throat of the male Anna's hummingbird and his green partner are a common sight in the not-so-cold cold months. But the real hot spot for winter hummingbirds is the Gulf Coast, where many western species head for a winter vacation.

- Anna's hummingbirds, like the one I first met in sunny southern California and the regulars that entertained me when I lived in Washington state, are a year-round treat along the entire Pacific coast. The species also turns up in the Southeast and along the Atlantic coast.

- Rufous hummingbird sightings have gone from rare to occasional along the Gulf coast—and they sometimes show up along the Atlantic seaboard and in interior areas, too, especially in the Southeast.

- Most ruby-throated hummingbirds leave the country, but some linger long into the cold season—even in cold areas. Others have taken to wintering in the tip of Florida.

- Even the tiny calliope hummingbird, our smallest North American species at $3\frac{1}{4}$ inches, may turn up far afield. This species seems partial to the area around New Orleans. Must be the beignets!

## Sugar for Survival

Not all areas along the Pacific Coast are exactly balmy, although the ocean does keep the climate relatively mild. And sometimes, winter settles in for real.

I'll never forget one winter in Washougal, Washington, when we were hit with days of highly uncommon snow and ice storms and a temperature that hovered around 15°F. Hard times for hummingbirds!

That's when I got to see, firsthand, how a hummingbird in a state of torpor behaves. At 4 inches from bill tip to tail tip, Anna's hummingbirds are larger than most species, which may give them a slight advantage in the occasional chilly weather along the coast. But this was severe cold, and my hummers reduced their metabolism to survive. They looked like they were in slow motion—and almost drunk. Their balance was poor when perched, they flew slowly and wobbly, and they blinked slowly, too, as if they were half asleep. In essence, they were. But every one survived the cold spell, with lots of help from our hummingbird feeders.

The moral of this story? Don't forget your hummers if your mild winter area gets hit with a dose of real winter. Nectar feeders can freeze, so invest in a few extras to have on hand; that way, you can swap them out while others are thawing. Sugar water spells survival for wintering hummingbirds.

## Windowpane Worries

Window glass is a huge danger to birds because they don't recognize it as a solid object; they see the reflection, instead, and fly right into the glass, often breaking their necks. During migration, millions of birds are killed flying into windows of homes and high-rises. But that's not all. When birds panic because of a predator, they often hit a house window with enough force to break their neck, or to stun them so that they become sitting ducks, so to speak, for the cat that scared them in the first place. You can take some easy steps to minimize the problem.

- Put a barrier between the birds and the window. A trellised vine will look pretty and still allow a view of the birds, as well as letting some light enter the window. In winter, the trellis and the dead stems will still serve their purpose.
- Place your feeders very close to your windows. Sudden panics are a way of life with feeder birds. When they get scared by a real or imagined danger, they fly off at top speed in all directions. Should they choose the wrong direction, help make sure they haven't gained much speed before they encounter the glass.
- Use feeders that attach to the window with suction cups; these can help birds become accustomed to treating the glass as a solid object.
- Tack plastic bird netting across the window, both to break up the reflection and to reduce the impact of the glass.
- Use window screens on the outside of the window to eliminate the reflection problem.

- Louisiana is queen of winter hummingbird sightings—perhaps because of dedicated observers and excellent record-keeping by its Audubon Societies. Folks there report black-chinned, broad-tailed, buff-bellied, and other species in their winter gardens.

In all of the regions where hummingbirds head in winter, there are at least some flowers that bloom year-round. If you're lucky enough to live in one of those spots, turn to "Winter Flowers for Hummingbirds" on page 281 in Chapter 15 for plant suggestions for your winter flower garden.

# BACKYARD DANGERS

It's not easy being a bird, especially in winter. Birds have to manage to stay warm and well fed, which is a full-time job in itself. But they also have to avoid other dangers that can threaten their survival.

A reliable source of food quickly attracts eager eaters, and not only those with a hunger for suet or seed. It's the suet- or seed-eaters that some backyard visitors are eyeing for a meal. Cats and hawks are the big two feeder predators. (In Chapter 5, you learned how much of a menace cats are to birds.) Owls may visit at night, but their menu consists mostly of rodents, since the birdies are sleeping.

# Tooth and Claw

Okay, you soft-hearted types (and I'd wager that's most of us—or we wouldn't be helping birds in the first place): It's time to take a look at the hard, cold facts of the situation our soft hearts create.

Feeding birds can create quite a dilemma. Consider this.

- A feeding station helps birds have an easier time surviving in winter.
- A feeding station bustling with birds is a tempting invitation to predators.
- The only sure way to keep feeder birds safe from predators is to remove the feeding station.

No, I'm not real fond of that solution, either. That's why I try everything else I possibly can before I resort to removing the feeders. In more than 30 years of feeding birds, I've only had to stop feeding them two times—both times because of a Cooper's

## Hawk Appreciation

It's very hard to appreciate a hawk when it's plucking the feathers out of one of our favorite feeder birds. But the predator/prey relationship is just part of nature, and the hawk itself is only doing what comes naturally. Of course we'll want to take steps to keep our feeder birds safe, but it's also fun to figure out what kind of hawk we've attracted. Here are the most likely suspects.

**Cooper's hawk.** "Blue death" was an old nickname for this superb bird hunter, which once stayed mostly in the forests. In the past decade or two, it learned that feeders offer easy pickings and adjusted its habits accordingly. Nowadays this once-reclusive forest species often patrols a regular route of feeders in cities and towns.

**Red-tailed hawk.** Big and bulky, red-tails hunt mostly by sitting and waiting, or by cruising through a feeder area. Doves are often a target, but small birds can fall into their clutches, too.

**Sharp-shinned hawk.** The sharpie is a slim, small hawk with a blue-gray back, reddish belly, and dramatically barred tail. (Young birds have brown backs and coarsely brown-streaked breasts.) At 11 inches long, this hawk is only an inch bigger than a robin. Look for the squared-off bottom of the tail; the look-alike but larger Cooper's hawk has a rounded tail tip.

Many other raptors have also been seen at feeding stations, including the American kestrel, the merlin, the broad-winged hawk, and others (no eagles—yet), so keep your field guide handy. I was thrilled to see a peregrine falcon dart through a few years ago, although it never made a return visit that I'm aware of. In recent years, though, peregrines seem to be adopting this food source more often, according to reports from backyard birders and nature centers.

**winter secret** By New Year's, which is when I met my first Anna's in California, these incredible birds are already beginning spectacular courtship flights, with the male climbing high before a daredevil dive that ends with a quick, slurred chirp so loud it makes you jump. That *Tewk!* sound has always mystified me. I could never tell whether it was the bird's voice or its wings that was making the noise. Now we know, thanks to high-speed video shot at the University of Berkeley, then slowed way, way down for examination. At the bottom of the dive, when the male hummer is zooming at an astounding 50 mph, it flares its tail for a split second (60 milliseconds, to be exact). The force of that wind makes the two outer tail feathers vibrate like a reed in a clarinet, producing that brief but startlingly loud chirp.

hawk that just wouldn't quit. The predator took to hanging around most of the day, grabbing breakfast, lunch, and dinner, and between-meal snacks whenever the feeder birds left the bushes.

My solutions depend on cover—and on chasing. In Chapter 15, you'll learn how to arrange cover near the feeding station to give birds a fighting chance.

As for the chasing, I find it a great way to get my exercise and to work off some tension. Kids and dogs take to it enthusiastically, too. The how-to is simple: Just run toward the offending predator, making as much noise as you can. The cats and hawks that have checked out my feeders can attest that loud hand-clapping and hollering *"Shoo!"* are remarkably effective.

# CHAPTER 14

# THE FEEDER SCENE IN WINTER

I T'S EASY TO SEE where the real heart of a house is: Just watch where people gather when a bunch of friends gets together. No matter how luxurious the leather couches, or how lovely the lighting in the living room, everyone eventually ends up in the kitchen.

Why do we tend to gather in the kitchen? I think it's because there's something comforting and connecting about food. Whether it's crackers and cheese or caviar on toast, the simple act of sharing food makes us feel closer to each other. And that feels good.

Offering food is also a way of sharing ourselves. The preparation of a meal is an act of love, to my mind. So no wonder it makes us feel bad when we put together a great dinner and then have folks say, "No, thanks, I'm not hungry," or "I grabbed a bite on the way home." We want those whom we cook for to appreciate our offerings.

Cold that be why some of us stop feeding birds in summer? When natural food is at its peak in summer, our feeders only entice birds to stop in for the briefest of visits. Most birds will say, "No, thanks; couldn't eat another bite after all those caterpillars."

Whether or not we take that summer slowdown personally, we all get excited when winter brings birds back to the feeder. Natural foods have dwindled from what was an all-you-can-eat banquet of summer to the bare bones of winter. Now it's way harder for birds to fill their bellies, so our offerings are eagerly accepted. Even if our feeders are stocked with a bargain blend instead of a high-priced seed-and-nut mix, the pickings are way better than seeking out a few stray seeds in the wild.

In winter, birds gobble up our feeder offerings as eagerly as we say, "Mmm, thanks!" to a steamy cup of cocoa. Without the demands of a young family, birds are free to linger for hours if they like, and many of them do. That kind of appreciation, plus the knowledge that our efforts are really needed, is enough to inspire us to keep refilling those feeders.

## RELY ON THE REGULARS

Fall brings plenty of surprises to the feeding station as migrants come and go, but winter quickly settles into a routine. The shifting scene of migration has ended, and birds are on their winter feeding territories, spending their days getting enough calories to keep warm. We may still have a few surprises in store for us, especially when winter storms cause birds from farther afield to seek sustenance. But in general, the cast of characters at our feeders is the same day after day.

Sound boring? Not at all! This is our chance to really get to know the crew of old faithfuls who keep us company through the winter months. In many cases, these birds are also year-round friends. Getting to know them now means we'll be better able to see how their behavior changes when they pair up for nesting season.

## Shared or Special?

As we talked about in Chapter 13, many of our winter birds are the same across wide areas of the country. Juncos, for instance, are a mainstay at most of our feeders. Chickadees are a constant from Atlantic to Pacific, and so are mellow groups of mourning doves. Native sparrows scratch under every winter feeder, and nuthatches comb the bark of trees just about everywhere. We don't all share the exact same species of our common birds, but we do get to enjoy our regional representatives of the same tribe.

Other winter birds are unique to particu-

lar areas. In the Southeast, for instance, a catbird may grace your winter feeder, while in the cold North, crossbills may come to call. Those regional specialties exist because the birds are adapted to whatever natural foods our little corner of the world has to offer—conifer cones for crossbills, for example, or warm-winter insects and berries for that catbird.

## Back to Basics

We don't all feed the same birds in winter, yet our menu mainstays are the same no matter where we live. That's because three basic bird foods are highly popular with lots of different birds. I think of them as the one-size-fits-all foods of the backyard scene.

Of course, we all know that "one size fits all" is sometimes not quite true. I've had my share of frustration trying to pull up a pair of one-size-fits-all pantyhose that didn't quite fit my "all"! So I bolster the Big Three with special foods that are more appealing to some species; you'll read about those foods in "Added Appeal" on page 258.

Still, these basic bird foods are as close to "one size fits all" as it gets at the feeding station. Nearly every species that stops in will at least sample them, and most birds will be happy to eat them day in and day out. They're the best place to start when you're setting up your winter feeding station.

### Black oil sunflower seed

- It's the most popular birdseed for the widest variety of birds.
- It takes very little effort to split the shell and get at the huge payoff: a supersize morsel of meaty, high-fat, high-protein food.
- Small and large birds alike can easily split the shell.
- Small birds can also pick up crumbs that drop when larger birds work through the seeds.
- It's relatively inexpensive to buy, although prices do fluctuate.
- It's a favorite of cardinals, jays, grosbeaks, finches, chickadees, titmice, and nuthatches.
- It's also eaten by sparrows, juncos, towhees, woodpeckers, blackbirds, and other birds.

## Foraging Friends

Birds use winter territories that are much bigger than their nesting grounds. They no longer stick together in pairs, either. Instead, it's usually small bands of birds that travel through an area, gleaning food as they go. You'll see foraging flocks travel through your own backyard in winter.

Watch for these feeding friends, who often loosely travel together to scour your yard as well as stop in at the feeder.

- Chickadees, titmice, and nuthatches will often band together, along with a downy woodpecker or a brown creeper to look for food. (See Chapter 16 for more about chickadees, titmice, nuthatches, and woodpeckers.)
- Ruby-crowned or golden-crowned kinglets sometimes join a mixed group of little gray birds, or LGBs, as I sometimes think of them.
- Sometimes a yellow-rumped warbler or two, or a Carolina wren, will be part of the patrol, too.
- Over winter, bluebirds band together in groups that may number a dozen or more birds and are probably extended family groups.
- Native sparrows often congregate in mixed flocks to feed on the ground. Look for groups that include white-crowned, white-throated, golden-crowned, field, tree, or song sparrows, depending on whether you live within these species' winter ranges.
- Towhees often join a group of native sparrows, although they usually keep to the fringes when the birds are feeding on the ground.
- Redpolls, pine siskins, and goldfinches often hang out together to nibble seeds from standing weeds or your thistle feeder.

## White proso millet

- It's perfectly sized for native sparrows, juncos, and other small birds that eat a diet mainly of small seeds.

- The round seeds have a good shell-to-meat ratio: They provide a generous bite of nutritious food for not much work.

- Because the seeds are small, a single scoop keeps a lot of birds busy.

- The amount of empty shells produced is much less than with sunflower seeds, and the light shells often blow away in the breeze, so feeder areas won't require as much cleanup.

- It's a favorite of sparrows, juncos, buntings, and towhees.

- It's also eaten by finches, blackbirds, varied thrush, and tanagers.

## Suet

- This is the high-fat staple for birds that normally supplement their seed diet with insects, or which mainly eat insects.

- Suet feeders require very little maintenance, since a refill can last for a week or more, depending on the amount of traffic.

- All of the suet is eaten, with no waste.

- It's a favorite of chickadees, titmice, nuthatches, woodpeckers, wrens, thrushes, bluebirds, thrashers, catbird, mockingbird, warblers . . . and starlings, grackles, and blue jays.

# ADDED APPEAL

The basics are great for most of the birds in our backyards in winter. But some species aren't suited to such a menu.

Some birds simply aren't big seed eaters. Their bills and bodies are adapted to eating other sorts of food—insects, say, or fruit.

Depending on where you live, you may

spot one of these species in your winter backyard.

- Robins, as every school kid knows, eat worms—and other insects and soft-bodied critters, plus plenty of fruit. We think of robins as spring harbingers, but many linger in cold regions during winter, getting by on the last of the berries and fruits, plus whatever else they can ferret out of the leaves.

- Orioles, thrashers, Carolina wrens, and the catbird have bills adapted to nabbing insects and slashing into fruit. They winter mainly in the Southeast and the South, where such foods can still be found in winter.

- Bluebirds and waxwings have bills made for grabbing insects and biting off berries. They may turn up across much of the country in winter, wherever they manage to find enough to eat.

- Kinglets, the brown creeper, and wood warblers have small, thin bills that suit their style of rapidly dabbing up little bugs. Cracking seeds? No can do. In winter, they seek overwintering insects at any stage of life, from eggs to adults.

## Special Menu

Birds that previously showed little or no interest in our feeders—those thrashers, catbirds, orioles, wrens, and other birds we mentioned—have begun to adopt a new attitude toward feeders now that mealworms and other foods that pique their interest are becoming more common on the menu. Only a few years ago, these birds stuck to the wild foods in our yards, happily gleaning insects off the branches or plucking berries off the bushes. But as we have added feeders and foods tailored to their tastes, including oriole nectar and jelly feeders and dishes of tempting mealworms, these non-seed-eaters are becoming more common feeder guests.

Just as hummingbirds did with nectar feeders a generation ago, these birds have learned to associate foods that they enjoy

**winter secret** Desperate times, such as winter ice storms, can cause birds to change their eating habits and sample just about anything of nutritional value. Robins, wrens, and other birds that don't generally eat seeds may visit a seed feeder when starvation is the only alternative. Often they can find bits of sunflower meats dropped by other birds among the mix.

The faster you get the feeders uncovered after a snow or ice storm, the better for your birds. You can use a stiff broom to sweep off snow. I also use a natural bristle broom to sweep beneath the feeders, a favorite dining area for sparrows, juncos, towhees, and doves. For ice or crusted snow, use whatever tool works best for you; my secret weapon is a long-handled ice scraper with a built-in brush. I hammer the ice or crust with the handle of the scraper so that it cracks, then lift or brush off the pieces to expose the seed.

**winter secret** Winter storms may drive very unusual visitors to your feeders. Birds from outlying natural areas, such as meadowlarks from farm fields or towhees from the woods, are a possibility. But even wild ducks, herons, or other "What's he doing here?!" birds may show up to see what your feeder has to offer when a blizzard hits. The usual seeds at a feeding station will suffice for these birds in such an emergency, but these big birds need a lot of food, so feel free to experiment with whatever you think they might eat. Bread is always a good emergency ration. You can also try whole-kernel or cracked corn.

eating with a feeding station. That means they are more likely to check out a backyard setup.

Try these foods to tempt birds that aren't interested in seeds to your feeding station.

- Mealworms

- Accessible suet (see "Suet Service" on the opposite page for info)

- Fruit

- Nectar

## Mighty Mealworms

The thought of a dish of mealworms makes many of us say, "Eew! Gross!" I used to feel a little queasy at the thought, too, until I saw how the birds responded—and which birds were attracted. As soon as I saw a bluebird and a beautiful cinnamon-colored brown thrasher perch on the mealworm

feeder, I forgot all about how revolted I once was.

Overwintering bluebirds, thrashers, and other species that usually don't eat seeds are a great incentive to investigate mealworms, one of the newest feeder foods on the scene. Mealworms are quickly becoming a real hit with bird feeders—the human kind—because of the more unusual birds they attract. As "nonfeeder" winter birds learn to associate mealworms with bird feeders, the birds visit feeders more often. We feeder-keepers respond by offering more mealworms, which reinforces the birds' behavior.

Offer live mealworms in a small, straight-sided container so they can't crawl out. Make sure the dish is heavy enough not to tip when a larger bird alights. Or try the roasted variety of mealworms (or other larvae), to eliminate the possibility of escapees. My birds eagerly eat both kinds, although live

**winter secret** Be sure that mealworms are highly visible when you begin offering them at your feeder. Tuck a small glass or crockery dish into the corner of an open tray feeder, where the wigglers can be seen by birds flying over. If starlings or other less desirable species take to gobbling up your precious mealworms, you can switch to a feeder that only smaller birds can access.

mealworms seem to be favored. The motion of the live worms seems to elicit an instinctive stab-and-grab behavior that requires no learning curve. Roasted mealworms, on the other hand, are usually sampled gingerly before being adopted as a menu item to be eaten with gusto. (See "Shopping for and Storing Mealworms" on page 42.)

## Suet Service

The pure, solid fat called suet is one of the most popular winter foods. It's sky-high in calories, so it provides plenty of fuel to keep birds going during the day and to help them survive cold temperatures at night. Almost every bird that visits your winter feeding station will eagerly eat suet—if they can get at it. Many birds aren't agile enough to cling to a hanging wire cage of suet, but they will gratefully accept a handout where they can perch and peck.

Bite-size bits of chopped suet are a huge hit with winter birds of many species. I buy blocks of plain suet packaged for birds, or fat from the supermarket meat department or butcher, then chop it into bits with a sharp chef's knife. Sprinkle it in small quantities on a tray feeder, on a garden bench, or right on the ground.

Don't be surprised to see sparrows, juncos, and other regulars sampling it, too; many seed eaters eagerly eat chopped suet. Set out the chopped suet at the same time each day, in the same place, and your birds are likely to start looking for it at the appointed time. I feed chopped suet in unusual places, away from the feeder, so that starlings don't devour it in seconds. My garden bench and a big rock in the flowerbed serve well as feeders for a daily handful of chopped suet.

## Winter Fruit Feeding

Fruit feeders that hold apples or oranges are popular in winter, especially if any lingering fruit lovers, such as a brown thrasher or Carolina wren, are in your neighborhood. Halved apples, laid on the ground cut-side up, are popular, too; this is a good way to offer fruit to robins, which prefer to eat on the ground.

Most fresh fruit is expensive in winter, so I look for bargains for my birds. Produce department managers are often happy to give me less-than-perfect apples or other fruits at a minimal price or, even better, for free.

If you find yourself with more fruit on hand than you can use before it goes bad,

**winter secret** A swinging suet cage requires that birds possess a certain amount of agility in order to balance on it. To help less-acrobatic birds such as the larger gray catbird or brown thrasher feel secure, make one of your suet cages stationary. Stabilize the wire cage by attaching it securely to a wooden post with a couple of screw-in hooks; space them about 4 inches apart, so that the wire grid of the cage can slip onto them.

## Starling Smarts

Serving suet in a way that all birds can access it can be as simple as finely chopping the fat and scattering it on the ground or in a tray feeder. What could be easier?

Not so fast, suet-choppers: There's a problem with that technique. Does the word "starlings" ring a bell? Squirrels can also be frustratingly fond of suet.

Nicely chopped suet makes the fat readily available to birds with big appetites, as well as to the daintier eaters you'd rather see eating it. Once starlings discover the handout, they'll gobble those precious bits down in minutes—or seconds, if word spreads fast.

Starlings can be a big frustration at a feeding station. They eat fast and furious, creating a commotion that keeps other birds away from the feeder. And they eat a lot, often gobbling down the suet or other soft food until it's gone.

Grackles, blackbirds, and pigeons can also fall into the category of feeder hogs. Jays aren't the most polite birds, either, but they generally don't take over feeders for hours at a time, as the other species are wont to do.

Starlings and the other birds that many of us think of as feeder pests are big and assertive. When they arrive, the less aggressive birds go hungry instead of shouldering their way in among them to fight for their share.

I don't like to deny any hungry birds the chance to fill their bellies, but I sure get annoyed when starlings scarf up the raisins I had intended for the much shyer robin, or gobble the grapes I'd hoped the Carolina wren could sample.

I depend on some simple tricks to minimize the frustration of feeder hogs.

- If starlings aren't regular visitors at your feeding station, count your blessings and keep doing what you're doing.

- A menu of sunflower seeds and niger seed isn't very appealing to starlings. Stay away from soft foods and special treats, and you might not have to deal with the hungry hordes.

- Starlings are opportunistic birds that go anywhere the eating is easy. When the food is gone, starlings depart, although they may come back to double-check for a day or two. If they vacuum up your suet, let the feeder stay empty for a few days, then move it to a new place, and refill it.

- Try a horizontally hanging suet feeder that holds the suet upside-down, which requires extra dexterity to cling to. It's not starling-proof, but it may slow down consumption and give other birds a chance to dash in and grab a bite.

- Decoy offerings work great—but they also attract starlings to your yard. So if you don't have the birds already, skip this trick. If starlings are pretty much a constant, use a lavish banquet of scraps to lure them away from your feeding station to a "Reserved for Starlings" spot. Leftover pasta, meat, dog food, PB & J scraps, crackers, bread, canned corn, cheese, apple cores, and similar foods will keep them busy.

## Dried Fruit

Dried fruit works well for winter bird feeding because it has a long "shelf life" in a feeder. Raisins, dried apples, currants, apricots, and other dried fruits contain far less water than fresh fruit, so they won't freeze as readily when the weather turns cold.

Many birds eat very small bites of fruit, so I take the time to chop dried fruit. Tiny dried currants are fine as they are, but dried apricots, peaches, and apples are more appealing to birds if you present them in very small pieces. It makes my offering stretch a little further, to serve more birds or to flavor a recipe for bird treats. You can use a sharp knife or a pair of scissors to cut larger dried fruits into small bits.

freeze it for later use. A little preparation before freezing will make it easier to add fruit to bird treat recipes or to serve it alone when needed.

- Bruised or withered fruit is fine for birds, but discard any fruit with visible mold, or cut that part off, if possible.
- Chop apples coarsely, into ¼-inch cubes. (Think bite-size for birds.)
- Slice strawberries into halves or quarters.
- Chop grapes and cranberries in half.
- Freeze blueberries, blackberries, or raspberries whole.

Line a cookie sheet with waxed paper, and spread out the pieces of fruit to freeze, so that they don't stick together in one big lump. When the fruit is frozen, pour the pieces into plastic zipper-lock bags so you can add them to bird treats or pour them into feeders or on the ground as needed.

## COLD-WEATHER CALORIES

Get out a map and draw a line across the middle of the United States, from coast to coast. Above that line, winter is severe, with frigid cold and often lots of snow. Below that line it's not so bad, relatively speaking. Birds that spend the winter in that top half of the country need all the calories they can get to keep their bodies warm in winter. Those below the line usually have an easier time fending for themselves.

Of course, Mother Nature doesn't always pay attention to general climate boundaries. And these days, when she seems to be feeling especially moody, it's hard to count on any established patterns.

So I take a clue from my own cold-weather preparations. If I have to bundle up to stay warm, with a thick winter coat, scarf,

**winter secret** Hang a bunch of red grapes over a twiggy branch so that it is well supported and resists falling off when you lightly tug on it. Orioles, thrashers, northern mockingbirds, catbirds, wrens, and other birds may adopt this fruit "feeder," even if the grapes freeze.

hat, and gloves, then I know my birds are going to appreciate all the high-calorie food I can dish out.

# FATS COME FIRST

Here's an easy way to figure out which foods to focus on for birds that are trying to keep warm in cold weather: If it's a food that we'd call "fattening," it packs plenty of calories. That's the place to start. Then, consider that birds eat mostly seeds, grains, insects, or animal products—not leafy greens or veggies—and choose foods that suit their style.

Make sure your winter menu includes some of these high-fat favorites.

**Plant-origin fats.** Corn oil or other vegetable or nut oils, margarine,

## Feel-Good Feeding

Every bird in town, it seemed like, came to my yard after the ice storm.

Three big flocks of blackbirds (one of red-wings, one of grackles, and one of cowbirds, Brewer's, and rusty blackbirds) covered most of the ground in my small yard. Mixed in were dozens of cardinals, finches, juncos, jays, tree sparrows, chickadees, woodpeckers great and small, and, of course, a full complement of starlings. With so many customers, I wasn't bothering with feeders. I was pouring sunflower seed, millet, niger, and cracked corn right on the ground.

I'd felt happy with my efforts. Until I saw the robin.

It was about an hour to sunset. Of course, the sun had never actually shown its face that day, so all that meant was that the gloom was a little grayer than it had been. But the temperature was dropping as night approached, and a fresh flurry of snowflakes was spattering against my cheeks. The birds in my yard were extra busy gobbling up whatever seeds they could find. They desperately needed those calories to help them keep warm during the coming night. Because I'd been feeding so many birds, I'd had to restock the birdseed a lot. The aluminum storm door had been opening and closing so often that the birds had become accustomed to it.

"Just Sally bringing us more food," seemed to be the look on their faces whenever I came back out.

Now, late in the day, the juncos, cardinals, goldfinches, and sparrows hardly flinched when I pushed the door open. My hands were full with the big but nearly empty sack of sunflower seeds, the coffee can of niger seed, and the last of my precious pecans for the chickadees. Just as I was bending down to park everything on the sheltered step for a minute, I heard the familiar chirp of a robin.

Oh, man. This was not exactly robin weather.

The temperature was somewhere in the low 20s and going down fast, now that the sun was setting. Every weed, twig, branch, and tree trunk was cased in heavy ice. The ice over the snow on the ground was so

peanut butter or other nut butters, and nuts.

**Animal-origin fats.** Suet, fat trimmings from meat, lard, hamburger, hot dogs, and sausage.

**Dairy fats,** such as butter or cheese, may attract the attention of a few species, such as wrens or the catbird. But plant-oil or animal fats are usually accepted more readily. Still, if you run short, it won't harm birds to experiment, if you can spare the human food. Butter in the suet holder? It's worth a try, if you have enough to share and nothing else to offer.

## High-Fat Handouts

It's gratifying to watch birds crack store-bought seeds that we've put in our feeders.

solid that all my weight wasn't enough to do more than make a slight dent, even when I stomped my feet to try to get a grip.

Ice storms bring the worst conditions a bird can face: Zero food is pretty much the score. Add cold temperatures when there's not enough food to keep a body warm, and you know the end of the story isn't going to be pretty. Bluebirds, robins, Carolina wrens, and waxwings can't get at cedar or sumac berries or other lingering fruits when they're covered in a layer of ice; they may as well be cased in glass. Dead weeds that might hide many an overwintering insect are off-limits to woodpeckers, chickadees, titmice, and kinglets. As for seeds, forget about it. From big tulip tree seeds to tiny pigweed seeds, ice-coated seeds are out of reach of the beaks of finches, siskins, and sparrows. Just getting around is hard for birds when ice coats the branches and covers the ground.

Now imagine you're a robin.

In winter, you depend on the last of the multiflora rose hips, sumac, and cedar berries. You hop about on the ground, searching under bushes or along creeks to find a few beetles, snails, and maybe even a worm or two, if you're lucky.

No wonder that robin in my yard looked so unhappy. He was starving.

I ran back inside to find the soft food that robins need. A can of dog food, my last slice of bread, ripped into bits, and a few chopped prunes: Perfect!

The robin was waiting on the icy ground, puffed up and holding one foot up in his feathers, when I came back out.

"Here you go, Robin," I said quietly, as I emptied the bowl.

Night was coming, and I felt the cold sneaking in through all four of my sweaters and my jacket. But as I watched the robin gobble down his food, my heart felt as warm as could be.

But just wait until birds give the seal of approval to your own homemade treats. You'll feel even more connected to your friends at the feeder when you nurture them with goodies you've mixed up with your own two hands.

"Mixed with your own two hands" is exactly right: Most bird recipes, at least in my kitchen, are best assembled using those all-purpose appendages. When I work with my hands, I can tell by "feel" whether I need another glob of peanut butter, or whether the treat feels skimpy on raisins or nuts. Since I usually work without measuring my ingredients exactly, that skill comes in handy (sorry!) when I'm evaluating the results.

It feels good to nurture our backyard birds by making them homemade treats. But it's also practical: Putting out pure peanut butter or other fats can get expensive, and making your own treats by adding some bird-approved fillers will stretch your bird food budget. The calorie count does drop somewhat, compared to the pure-fat product, but your treats will serve more birds, and the high-calorie handout is still excellent insurance against the ravages of cold weather.

## Mixing by "Feel"

The birds at our backyard restaurants are way less fussy than we are when we dine out, so there's no need to worry about exact measurements when you're cooking for birds. I mix up my recipes more by "feel" than by markings on a measuring cup.

Usually I'm aiming for an end result that holds together in the feeder but is easy to peck apart. If I plan to spread it on bark, stuff it into the holes of a suet log, or fill a recycled plastic tub, then I aim for a result that's stickier.

Generally speaking, ¼-cup more or less of any ingredient will make very little difference to the ultimate eaters of the treat. It's the greasy ingredient that's the main attraction—and peanut butter is the most appealing, so try to include at least some of this beloved bird food.

If you discover that you're ½ cup short of peanut butter or cornmeal or that your cupboard is bare of some ingredient, go ahead and improvise. If the result is too gooey or too liquid, add a similar dry ingredient. Too dry? Scour the shelves for another source of fat.

## Basic PB Treat, and Variations

My favorite high-fat bird treat is one that I've been using for more than 30 years of feeding birds. It's not the same every time because I vary it according to what I happen to have available in my pantry or fridge.

One reason this recipe is my favorite is because I usually have the ingredients on hand, so I can mix it up whenever I want to from the staples on my shelf. But more important, it's a favorite because the birds really like it. Have fun making it your own!

### Basic PB Treat

**About 1 part peanut butter**
**About 3 parts cornmeal**

Peanut butter varies in oiliness, so adjust the dry ingredients as needed until you have a dough that forms a ball. I aim for a texture like that of cookie dough: somewhat crumbly, but not too sticky, so that birds can easily peck off small bits of material.

If you plan to serve the treat in an open tray feeder or on the ground, add more cornmeal (or other dry ingredients) so that you can crumble it into bits. That way, more birds can feed on it at the same time.

Spread it on a tree or stuff it into the holes of a suet log for chickadees, woodpeckers, and other agile birds; crumble it in small amounts into a tray feeder or on the ground, for bluebirds, native sparrows, robins, and other birds.

### Variations

- Substitute steel-cut oats, old-fashioned oatmeal, or quick-cooking oatmeal for 1 part of the cornmeal.
- Substitute flour, any kind, for 1 part of the cornmeal.
- In a pinch, use flour or oatmeal of any kind in place of the cornmeal.
- Really scraping the bottom of the barrel? Pad out the peanut butter with stale cracker crumbs, bread crumbs, crushed dry dog food, or cereal.
- Substitute almond, hazel, or any other nut butter for any or all of the peanut butter.
- Substitute sunflower seed butter for any or all of the peanut butter.
- Low on peanut butter and gourmet nut butters? Add a dollop of solid vegetable shortening, such as Crisco, to fill out the recipe.
- Substitute liquid fats, such as peanut oil or corn oil, for part of the peanut butter. You'll need more cornmeal or flour to balance an oil than you would semi-solid peanut butter, so be sparing with it until you get a feel for proportions.
- Add raisins, currants, chopped apples, or other fruit.
- Add chopped nuts.

# Christmas Pudding

The famed English Christmas pudding (plum pudding) that tugged at our heartstrings in the feel-good finale of *A Christmas Carol* is held together by an ingredient we Americans rarely cook with: suet. I've only tasted a suet-free plum pudding, so I can't vouch for the real thing. But, in the spirit of the season, I do enjoy mixing up a version for the birdies, which I can serve in a suet log or spread on corncobs or pinecones. Or I can set a piece in a corner of the tray feeder for the birds to peck at.

> 1 pound lard
> 1 cup peanut butter, chunky or creamy
> 1 cup quick-cooking oats
> 1 cup coarse yellow cornmeal
> 1 cup dry bread crumbs (unseasoned store-bought or homemade)
> 1 cup whole wheat flour
> 1 cup raisins or currants
> 1 cup chopped nuts or sunflower seed chips

Put the lard into a large saucepan, and melt it over low heat. Remove the pan from the heat and stir in the peanut butter until it's melted.

Use a spoon with a strong handle to stir in the oats, cornmeal, bread crumbs, flour, raisins or currants, and nuts or seed chips.

Scrape the mixture into a casserole dish and let it cool. Stir occasionally so that the nuts and fruit stay well distributed, instead of settling to the bottom.

Serve when cool. Store extras in a covered container in the refrigerator.

This treat keeps for weeks in the fridge, or you can freeze the extras in zipper-lock bags. In winter, it'll attract soft food eaters including Carolina or Bewick's wrens, thrashers, mockingbirds, bluebirds, and robins—as well as seed-eating birds that favor your suet, such as woodpeckers, chickadees, titmice, and yes, I'm sorry, starlings. That's why I usually serve it in a suet log, an upside-down suet feeder, or a feeder enclosed in metal bars: All of these make it more difficult for starlings to gobble up my home cooking. On the other hand, when winter's at its worst, I sometimes add Christmas pudding to my kitchen-leftovers starling spread (placed well away from the other feeders), just to share the spirit of the season.

# SETTING THE TABLE

Impromptu dinner parties are one of my favorite pleasures. My human friends know they are welcome to drop by anytime. Often, as it starts to get near to dinnertime, I start to pull out food to put together for a spur-of-the-moment feast.

Those meals can be interesting, to say the least, depending on how long it's been since I visited the grocery store. One memorable evening, we shared delicate shrimp spring rolls and belly-filling mac-and-cheese, with a side of salsa, a few bites of Brussels sprouts, and a big bowl of spinach. Dee-lish, if a little different.

That's the great thing about friends. They'll adjust to whatever you offer, if they're hungry enough. Of course, they like it even better if your table is full of their favorite foods.

It's the same way with birds. As winter settles in, you'll get to know the eating habits and behaviors of the birds that spend this season in your backyard. Here are some things to keep in mind.

- A reliable source of plentiful seed is a powerful attraction in winter. Generosity will reward you with great bird-watching: The more seed you put out, especially during stretches of snowy weather, the more birds you're likely to attract.

- Traffic peaks at feeders in the morning, when birds arrive to replenish the stores of energy their bodies consumed during the night.

- There's a second peak in late afternoon, when birds fill their bellies for the coming night. Be sure to restock your feeders as needed between times.

- Winter can bring so many birds to our backyards that the birds overflow the feeders. Accommodate the masses by scattering seed directly on the ground. Start with a small amount, until you can gauge how quickly it will be eaten; too much of a good thing may attract rodents.

- As winter turns toward spring, gigantic flocks of red-winged blackbirds, grackles, and other blackbirds may arrive en masse, especially when bad weather buries natural food. I've hosted hundreds at one time, when big flocks that usually range the farm fields in winter got caught short in a snowstorm. Good thing a sack of whole-kernel corn is so inexpensive that I can keep an extra on hand!

**winter secret** An easy solution to serving your greasy treats is to spread them on pinecones. First, wrap a string or wire tightly around the cone under a row of scales so that it doesn't slip off. Then use a butter knife or hors d'oeuvres knife to spread the treat onto the cone, working the food into the openings between the scales. Hang the pinecone from a tree branch 5 feet off the ground or higher.

**winter secret** Because birds are so vulnerable to predation, they gobble a lot of food in a short time, then digest it elsewhere. That way, a cardinal, say, needs to spend only a few minutes out in the open eating weed seeds. When its crop is full, it can retire to a safe, brushy place where it remains well hidden while it digests its meal.

## Turkey Trot

Most of our efforts at the feeding station are directed at small birds. So let's finish our feeder talk with the biggest of the bunch: backyard birds that can top out at more than 20 pounds, instead of a couple of ounces!

Wild turkey populations are growing by leaps and bounds in many regions of the country, and the big birds are showing up in backyards in winter much more often than they used to. They may scratch for seeds around your songbird feeders, but you can make them a setup that suits their style even better, in just a few minutes.

Set up a lean-to arrangement for them by leaning a half-sheet of plywood against a post or tree. You can nail a stake to the front edge of it, so that the plywood is held off of the ground and serves as a slanted roof, or you can set it against the ground, so that it forms an A-frame that's open at the sides. Brace it with a rock or two at the bottom edge, to help keep it in place, and cover it with a layer of evergreen branches to make it look more natural. Use evergreen boughs that are long enough to cover the roof and as wide as possible, so that you only need two or three, or maybe even just one, to cover the roof. Secure the ends of the branches to the post or pole with garden twine or florist wire, and let the roof support the bough.

This simple shelter will protect your friendly flock of turkeys from cold, wind, and snow while they feast on the cobs or kernels of corn you put inside. Pheasants and quail may join in, too. Unfortunately, so may less desirable feeder visitors, such as squirrels and rodents. If rats are a problem in your area, avoid ground feeding altogether.

## The Nitty Gritty

Next time you're ready to pour a scoop of sunflower seeds into the feeder, sample a few yourself. Nibble off the seed coat, and you're left with a nice meaty morsel. What do you do next? You chew it, of course.

Notice how much chewing you have to do to make that seed slide down the hatch? Now, imagine you don't have any teeth at all. How are you going to grind that seed, and all the others that fill your belly, into a form that your body can digest?

For many birds, the answer is grit. Here's how it works.

1. In the bird's chest is an organ called the crop, a kind of pouch that works as a takeout container when birds eat—they can gobble fast, fill the crop, and then move to a safer perch to continue digestion.

2. Seeds leave the crop a few at a time and move into the first chamber of the two-chambered stomach. Here they're exposed to stomach acid that breaks down the food. (A predatory bird called a shrike, which eats small rodents and birds, has superstrength stomach acid that can break down a mouse in as little as three hours!)

3. The food, which still contains some undigested parts, moves on to the second part of the stomach. You may have actually eaten a chicken's version of this stomach part. It's the gizzard—a tough, muscular organ that grinds the food.

Muscles alone can't totally break down the food, so birds eat small particles of grit, which settle in the gizzard to work as grinders. Without grit, birds can't digest efficiently. You may notice birds in winter pecking up grit along the melting edges of roadsides after they've been sprinkled with sand.

They'll peck up sand in your backyard, too. The simplest way to add grit to their diet is to do just that: Pour a small amount of sand in your tray feeders. Washed sand or fine gravel sold in pet stores for aquariums or caged birds will be welcomed by your native sparrows, finches, and other winter birds.

## WARDING OFF DISEASE

Bird feeding stations attract a lot of birds, and those birds are concentrated in a very small area. Such a concentration of birds is an unnatural situation, and it can lead to problems as birds brush against each other or come in contact with or even ingest each other's droppings.

If a bird visiting the feeder is infected with a contagious disease, the problem can spread like wildfire.

In 2007, the state of Washington strongly urged that all residents empty and clean their backyard feeders, to stop the spread of salmonellosis, a usually fatal bird disease that affects finches, grosbeaks, siskins, and other species. Birdfeeding wasn't officially banned, but many folks helped out by keeping their feeders empty until the state announced that it was safe to refill them because the spread of the disease had been halted.

**winter secret** We all share some winter birds, but we may not see the exact same species of that kind of bird. Look out your window in winter nearly anywhere across the country, and you're likely to see a chickadee. But which chickadee? Bird-watchers in Wisconsin won't see Carolina chickadees, for instance, because they winter in more southern states. Meanwhile, South Carolinians are bereft of the boreal chickadees that brighten Wisconsin winters. But wherever you live, some sort of bright-eyed little chickadee is likely to be stopping by your feeder to liven up a winter day.

## Contagious Conjunctivitis

Many feeder keepers saw the effects of contagion firsthand several years ago, when an eye disease affected house finches, mostly in the eastern part of the country. The disease, mycoplasmal conjunctivitis, causes red, swollen eyes—a condition that limits sight. Sadly, a bird that can't see doesn't last very long in the wild.

House finches are gregarious, flocking birds by nature, and it wasn't unusual for 50 or more of the pretty, cheerful birds to gather at the same feeder.

Then conjunctivitis hit. It spread rapidly in the crowded conditions at feeding stations. It also affected a few other individuals of related species, such as purple finches and goldfinches, though, thank goodness, it seemed to be less severe in those birds.

In recent years, finch conjunctivitis has simmered down, or, as biologists say, "equilibrated." No large die-offs are expected, and the dramatic spread has eased immensely.

## Cleanliness Rules

Keeping your feeding station clean may help keep outbreaks of disease to a minimum. Here's how to ensure the healthiest conditions for your feathered friends.

- Empty the feeder about once a month, scooping out all of the loose seed.
- Wearing disposable gloves, pour a bucket of hot, soapy water over the feeder and scrub vigorously with a scrub brush.
- Follow up by rinsing with a 10 percent bleach solution, to kill germs. Use 1 part liquid household chlorine bleach to 9 parts warm or cold tap water, and mix well.
- Wait a few minutes, then rinse the feeder thoroughly with a hose, or pour a bucket of warm or cold water over it if your hose has been put away for winter.
- Let the feeder dry in the sunshine (which will also help reduce any lingering germs), then remount and refill it.
- Rake up shells and other debris beneath feeders periodically.
- If you notice a sick bird in your yard—a bird that is slow to fly away, with puffed-up feathers and perhaps a wobbly stance—remove your feeders temporarily, so that other birds aren't as likely to encounter the sick bird or its droppings.

## WATER IN WINTER

Fresh water isn't always easy to provide in winter—but that's exactly what makes it such a tempting attraction for birds. When cold weather covers puddles and creeks with ice, birds are hard put to find a place to get a drink, let alone a handy bathtub.

Check bird supply stores and catalogs to find birdbaths that heat water in one of two ways.

**winter secret** Electric heaters for birdbaths cost more to buy and more to operate than passive solar birdbaths, which are free to use. Maybe, with the new interest in alternative energy, we'll be able to buy a birdbath heater that is powered by solar energy. Then all we will need is some winter sun to provide the power—not always an easy order in the gray days of the season.

- **Passive solar energy.** Passive solar birdbaths depend on a dark colored interior to soak up the sun's rays and delay freezing. Most are made of plastic that resists cracking.

- **A birdbath heater.** These may be built into a particular birdbath model, or you can simply buy the attachment and lay it in the basin of any birdbath you already own. All you'll need is an electrical outlet where you can plug in the cord.

At $30 to about $200, a heated birdbath may seem like a big investment. But you'll be amazed at how effective this reliable source of winter water is for drawing birds to your yard. Overwintering orioles are especially fond of a good, vigorous bath on a winter's day. But many other birds also are likely to drop in to take a sip or dip their wings.

Consider a solar or electrically heated birdbath that clamps to the railing of your deck for winter use. You'll be able to reach it easily for refilling or cleaning, even when snow is deep in the yard. And you'll get to enjoy a close-up view of the happy bathers.

# CHAPTER 15

# NATURAL FOODS
# AND COVER FOR WINTER

I**T'S EASY TO** get so distracted by our busy feeders in winter that we forget to take a look at what's going on elsewhere around the yard. Birds at the feeder are in plain view, and it warms our hearts to watch them help themselves to the food we've put out just for them. So it's no wonder that most of us get a case of feeder "tunnel vision" in winter.

But if you can manage to take your eyes away from those unbelievably red cardinals cracking sunflower seeds, or that elegant Steller's jay that just swooped in for a peanut, or that—Wait a minute! What's that giant Woody Woodpecker bird that just flew in to the suet feeder? Could it be a pileated? Hold everything!

Sorry, what were we saying? Oh, yes: If you can manage to yank your focus away from the feeder for a few minutes, you'll see all kinds of bird activity taking place around your backyard.

Natural foods, all-important cover, and cozy nooks where birds can keep warm are vital additions to the food and fresh water that you're offering at the winter feeding station.

## LAST CALL

By the time winter rolls around, seeds are in short supply. Birds need to work harder to find them than they did in fall, when every roadside, field, and woods' edge was beckoning with billions of nutritious seeds.

In most regions of the country, fruit, too, is much harder to find in winter than it was a few months before. The orchard is

The slate-colored junco "snowbird" and its kin are natural-born ground feeders.

almost bare, and wild berries are mostly gone.

Some plants, though, still supply seeds or berries to help birds get through the months when the cupboard is bare. Insects, too, can still be found, although it takes a sharp eye to spot them in their winter hiding places.

Winter is when you will get a big pat on the back from your backyard birds; this is when you'll be truly rewarded for all the effort you've made to make your yard more suited to their needs. No, they won't be spelling out "Thank you" in the snow, but they will be showing you in other ways how welcome your efforts are.

Here are some of the thank-you notes you may notice being acted out in your own backyard.

- Native sparrows congregating among the still-standing stems in your flowerbeds for cover while they feed on weed and flower seeds.
- Doves and quail visiting the remains of your vegetable garden for seeds.

Cardinals approach by moving from perch to perch, so place your feeder near a shrub or tree.

- Woodpeckers tapping at your trees for burrowing insects.
- Nuthatches busily examining the bark of your trees for insect eggs.
- Chickadees, titmice, and kinglets swinging from the twigs of your trees and shrubs.

## Winter Changes

Finding natural food in winter requires more searching than it does in summer or other seasons.

- Insects are sleeping or waiting for next year to hatch, so they're much harder to find.
- The ground is frozen, so earthworms aren't available.
- Fruits (including berries) have pretty much been cleaned off the bushes and trees.
- Seeds are dwindling, too, and require more energy to find.
- Snow covers up seeds that have fallen off the plant to the ground.
- Ice storms can coat any remaining tree seeds, cones, or berries, making them impossible for most birds to access.

**winter secret** Natural food won't help winter birds if it's buried under snow. That's why it's a good idea to let weeds and garden plants stand over winter, so that birds can pick the seedheads clean of seeds and insects, even when snow lays deep.

- Jays and woodpeckers pecking at the last apples still hanging on the trees.
- Wild turkeys or pheasants scratching beneath your oak trees for acorns.
- Juncos, native sparrows, titmice, nuthatches, chickadees, jays, cardinals, and every other bird on the block investigating the ground beneath pecan and other nut trees.
- A lone robin or brown thrasher visiting the compost pile for beetles, worms, or other critters drawn by the warmth.
- Carolina wrens, chickadees, and titmice patrolling the eaves of your house or outbuildings, looking for spiders.

## Finding a Balance

Nature often seems way out of kilter to me in winter. That's when birds need the most calories—but that's when food is least abundant.

Of course, it's my own human compassion that is getting in the way: Paring down the population in winter is just a natural part of the cycle. Not all insects, birds, or plants will survive the hard times of winter to start a new generation next year. Limited food is one of the main factors that keep various species in balance.

Sometimes I wonder how that balance might've looked two or three hundred years ago, before we cleared the vast forests, dammed the rivers, and carved up the land with concrete and asphalt. I've read about the immense flocks of millions upon millions of passenger pigeons that darkened the skies for days. I've found old diaries that told of squawking flocks of green Carolina parakeets—in New York! I've listened to my mother tell of a time when American chestnut trees in bloom made the mountains look like a summer snow.

In my own lifetime, I've seen birds that I once took for granted become rare finds. If you had told me years ago that one day I'd be thrilled to hear a red-eyed vireo sing, I would have laughed. The birds were once so abundant that their loud, constant song was part of the scenery. On the other hand, if you had told me that one day I'd be routinely hosting rufous hummingbirds—once a strictly Western species—at my feeder in Indiana, I would have laughed at that notion, too.

The moral of this story? Things change. And because everything is interconnected, a change in one part of the natural world affects everything else.

## Human Effects

Our own activities have a huge impact on plants and insects, and on the birds that rely on them. In winter, when food is naturally scarce, those effects are magnified.

Here are a few of the ways our species has tilted the natural balance in winter.

- Pesticides, including organic ones such as Bt and milky spore disease, reduce the number of insects available to birds—including overwintering adult insects and insect eggs.

- Herbicides and tidy yards reduce the number of weeds, which are valuable seed sources for birds in winter.

- Big agriculture, with huge fields that lack brushy places in between them, greatly cuts down on bird habitat and on winter seeds and insects.

- Roads, shopping malls, sprawling cities, suburbia—anytime we pave paradise, we reduce the natural places for birds and decimate the foods they depend upon.

On the other hand, we've also made life easier for winter birds in some ways.

- Birds that were once thought to be rare strays, such as the varied thrush and rufous hummingbird in the East, or the cardinal and blue jay in the West, are turning up with increasing frequency. Although there's no way to prove it, one of the reasons is probably that there are more birdfeeders. Sales figures of

Cedar waxwings patrol for miles in winter, stopping wherever they find lingering fruit.

birdseed, feeders, and related supplies show that the hobby has grown by leaps and bounds.

- Dumpsters and parking-lot trash cans favor opportunistic birds, including

**winter secret** Not being seen is key to survival for many insects. In summer, caterpillars and other bugs mimic the colors and shapes of leaves, stems, and flowers, in the hope that birds will fail to notice them. In winter, insects hide in crevices or under loose flaps of bark, or overwinter in cocoons that mimic dead leaves. Watch a chickadee search your yard for a few minutes, and you'll see how intently it examines everything in its path, pecking at anything that offers even the most remote possibility of food.

Hungry birds investigate anything that's not buried under snow. In the countryside, old hay bales with sleeping insects are targets for bluebirds.

starlings, English or house sparrows, crows, and gulls.

- Many fast-food places, I've noticed, have a resident mockingbird, ready to dive for any scraps of burgers or fries that come its way.

- Weeds that came along with European settlers, including ragweed, Queen Anne's lace, chicory, foxtail grass, chickweed, and others, now supply a big part of the winter menu for finches, native sparrows, and other birds.

- The use of viburnums, pyracantha, and other berry bushes in home and commercial landscaping have added winter food for mockingbirds, catbirds, robins, and waxwings.

- Street trees with small fruits, such as Callery pear, hawthorns, and palms, provide abundant food for winter birds, including mockingbirds, robins, flickers, and waxwings.

## Tipping the Scale

We humans have introduced so many changes into the natural cycle that Mother Nature sometimes has a hard time keeping up. Our big brains let us adapt quickly and create the kind of surroundings we want—but that often leaves other species in the dust.

I think of us humans as kids standing on the edge of a great big pond, our pockets bulging with pebbles. As we toss stone after stone into the pond, the ripples spread outward, affecting everything they touch. But the natural world is always seeking a balance. So, no matter what we do, those ripples will eventually even out.

The big question is, what will get lost along the way? Will it end with the loss of the wood thrush and the cerulean warbler, two species that don't seem to be able to adjust their specialized habits fast enough to compensate for our footprint on the earth? Or will it end with our own species causing ripples that are so big that they wash us away, too? It's a sobering thought, and one that makes me think twice about my own actions—and help other species any way I can.

• Home landscaping has increased winter cover, thanks to the conifers we're so fond of. Conifers provide sheltered roosts as well as protection from hawk attacks. (You'll find more on conifers later in this chapter.)

At long last, we seem to be learning that every action we take can have an effect on our fellow species, and many of us are changing our habits. That's why I'm such a big fan of turning our backyards into sanctuaries for birds and other living things. It's way more fun to watch wildlife than it is to mow the lawn; it feels great to nurture fellow creatures, especially in wintertime; and we can take comfort in making at least a small difference in their survival.

## LINGERING SEEDS

Plants that hang on to their seeds through winter will nourish native sparrows, juncos, cardinals, and many other seed-eating species through the cold months to come. The larder includes three main types of plants, some of which are probably already growing in your yard.

• Garden flowers

• Weeds and wild grasses

• Trees

Let's take a look at how you can take advantage of these seed-bearing plants to attract birds to your winter landscape.

## Flowers for Seeds

A flower garden for the birds starts in summer and continues nonstop right through winter.

By late summer, seeds are already ripening on some garden plants. Sunflowers

Sunflower seeds dropped by summer goldfinches become winter food for sparrows and juncos that scratch along the ground.

are beckoning to chickadees, cardinals, titmice, jays, woodpeckers, and a host of other sunflower seed lovers. The seeds of Sensation cosmos (*Cosmos bipinnatus,* Sensation-type), colorful zinnias (*Zinnia* species), and purple coneflowers (*Echinacea purpurea*) are getting gobbled up by goldfinches as fast as the seeds ripen.

The feast continues into fall, as native sparrows and juncos move through on migration or settle into winter residence. They, too, will happily pluck seeds from ripe seedheads or glean them from the ground beneath.

As winter settles in, birds that had been making do in their wild habitat begin making regular visits to the flower gardens, where standing stems offer cover and a wealth of seeds still awaits. Doves, quail, towhees, and woodpeckers mingle with sparrows, juncos, and finches, in search of seeds and any insects they can find.

As you watch the winter birds in your yard, you'll soon discover which of your garden flowers hold the greatest appeal because of their lingering seeds. In general, plants with many small "florets," either in clusters, like goldenrod, or in daisy-type heads, like cosmos or coneflowers, produce a better crop of birdseed than flowers with large, single blossoms.

## Weeds for Seeds

Birds know what's good for them. That's why you'll see them eating weed seeds in winter just as avidly as they would your best birdseed. Weed seeds can be even higher in nutritional value than the usual seeds at our feeding stations.

Weeds sure don't fit into that tidy, manicured look that many folks strive for in their home landscapes. Weeds can be big and unruly, pushy and prolific. Some weeds, though, are worth tolerating, because their seeds have immense value to winter birds.

## Winter Seed Supply

Many garden plants produce seeds that make a good food source in winter. You can use this list as a starting point or experiment on your own to see which flower seeds your birds like best.

These plants have sturdy stems that persist into winter, instead of collapsing soon after frost kills them. And they hold their seeds at knee height or above, so they'll be exposed unless the snow is very deep. They never fail to attract birds in winter in my gardens.

Cockscomb (*Amaranthus* species)

Native asters (*Aster cordifolius* and many other species)

Purple coneflower (*Echinacea purpurea*)

Sunflowers, annual types (*Helianthus annuus*)

Gloriosa daisy (*Rudbeckia hirta*)

Goldenrod (*Solidago* species)

Tall marigolds (*Tagetes* species)

Zinnia, large flowers (*Zinnia elegans*)

# Winter Flowers for Hummingbirds

In sections of the country with warm, sunny winters, all sorts of flowers bloom in winter. Hummingbirds that winter in Florida or California, or the desert hot spots of Arizona, Texas, and New Mexico, have plenty of nectar flowers to visit.

But in my rainy Zone 8 Washington garden, only a few flowers bloomed all winter, mostly native shrubs of the heath family. These included the evergreen salal (*Gaultheria shallon*) and ground-covering kinnikinnick (*Arctstaphylos uva-ursi*), which grows thickly in the understory of the wet, mossy woods. In late winter, there's a real burst of bloom from red-flowering currant (*Ribes sanguineum*), which is always well attended by hungry hummers. But in my neck of the woods, where winter-blooming flowers weren't as plentiful as in sunnier climes, hummingbirds were happy to visit nectar feeders for supplemental sugar water in winter.

I'm perfectly happy to adjust my vision of a perfect yard if it means I get to watch lively birds every day in winter.

Letting weeds grow in our yards, let alone our garden beds, goes against the grain of everything we've been taught. But before you reject the idea of intentionally growing weeds, consider some of the benefits they offer.

- Weeds provide excellent winter cover because the plants grow close together, shielding birds from hawks overhead.

- Weeds produce enormous quantities of seeds that will help take the pressure off your feeders, reducing competition for perching space, saving you money, and still boosting the number of birds in your backyard.

- Many weeds hold their seeds above the snow, so they'll nourish birds even in the worst winter weather.

- You can pick and choose which weeds you grow, selecting only those with attributes that go with the rest of your garden.

- You can grow weeds in groups of all one kind in your beds, which gives them an intentional appearance, instead of letting single plants grow as rogues that look like . . . well, weeds.

Pesky weeds produce thousands of seeds—but that's good news to winter juncos.

## Winter Weed Supply

Weeds can be just as pretty as flowers, so I incorporate patches of them into my flower gardens. Once you gain an appreciation for what weed seeds can do to attract birds in winter, you won't mind the many seedlings that sprout in spring—one of the traits that relegate a plant to the category of "weed."

Here's a collection of weeds that stand tall in winter, holding their heads above moderate snow. They'll also sprinkle plenty of seeds on the ground (or snow) so that ground-feeding birds can peck them up.

| | |
|---|---|
| Chicory | Pigweed amaranth |
| Dock | Queen Anne's lace |
| Fleabane | Ragweeds |
| Foxtail grass | Smartweeds |
| Goldenrods | Waterhemp (*Amaranthus rudis*) |
| Lambsquarters | Wild asters |

- Many weeds are ornamental—even pretty. Once you get over the psychological hump of thinking of them as undesirables, you'll find a lot to like.

## The Riches of Ragweed

Ah-choo! If you suffer from pollen allergies, you might want to skip this section—we'll be extolling the glories of ragweed. Yes, the very same weed that makes you feel miserable for weeks, thanks to its incredibly irritating pollen, is one of the best bird foods around. The several species that blanket the United States and put allergy sufferers over the edge in summer supply vital nourishment with their abundant, supernutritious seeds throughout winter.

Ragweeds belong to the genus *Ambrosia,* although only birds and other wildlife find the plant a delicious food. We're blessed with many species of ragweeds in the United States, including 10 species in the Sonoran desert alone and a couple—giant ragweed (*Ambrosia trifida*) and common ragweed (*Ambrosia artemisifolia*)—that are ubiquitous across at least half of the country. All have seeds that are high in fat and protein.

Ragweed gets its start as a single plant that sprouts from a seed passed along by a bird. But birds don't eat every seed, so that single plant becomes a patch the following year, as seedlings sprout by the dozens.

All ragweeds have skinny fingers of greenish flowers dusted with plenty of yellow pollen, but in winter, all that remains are frost-browned stems and leaves. Those dead remains give ragweed another big benefit in birds' eyes: They offer protective cover while the birds are foraging for some of those lingering seeds.

Allergies are no fun, so if you get the

# A Clear Winner

No wonder ragweed seeds are such a big draw in wintertime! Look how they stack up against favorite feeder foods.

| SEED | CRUDE PROTEIN | CRUDE FAT |
|---|---|---|
| Giant ragweed (*Ambrosia trifida*)* | 47% | 38% |
| Whole peanuts** | 25% | 36% |
| Hulled sunflower chips** | 24% | 40% |
| Canola (mustard, rapeseed)** | 23% | 38% |
| Flax** | 23% | 34% |
| Amaranth*** | 13–17% | 6–8% |
| Black oil sunflower** | 16% | 25% |
| White proso millet** | 11% | 3.5% |

* Harrison, et al., "Postdispersal predation of giant ragweed seed in no-till corn," Weed Science 51:955-964, 2603; Ohio State University.

** Birdseed figures are from the Commodity Marketing Company (www.commoditymarketing.com), a member of the Wild Bird Feeding Institute and the leading seller of U.S. birdseed commodities.

*** Ecological Agricultural Products, www.eap.mcgill.ca/CPAT_1.htm.

## Ragweed by the Acre

Quail management biologists have become huge fans of ragweed. Sowing fields of ragweed for nesting habitat, a practice that began in about 1992, has doubled or even tripled the quail population in studies.

"Farmers think we're crazy," says biologist Clay Sisson, coordinator of the Albany Quail Project at Auburn University in Georgia, but the results have been astounding. If you have a spare acre or two, you can give it a try yourself by sowing ragweed seeds at about 7 to 10 pounds an acre. You can buy the seeds in 20- and 40-pound sacks at www.quailrestoration.com.

In winter, that acre of ragweed will make for some superb bird-watching. The high-calorie seeds will draw flocks of hungry native sparrows, juncos, doves, quail, cardinals, woodpeckers, and other birds to the banquet.

**Ragweed often sneaks into flower beds, thanks to birds that drop a few undigested seeds.**

sneezes, keep ragweed out of your garden. But if you're not susceptible or if you have a very large yard, why not let a few plants grow, so that birds can enjoy their bounty in winter?

## Tree Seeds

Any kinds of seeds that are still around in winter are likely to be on the list of natural bird foods. Weeds and garden seeds are the targets of many birds, including the flocks of native sparrows and juncos that fill our yards in winter. Other birds seek out seeds at higher levels—in the trees.

Nuts and acorns will be gone by the time winter comes around, as birds, squirrels, and other wildlife quickly eat and store them. But other deciduous trees and conifers may still have a bounty of seeds waiting for winter birds. Evening grosbeaks may seek out catalpa pods or nibble apart the cones of tulip trees. Pine siskins pry out the seeds of western red cedar, while chickadees work at extracting seeds from redbud pods.

**winter secret** Finches large and small are the biggest fans of tree seeds, perhaps because their bills have enough leverage and strength to crack the hard shells or enough finesse to extract seeds from cones. Grosbeaks, crossbills, purple finches, goldfinches, redpolls, and pine siskins are all regulars at the treetop café. Nuthatches, chickadees, and titmice are also big fans of tree seeds. So don't forget to look to the treetops when you want to spot birds in winter.

Crossbills employ their unusual bills to neatly scissor out seeds from the cones of spruces and other conifers.

## WINTER FRUIT AND BERRIES

Most birds that depend mainly on fruit to fill their bellies depart for the winter months, with one notable exception: waxwings. Cedar waxwings and their much less common cousin, the Bohemian waxwing, are huge fans of fruit. Both have been nick-named the "cherry bird" because of their fondness for fresh cherries.

Fresh fruit is just a fond memory in winter. But withered, weathered, or frozen fruit can still sometimes be found. Waxwings are usually first on the scene where fruit still lingers, but wintering bluebirds, robins, thrashers, catbirds, mockingbirds, or wrens may also snag a few bites.

## The Precious Few

Any lingering fruit or berries won't last long once winter birds start cleaning up all of the edibles in your area. The abundance of summer is long gone, but a few bites of fruit may still be hanging on trees, begging for attention.

## Winter Tree Seeds

Another good reason to go native: The seeds of native trees are appealing to winter birds, while those of many imported ornamentals go uneaten. Ask a local nature center or chapter of the Audubon Society to suggest of native trees for your region. Here are some widespread native trees that supply birds with seeds in winter.

Fir (*Abies* species)

Boxelder (*Acer negundo*)

Alders (*Alnus* species)

Birch (*Betula* species)

Catalpa (*Catalpa* species)

Redbud (*Cercis* species)

Ash (*Fraxinus* species)

Tulip tree (*Liriodendron tulipifera*)

Spruce (*Picea* species)

Pine (*Pinus* species)

Western red cedar (*Thuja plicata*)

Hemlock (*Tsuga* species)

A winter visit from a white-winged crossbill is a red-letter day. The birds hang like parrots to extract seeds from conifer cones.

Alder and birch cones are favorites for chickadees and titmice in winter.

Here are some of the possibilities that might exist in your backyard.

- Juniper trees (*Juniperus* species) may be decorated with gray-green berries that birds adore.
- Grapevines may still have some withered bunches.
- Apples may still hang from the branches or lay waiting on the ground.
- Rose hips on the branches of multiflora and other roses may beckon birds from thorny hedges.
- Barberries (*Berberis* species) and burning bush (*Euonymus alatus*) may dangle small berries.
- Persimmon trees may still hang on to a few frost-bitten fruits.

## ALL-IMPORTANT COVER

Winter is the hunger season, and not just for feeder birds. Predators, too, need calories to keep warm, and they work hard in winter to keep their bellies filled.

Many folks who keep feeders eventually gain the attention of a resident winter hawk. Hawks range over big territories, often scouting several backyards or a few blocks in their quest for food. A chickadee here, a junco there . . . it's a sad but natural part of the equation. Mercifully, the kill is swift. A puff of feathers, a few drops of blood, and the hawk retires to pluck and eat its dinner.

When plants drop their leaves after frost,

## Southern Trio

In the Southeast and Florida, I've seen thrushes feasting on three plants that are well worth inviting into your garden: yaupon or yaupon holly (*Ilex vomitoria*), Carolina cherry laurel (*Prunus caroliniana*), and southern bayberry or wax myrtle (*Myrica cerifera*). These adaptable, easy-care shrubs or small trees are gaining popularity and are turning up in more garden centers.

- Yaupon or yaupon holly (*Ilex vomitoria*) is an evergreen shrub or small tree that was known to native Americans for the purgative effect alluded to in its Latin name. Birds are drawn to them in late winter.

- Carolina cherry laurel (*Prunus caroliniana*) can eventually grow to 20 feet or more, but it often forms a shrubby clump and is easily pruned to keep it at a lower height. Fuzzy, fragrant white flowers show off against the dense evergreen leaves and are followed by blue-black berries that are eagerly eaten by many birds.

- Southern bayberry or wax myrtle (*Myrica cerifera*) is the southern version of bayberry (*Myrica pensylvanica*). Usually evergreen, it sends up shoots to form a dense thicket. Small, waxy, pale blue berries crowd the stems.

All three of these natives are fast growing, trouble free, and just the ticket for berry-eating birds in the Southeast and Florida. Thrushes, mimic thrushes, warblers, and many others seek them out. Plant them as a hedge or in a group, and the vigorous plants will quickly knit together, providing abundant cover and food for birds and other wildlife.

**Pretty, fragrant Carolina cherry laurel provides a plethora of bird-favored berries, as well as winter cover among its evergreen branches.**

Wait long enough near a juniper in winter, and you're likely to spot a flock of foraging cedar waxwings.

backyard birds become more vulnerable. Predators can spot them and chase them down much more easily than they can in summer, when greenery interferes with the hunt. Give your backyard birds a fighting chance by providing plenty of cover in winter.

## Running Interference

Bare stems and branches can be surprisingly effective at keeping birds safe from predators. Groups of deciduous shrubs and hedges provide good cover for birds, as do garden beds with dead stems still standing.

Here's why they work.

- Hawks attack from above, dropping down upon their prey suddenly. If birds are deep within the branches of a shrub, the hawk will have to take another tack; usually, it tries to frighten the birds into flying out into the open.

- Hedges of deciduous shrubs allow birds an escape route if a hawk frightens them. It's hard for a predator to corner a bird when the bird never hits a dead

## Role Reversal

Winter is more like spring in the southern tier of the country, where fresh fruit starts with citrus season. To the rest of us, it's the dead of winter, but if you're lucky enough to live in Florida, you might spot orioles at your orange trees. The Southwest, too, gets a taste of spring in winter; you are likely to see thrushes or wrens dining at cactus fruit or other goodies. Meanwhile, the rest of us may be watching a mockingbird plucking a few rose hips or a very cold robin pecking at the last frozen apple.

Wherever you live, it's worth offering winter fruit of whatever kind suits your region, to entice those fruit-eating birds. They're usually among the species that are hardest to tempt to a feeder, so fruit is a natural food that offers a great incentive for them to come to your yard. Bluebirds, anyone?

Even when they're bare of leaves, twigs and branches provide some predator-protection cover to cardinals and other birds.

end. Large hawks, which can't get into the interior of a shrub, often try to reach a taloned foot down inside to nab a bird in a bush; if the bush is actually a hedge, the intended prey can make its getaway.

- Hawks aren't fond of getting their wings tangled; interfering branches or standing stems can break a flight feather if a hawk gets in too deep.
- Cats have an easier time ambushing birds if they can slink up silently. A garden full of dead stems and crinkly leaves works like an early warning alarm system, letting birds know that an enemy is on the prowl.

## Evergreen Appeal

Trees and shrubs that retain their leaves in winter are an enormous draw for birds. They serve as shelter from the weather, protection from predators, sleeping spots at night, and sources of food.

Conifers are hands-down the best plants for winter cover and roosting spots. Here's why.

- Their needles and dense branches protect birds from predators that prefer not to get mixed up in the prickly foliage.
- Their overlapping branches shed water and snow, so birds stay dry inside.
- Their dense branches create lots of little nooks, with "walls" of needled foliage that help retain the body heat of roosting birds.

Include evergreens in your bird-friendly backyard so birds can seek shelter from snow and cold.

Seed-bearing cones are a bonus with conifers. The trees often begin bearing at a young age, which will give your chickadees and nuthatches another source of natural food.

## Keeping Cozy

It'd be nice if autumn slid gracefully into winter, with the temperature sinking so gradually that we hardly notice it. Maybe it works that way in your neck of the woods. But for most of us, winter moves in with a sudden blast of cold that leaves us shivering even in our warmest clothes.

Cold weather takes some getting used to. Our bodies become acclimatized to the cold, "adjusting the thermostat" by regulating the burning of calories so that we feel comfortable. The process can take several days to fine-tune. But after we've adjusted, a cold day doesn't feel nearly as uncomfortable as it did before. The same thing happens when we get used to hot weather.

Plants go through an acclimatization process, too, as fall shifts to winter. You may have noticed that some of your plants tend to "toughen up" in autumn, so that they shrug off light frosts. They develop a natural antifreeze in response to cooling temperatures by decreasing the water and increasing the sugar content in their tissues, which lowers the freezing point of their sap. But if a sudden blast of cold follows close on the heels of Indian summer, plants won't be as hardened to the cold as they would be if they'd had time to acclimatize, and they will suffer.

Birds are just as sensitive to changes in temperature as people and plants are. They, too, need time to get used to the cold. That's why winter is the time to pay special attention to helping birds conserve every bit of body heat. Providing suitable shelter, in the form of roosting places, is the way to help them out.

## Roosting Places

Most people who live in a mild climate count their blessings. But I never stopped wishing for a "real winter" when I lived in USDA Zone 8, where a fleece jacket is all you need to stay cozy.

I'm one of those odd ducks who actually likes snow and cold. Maybe it's a legacy from growing up in the East, or maybe it's just my nature, but cold weather makes me feel alive. And snow—well, let's just say that my neighbors in the Pacific Northwest, where flurries were a rarity, didn't seem to get nearly as excited as I did when I saw those precious flakes.

Flakes indeed, I could hear them muttering, as they hurried from their car to the house, waving politely while I gaily called, "It's snowing! It's snowing!"

Winter weather is one of the reasons I'm happy to be back in the Midwest, where my cross-country skis stand ready by the door and extra sweaters hang on the backs of the kitchen chairs.

It's easy for us to pull on an extra sweater when the house feels chilly, or to nudge that thermostat up a notch. Even a Wisconsin or Idaho winter is tolerable when you're dressed right—and of course, we can come in out of the cold.

But birds are left to their own devices when the temperature starts to sink. How can we help? Two big ways: Plenty of high-calorie food, and snug places to sleep at night.

## Places to Sleep

Perhaps your spouse is one of those dastardly types who steals the covers while you're sound asleep. After vivid dreams of trekking across the Arctic in a blizzard, you wake shivering, reach to pull up the blankets—and find them wrapped snugly around your sleeping partner. Grrr.

## Theory of Relativity

If you want a good laugh, Minnesota or Montana readers, try this description of weather in Portland, Oregon, as described by Bruce B. Johnson, a photographer and climatology buff, on his Web site (www.oregonphotos.com/pagetwentyone-Q.html).

*The winters of both 1949 and 1950 provided residents with two back-to-back horrific winters, which shattered many records for both extreme cold and deep snowfalls. Most of those marks were so extreme that they are still standing today, e.g., the average daily low in January 1949 was 21.0 degrees, and in January 1950 it was 21.2 degrees. . . .*

Twenty-one degrees! Horrific!

Chickadees, titmice, and bluebirds often hole up in old woodpecker homes during the long, cold nights of winter.

A standing clump of ornamental grass provides shelter from wind and snow for juncos and native sparrows.

A snug place to sleep is just as vital for winter survival as a full belly is. You can't offer your backyard birds an extra blanket on a cold night, but you can add safe and secure sleeping places to your yard, where birds can conserve their precious body heat during the long winter nights.

- Put up roost boxes, which look like simple wooden birdhouses but have cleats or perches on the inside walls. Chickadees and titmice often sleep communally in a roost box; so do bluebirds. Nuthatches and wrens may also use the boxes.

- Your backyard trees probably have more dead limbs than you're aware of, and birds have most likely already been making use of them. A natural cavity is

## Roosting Spots and Secondhand Homes

It's thanks to woodpeckers that many other birds have a snug place to sleep on a winter's night or a tidy hole to call home. The beaks of chickadees, titmice, and others aren't stout enough to do heavy construction work on a roosting or nesting cavity, so they often adopt a woodpecker's former home.

The bufflehead duck, an adorable black-and-white butterball, depends mainly on flickers for its housing needs. This is one of the duck species that, incredible as it seems, nests in holes in trees, and a flicker's old nest cavity is just the right size for this small duck and its brood. When the ducklings hatch, they hop out and tumble down to what we hope isn't too hard a landing, then skedaddle after the mother to reach water.

**winter secret** Most heat loss occurs around birds' eyes and bills, where the skin is unprotected by the dense feathers of its body. To increase its chance of survival, a bird in extreme cold will fluff out all of its feathers, including those on its head, and tuck its head under its shoulder feathers to protect those vulnerable areas.

the most common nighttime roost for chickadees and other cavity-nesting birds.

• Other backyard birds, such as sparrows and cardinals, seek a secure spot within a dense conifer, out of the wind and weather and protected from predators.

• Consider leaving the door of a backyard shed slightly ajar, so that Carolina wrens and other birds can seek shelter inside the structure.

• Mount birdhouses early—in winter— so that birds can use them as roost boxes.

Winter is when all of our efforts can really add up to make a difference to birds. With enough high-fat food, birds can survive the cold temperatures and winter storms that lie ahead. Roosting boxes and evergreens will help them weather the long, cold nights. And with plenty of cover, they can stay safe, protected from the predators whose appetites are mighty keen in winter.

In the next chapter, we'll take a look at some of the birds that are likely to benefit from your backyard sanctuary in winter. These active, loyal friends will do a lot to brighten the dark days of winter.

# CHAPTER 16

# SPECIAL BIRDS
# OF WINTER

**B**IRDS THAT SPEND TIME with us in winter quickly become a bright spot of the season. They bring a welcome dash of life to the sleeping winter landscape. We soon settle into a routine of looking at the feeder a dozen times a day, just to see who's there.

At almost any time of day, the winter feeder scene will include woodpeckers, chickadees and titmice, and nuthatches. They're among the most loyal customers at the winter feeder, as well as excellent caretakers of our trees in winter, when they pick countless insect eggs, larvae, and adult insects from the bark and branches. Here's a closer look at the habits of these faithful winter friends.

A year-round friend, the small downy woodpecker is one of the most common backyard visitors across the country.

## THE WOODPECKERS

Do you keep a suet feeder? If you do, then I'm going to go out on a limb here (okay, you can stop groaning now) and bet that you have already met at least one member of the woodpecker family. Woodpeckers are among the likeliest visitors in any backyard across the country—any yard with a suet feeder, that is.

Every species in the woodpecker family pecks at wood, but not all are named "woodpeckers." Flickers show a flickering patch of white when they fly, and sapsuckers—okay, take a wild guess. Yep, they sip up sap. Couldn't be simpler.

When you watch woodpeckers, you'll see them doing things you never imagined— like "bathing" with ants, perhaps, or playing peek-a-boo with their mate, or finding dinner in ways you've never dreamed of.

## Built Like a Hammer

Woodpeckers' bodies are a perfect fit for their natural eating habits. Pounding into a tree requires not only the right tools, but also a sturdy system of support. Here's how the special adaptations of woodpeckers make them highly efficient hammerheads.

- They have stiff, pointy tail feathers to help prop them up when they're clinging to tree trunks.

- Their legs are short and their feet have long, strong toes with good-size claws: All the better for clinging to bark with, thank you.

- Their feet have two toes in front, two toes in back, instead of the usual three in front, one in back arrangement of songbirds. That two-pronged stance gives them solid balance with a better grip on the bark.

- Their skulls are designed to snugly cradle their brains without any extra space, so that the birdbrain can take a pounding without colliding with the skull and causing concussion.

- Their neck muscles are strong and efficient, to provide that fast back-and-forth stroke.

- Inside that straight, strong beak is a remarkable tongue that the bird can stick out fast and far. It can extend several inches beyond the bill tip!

- That super-duper tongue is not only extra long, to better penetrate insect tunnels in wood, it's also tipped with a sharp, hard point, to impale insects with. Plus it's barbed, to better collect any wiggly larvae along the way. Bad news for bugs!

## Which Woodpeckers?

Ready to go try our luck finding an ivory-billed woodpecker in the Big Woods of Arkansas? I am! Okay, okay, before we tackle the rarest of the rare (the ivory-billed woodpecker was thought to be extinct until a possible sighting a few years ago; experts

## Big Bird, or Big Drum?

I like to track down drumming woodpeckers to hear who's who. One afternoon, I clawed my way through briers and poison ivy toward the tree where I was sure a pileated woodpecker was sounding off. The drumming was so loud and deep, it simply had to be the crow-size pileated, a bird I'll grab any opportunity to see.

Doing my best to be sneaky, I finally got to the tree, wiped the steam off my glasses, and pinpointed the bird. I couldn't believe my eyes. It was a cute little downy woodpecker. What I learned that day, and what I have to keep reminding myself every time I think "Pileated!" is that the resonance has more to do with the drum itself than with the drummer. A big drum makes a deeper sound. This guy must've had himself a bass drum branch.

❄
❄

**winter secret** Woodpeckers aren't technically classified as songbirds, although they do vocalize. Most of them have loud, raucous or harsh calls and *chirrs*. Many are pretty easy to mimic, and it's fun to call back by making the sounds in your own voice. Just go ahead and whoop it up! Woodpeckers are often vocal, even in winter. In spring, your efforts could draw a territorial male to see the new "bird" in his neighborhood.

disagree over the video footage that was shot, and the world still awaits definitive confirmation), let's start with a quick overview of some of the species that we have a chance of actually seeing.

- The diminutive black-and-white downy woodpecker is one of the most common and widespread backyard birds. You might see it year-round in any part of the country except for the Southwest.

Recycle the plastic net bags from your onions into suet feeders—even the big red-bellied woodpecker finds them easy to cling to.

- The eastern half of the country is home to only a handful of woodpeckers, including the very common red-bellied woodpecker, plus one flicker and one sapsucker—the much-mocked yellow-bellied version. Counting the eastern species of the Far North, the possibilities number about nine.

- The West is home to nearly double the number of woodpecker species as are found in the East. Seems a little unfair, but most of these birds stick to separate niches: for instance, gila woodpeckers in the saguaro desert, Arizona woodpeckers in oak woods, white-headed woodpeckers in redwoods and other mountain conifers.

## Year-Round Friends

Most woodpeckers are year-round birds. They don't take seasonal vacations to warm climates or depart for far-away nesting grounds when spring rolls around. Some individual birds may make short trips in winter, but incoming birds quickly fill the gap, and others, even of the same species, don't relocate at all.

That's one reason woodpeckers are so rewarding to tempt to your yard. When your

winter secret Woodpeckers are famed for straying outside the lines. No matter how carefully scientists try to plot their ranges, the birds often disregard them and show up elsewhere. Weather is often a factor, with the birds getting off-base during storms.

When I went outside to uncover the feeders after a blizzard one year in eastern Pennsylvania, I found a red-shafted flicker, a bird whose range begins in the Great Plains a thousand miles away. Unfortunately, he hadn't survived the storm.

yard is full of the plants they like, plus a well-stocked feeder, you're likely to see them year-round.

A few woodpeckers do migrate beyond short hops: All sapsuckers go to milder areas in winter. The red-bellied and Lewis's woodpeckers leave the colder parts of their range in winter, and the northern flicker withdraws from some northern areas.

But everybody else pretty much stays put, so they're possible customers for the winter handouts in your yard. And if migrant woodpeckers leave your area for the winter, you can count on them coming back in spring, hungry and hopeful.

## Sedentary Style

Got any couch potatoes in the family? Then you'll already be familiar with the slow-motion habits of woodpeckers. Compared to energetic chickadees and other birds, woodpeckers are slowpokes. They stay in one location for long periods of time, rather than frenetically covering ground. Think of a dead tree full of beetle larvae or carpenter ants as a big bag of potato chips, and you can see why woodpeckers aren't in a hurry to leave the "sofa."

But that doesn't mean they're not industrious. Woodpeckers are constantly and tirelessly searching for food; they just don't cover as much ground as other birds need to when they do it.

## Spring Shift

When flying insects become active, wood-peckers come alive. Their habits switch from sit-and-peck to behavior that's more like that of a flycatcher. They perch on a good lookout branch, fly out to nab a passing insect, return to the perch, and do it again, over and over. That's one of the best ways to spot woodpeckers in summer, especially the red-headed—just look for a bird "flycatching" from the tip of a tree or utility pole.

winter secret As a general rule, the bigger the woodpecker, the more secretive it is. The downy, for instance, has very little fear of humans, so you can get fairly close to it without causing it to hide or fly away. But its larger look-alike cousin, the hairy, as well as other larger woodpeckers such as flickers, red-bellieds, and pileateds, are likely to fly off when you come near.

## Making It Feel Like Home

Trees: That's the short answer to what makes woodpeckers feel at home. Most members of this family live in places with good-size trees, whether it's a city park, your backyard, or a national forest.

Woodpeckers not only eat in trees, they nest in them, too. These are cavity-nesting birds, and they peck out a home to fit their needs in a dead or living tree.

Most woodpecker species make use of whatever trees grow within their natural range, whether they're natives or nursery types. As long as there are plenty of insects to be found by pecking into tree trunks and branches, woodpeckers are right at home. And, by the way, the classic saguaro cactus of the Southwest, with its stout trunk and arms, serves perfectly well as a "tree." It's fun to look for woodpecker holes in the cactus when you're visiting or driving through the Southwest desert—you may even spot a cactus wren or a tiny elf owl peeping out of the former woodpecker home!

The acorn woodpecker definitely needs oaks to supply the food it collects for eating later. Its storage areas look like an odd Chinese checkers game board, with an acorn stuffed into each hole.

## What's for Dinner?

Insects, fruits, berries, and nuts are the big four for woodpeckers, with insects making up about two-thirds to three-quarters of the menu. Add a sampling of seeds and suet on the side, and woodpeckers will be happy.

Think about where you usually see woodpeckers—tapping at trees—and you'll have a big clue as to what they eat most of: insects that live in trees. Most woodpeckers dig for insects buried in the wood or hidden beneath the bark. Many kinds of wood-boring beetles (and their grubs and eggs) are cleaned up by woodpeckers. So are countless ants, including hefty black carpenter ants that may infest houses. On the ground, woodpeckers also zero in on grasshoppers, crickets, and beetles.

Woodpeckers love mulberries, apples,

What a face! And the acorn woodpecker has a raucous laugh that's just as clownish.

and other fruits. The berries of native plants, especially hackberry (*Celtis occidentalis*), blueberry (*Vaccinium* species), staghorn sumac (*Rhus typhina*), and Virginia creeper (*Parthenocissus quinquefolia*), are popular fall and winter foods. Poison ivy and poison oak berries are favored, too, which is one of the reasons these plants pop up all over the place—from seeds that pass through birds.

Acorns, beechnuts, pecans, and all other nuts are eagerly sought. So are corn and giant ragweed, by some species.

Sapsuckers have a sweet tooth. They drill a series of small holes, just enough to puncture the tree so that the sap flows slowly into the holes. Then the sapsucker returns to drink the sap and snatch up insects that have been attracted to it.

Woodpeckers are at a disadvantage when it comes to eating the seeds of many plants, because they need a secure perch for their big bodies. The seeds they eat in the wild are usually on plants with stout stems, where they can get a grip without bending a delicate stem to the ground.

But when food is the draw, woodpeckers can be surprisingly acrobatic. A woodpecker

Red-breasted sapsuckers hammer off outer bark so the sweet sap can flow. Hummingbirds often visit sapsucker works when flowers are scarce.

can contort itself into amazing positions, often using its tail as a counterbalance so it can reach the prize. At the feeder, they appreciate foods that mirror their natural favorites. (See "At the Feeder" on page 304 for more info.)

## Bad Press

Woodpeckers take plenty of interest in nonnative trees—sometimes a little too much interest. Orchardists and nut growers often consider the birds pests because they devour nuts and fruits by the bushel.

Sapsuckers, especially, are often maligned as undesirables because growers believe their feeding habits weaken orchard trees.

It's simply not true. In healthy trees, the bark soon heals, although the rows of scars will remain.

Personally, I like to see those neat lines of little holes, the evidence that sapsuckers have been sipping at my trees. And I've never seen a loss of vigor in a tree, no matter how heavily woodpeckers have been working at it.

## Woodpecker Harvest

Some years ago, I thumbed off a few kernels from a leftover ear of Indian corn into a back corner of a flowerbed, just to see what would come up. What came up were sturdy plants with foliage tinged with purple and red, a statuesque backdrop to the zinnias in front.

When a few ears started to form, I got pretty darn excited. I was dying to know what colors were hidden under those husks, but I didn't want to wreck anything before they ripened, so I let them alone.

Then I got distracted by other garden goings-on and forgot all about the Indian corn for a while. I was looking out the window one morning when I saw a red-bellied woodpecker fly into the patch and make himself at home, bracing his tail against a cornstalk. Bending over, he grabbed a piece of husk and firmly pulled it away from the ear. While I wavered between watching and running out to chase him away, the bird extracted one kernel after another from my lovely red-and-purple ear of Indian corn, which was now looking pretty moth-eaten.

Corn is a beautiful plant, adding an almost tropical feel at the back of a flower garden. If you can shoehorn a few corn plants into your yard, woodpeckers may visit the ears from the time the corn is still fresh until it's hard and dry. They'll keep coming back all winter, until every last kernel is eaten.

That kind of entertainment makes it worth buying your own Indian corn for decorations at the farmers' market and leaving the garden corn to the birds.

### In the Yard

- Trees are the main attraction for woodpeckers. Any trees in your yard may already be harboring wood-pecker-attracting insects beneath the bark.

- Trees, dead or alive, and the utility poles around your house make great stepping stones for woodpeckers on their daily travels.

- Plant a butterfly garden to provide snacks on the wing or juicy caterpillars. My mother's big clumps of heavy-headed peonies drew flickers every spring, thanks to the ants—a favorite flicker food—that climbed around the flowers.

**winter secret** Yellow-bellied sapsuckers winter in warm areas, but this season is still a great time to look for the calling cards they leave behind: rows of holes that mark their feeding places on tree trunks. Walk your yard and take a close look at any trees in it, to see if you can spot a tidy horizontal row of equidistant holes, each about ¼ inch in diameter and spaced about ¼ inch apart. Those are the places to look for sapsuckers, come spring—and for hummingbirds and kinglets that may sneak a sip of the seeping sap the drilled holes release.

- Add a fruit tree, or two or three. Cherries (*Prunus* species), mulberries (*Morus* species), apples and crabapples (*Malus* species), and plums (*Prunus* species) are popular.

- Elderberries (*Sambucus nigra*), staghorn sumac (*Rhus typhina*), and wild or native plums (*Prunus* species), which you can find at specialty nurseries or through mail-order catalogs, send up suckers that expand the planting over time. They make a good hedge or naturalistic thicket, with clouds of fragrant white flowers followed by bite-size fruit for woodpeckers.

- If you can put up with its fast-spreading ways, let Virginia creeper (*Parthenocissus quinquefolia*) cover a freestanding trellis that has room for a woodpecker to get a grip, or let the vine scramble up a tree to

Flickers are year-round residents, so watch for these large brown woodpeckers even in winter.

## Snacking on the Siding

Wood siding on your house usually attracts woodpeckers for the same reason that trees do—there are bugs in your belfry. Or, to be more exact, some kind of insect has moved into your wood siding and is beginning to eat you out of house and home.

If the hammering is annoying, or if you fear it's damaging your house, check your Yellow Pages for a pest-control company that specializes in woodpecker antidotes. Using pest-control measures that don't involve woodpeckers, such as replacing the affected areas of wood, should restore your peace and quiet. Once the insects are gone, the woodpecker will quickly lose interest.

Sometimes, woodpeckers will pound away at metal roof flashing, chimney caps, or other resonant parts of the house for the purpose of making noise, not for finding food. As you're pulling that pillow over your head at 6 a.m. to block the sound, it probably won't be much consolation to know that your home has been given the Best Drum in the Neighborhood Award. Luckily, the sounding-off usually stops when nesting season is over and territorial behavior subsides.

# Planting for Future Woodpeckers

Insects are the main menu item for woodpeckers, but that doesn't mean they don't like some variety in their diet.

| PLANT | TYPE OF PLANT | DESCRIPTION | HARDINESS ZONES |
|---|---|---|---|
| Apple (*Malus*, any cultivar) | Deciduous trees | Can grow 25' or more, depending on the cultivar. | Vary; most 5–8 |
| Common mullein (*Verbascum thapsus*) | Biennial | A rosette of soft gray leaves at ground level, from which emerges a flowering stem about 4' tall in the second year. | 3–9 |
| Oak (*Quercus*, any species or cultivar) | Deciduous or evergreen trees | Columnar forms available for smaller spaces. Some grow to 80'. | Vary with species |
| Staghorn sumac (*Rhus typhina*), species form; not cutleaf varieties. | Deciduous shrub or small tree | Vivid red fall foliage and fuzzy clusters of small berries. Grow to about 10' tall. | 3–8 |
| Virginia creeper (*Parthenocissus quinquefolia*) | Deciduous vine | Grows to about 30'. Gorgeous red fall leaves. | 3–9 |

add a flash of red fall color and a built-in perch. Virginia creeper is best in a naturalistic setting, where it can ramble along the ground and climb any tree or stump it wants to; in a more controlled setting, you'll have to uproot stray shoots that crop up away from the parent vine and snip the stems whenever they outgrow their allotted space.

- Try an arbor of grapes, such as hardy, trouble-free 'Concord'.

- Stout-stemmed mulleins (*Verbascum* species, especially common mullein, *Verbascum thapsus*) are beautiful in a flower garden, thanks to their rosettes of soft, felted gray leaves and tall, erect spikes of yellow flowers. Let the finished flower stalks stand through winter, and you're likely to see woodpeckers examining them for any insects in hiding.

- In desert gardens, cactus fruit, including

This family can't resist nuts and fruit. Try these plants for future crops of fruits, berries, nuts—and woodpeckers.

| USE | COMMENTS | OTHER BIRDS ATTRACTED |
|---|---|---|
| Fruit, nest holes, sap | If you want a few apples for yourself, try disease-resistant cultivars such as 'Liberty' or 'Yellow Delicious'. | Finches, jays, orioles, tanagers, thrushes, mimic thrushes, vireos, and warblers |
| Insects and possibly seeds in winter | Self-sows moderately. Transplanting can be difficult because of the taproot; move only young plants. | Finches, hummingbirds, native sparrows, and other small birds |
| Acorns; insects; possible nest sites when mature | Oaks are useful to birds even when young because of the insects attracted to them. Try one of the species native to your area. | Chickadees, grosbeaks, jays, nuthatches, tanagers, titmice, vireos, warblers, wild turkeys, and many other birds |
| Berries | The fruit of last resort, sumac berries usually don't get eaten until winter. Flickers are fans of the berries. | Bluebirds and other thrushes |
| Berries | Grow on a wood arbor so that woodpeckers have an easier time getting to the berries. | Grosbeaks, thrushes, mimic thrushes, and others |

that of prickly pear (*Opuntia* species) is popular with gilded flickers and other woodpeckers. Woodpeckers also approve of figs.

- In the Southeast, the fruit of saw palmetto (*Serenoa repens*) will tempt woodpeckers to your yard.

- Even your vegetable garden can be a hot spot for woodpeckers. You may see red-headed and red-bellied woodpeckers checking out the corn or tall sunflowers, or giving you a hand by picking off beetles and caterpillars, or cabbage butterflies in flight.

- Your lawn is an inviting place for flickers. Take a closer look when robins, starlings, or grackles are poking around in your grass, and you'll often spot a big brown flicker or two—or a dozen, during spring or fall migration. They're extracting grubs of Japanese beetles, plus the larvae of other insects.

## Acid Bath

When I see ants swarming out of a crack in the sidewalk in spring, I don't rush for the kettle of boiling water. Instead, I watch for woodpeckers to arrive—flickers, to be exact. They not only eat ants, they also "bathe" in them. If you catch them in the act, it's an amazing sight.

You may see the bird settle in the midst of the ants, raising its wings and fluffing its feathers to allow the ants to crawl all over it. Or you may see a woodpecker with an ant in its bill, wiping the insect over its own body like a bath sponge.

What's the point? Ants contain formic acid—that's what makes their bite so irritating—and scientists theorize that the substance repels or controls bird lice and other feather pests.

### At the Feeder

- Suet
- Insect foods, including mealworms, waxworms, and bug-enriched suet
- Nuts and nut spreads, including peanut butter, almond butter, and others
- Corn
- Sunflower seeds

## Staying Safe

Woodpeckers may fall prey to hawks, cats, and nest-raiding coons, snakes, and opossums. There's little you can do to help, beyond these usual steps.

- Use your noggin when placing feeders and birdbaths, so that birds can dash to safety if it's required.
- Keep stray cats out of your yard.

## A Good Word for Short-Lived Lombardies

Oaks, maples, and other classic shade trees require decades to gain size—and even longer to sport some dead wood. But Lombardy poplars (*Populus nigra* variety *italica*), which are notoriously short-lived trees, can be just the ticket for woodpecker fans.

Lombardies are upright, columnar trees that grow superfast from cuttings or rooted plants. Just 3 to 5 years after planting, the trees may be 30 feet tall. And that's the beginning of the end. Their weak wood is attacked by insects (read: woodpecker food!) and disease, and before you know it, dead branches and dead trunks are poking up amidst the surviving greenery.

You can buy Lombardy poplars at reasonable prices, but why waste even a few bucks? In early spring, cut a few live branches from a neighbor's tree, strip off the bottom foot of leaves, and stick the bare part in moist soil. Keep them watered, and they'll root fast and take off like lightning. Of course, you'll want to plant these soon-to-be sad sacks away from parking areas and streets. But they make a great fast hedge, or a single specimen. And, before you know it, they'll be attracting woodpeckers to chomp on bugs and chisel out homes.

## Hunting by Ear

Late at night, when our 100-year-old family home was especially quiet, I would often hear a steady, rhythmic gnawing noise. It was way too soft to be a mouse, but it was definitely the sound of something chewing.

My mother and father couldn't hear it. "Put your ear against the wall," I suggested. "It sounds louder, then." They tried, but they still couldn't detect anything.

Months later, my father was poking around in the cellar, two stories below my bedroom, and stumbled across a tidy pile of fine sawdust. He hurried for a brighter light and his big folding pocketknife. When he poked the knife into one of the floor joists, the wood crumbled away, revealing the tunnels of a busy colony of powder-post beetles, a scourge that does exactly what their name says—turns posts to powder.

My parents ended up replacing beams. But I was enthralled by the notion that I had actually heard the beetle larvae chewing.

For humans, those tiny noises are easy to overlook. But for woodpeckers, they're the clue that food is nearby. When their sharp ears pick up the sound of insects active in the wood or beneath the bark, it's time to hammer away to get at the goodies.

- Keep your own cat confined to the house.
- Hang suet and nectar feeders under a tree, to guard against aerial attacks from hawks, and high enough that a lunging cat can't reach the clients.

## CHICKADEES AND TITMICE

Who doesn't love these small, friendly, faithful birds? They're reliable winter visitors to our backyards and feeders, day in and day out. They're not shy, but they are polite, never grabby or aggressive. And they have small appetites, so they never become pests.

Add in the entertainment factor of their acrobatics, and no wonder bird lovers proudly wear sweatshirts decorated with their pictures. These little gray guys feel like our best friends.

Chickadees and titmice are friendly at the feeder and in the yard. Even in their natural habitat of the woods, they're unafraid and often come close to us.

## Sorting Them Out

All chickadees and titmice are small, gray birds, many with jaunty black or dark brown caps or stripes on their heads. Some show a wash of pale rusty orange, usually along their sides; the well-named chestnut-backed chickadee is mostly rust instead of gray.

No matter what color their markings, chickadees can look like little butterballs in cold weather, with their feathers fluffed up for better insulation.

Various chickadee species cover just

## Nary a Titmouse

How does that old Joni Mitchell refrain go: "you don't know what you've got till it's gone"?

I was so used to seeing titmice everywhere, in my Pennsylvania and Indiana backyards as well as when traveling across the country, that it never dawned on me that they might be totally lacking in some areas.

It wasn't until I put up my feeders in southwest Washington state a few years ago that I noticed my perky pals weren't around. There were chickadees galore, sure. But nary a titmouse.

Flipping open a field guide, I discovered that I wasn't the only one who had to live without titmice— they're not in the Far North or the Plains, either.

Now that I've learned that these common, friendly birds can't be taken for granted, I treasure them all the more. And I'm thrilled to be back in southern Indiana, where tufted titmice keep me company all year long.

**Appreciate the everyday visits of your titmouse—some parts of the country don't get to enjoy these perky little birds.**

about every part of the country (sorry, little corner where California, Oregon, and Nevada come together—you don't have them). But titmice aren't quite as expansive—they have never moved into the Pacific Northwest, the tier of northern states, and a big part of the Plains.

Each of the five species of titmice and the seven kinds of chickadees (that number includes the gray-headed chickadee of Alaska) has its own niche, but there's plenty of overlap. It's common to enjoy the antics of two or three species in your yard.

## Year-Round Feeder Friends

Chickadees and titmice live year-round within their range. They do migrate, but they stick within the borders shown on field guide bird maps. So, if you live in an area outside their range, you don't even have a chance of seeing them when they're passing through, as you would with warblers, vireos, and other migrating birds.

The good news is that, because the birds can be seen in all seasons, you'll get to watch every bit of their behavior, including courtship and family life.

"Your" birds will probably relocate in winter, returning to nesting grounds in spring. But others soon move in to fill any gaps. Even though I like to believe I really "know" my individual birds, I can't tell the difference. It's darn hard to distinguish one titmouse or chickadee from the next.

## Did You Say "Chickadee"?

Chickadees are real chatterboxes. Most of them say some variation of their own name in all seasons. And they touch base with each other when foraging by using high-pitched buzzy calls that sound a lot like

Adorable, friendly chickadees are one of the big pleasures of winter. They're easy to hand tame.

## Fooled by a Friend

For years, I tried to track down the owner of a loud, clear whistle that I heard every year, beginning in late winter. It was a distinctive call, a repeated "*Pee-ter!*" So easy to imitate that I couldn't resist.

But the only bird I ever saw anywhere nearby was a little gray tufted titmouse, one of my favorite feeder friends.

Couldn't be him, I reasoned, because he was such a small bird and this was such a big, loud whistle. So I kept looking for the mystery singer I was sure must be concealed in the treetop.

You may already know the humbling end to this story. Sure enough, one day I actually caught the titmouse in my binoculars just as he opened his beak to whistle.

I'm still convinced that the titmouse planned it that way, clamping his beak shut whenever he saw I was looking at him and flitting from branch to branch or tree to tree, just to keep me guessing. Not to mention getting a good laugh out of making me climb through brambles and trip over branches while I was trying to get closer. Grrr. Little joker.

But the quest was worth it because now I had a new behavior to put with what I already knew about titmice from watching them at the feeder. That later-winter whistle is the overture that announces the beginning of breeding season, when the birds leave their winter foraging groups to pair up for nesting.

*(continued on page 310)*

# Plants to Attract Chickadees and Titmice

These little gray birds are faithful year-round friends, so add plants for food in all seasons, and tickle them with

| PLANT | TYPE OF PLANT | DESCRIPTION | HARDINESS ZONES |
|---|---|---|---|
| Birch (*Betula* species) | Deciduous trees | Graceful, multi-trunked, with beautiful bark; appealing catkins; yellow fall color; fast-growing, to about 30'. | 2–9, depending on species or cultivar |
| Cinnamon and royal ferns (*Osmunda cinnamomoea*, *Osmunda regalis*) | Perennial, deciduous ferns | Both have brown-felted stems and lush, beautiful fronds. Grow to 3–5'. | Cinnamon fern, 4–8; royal fern, 4–9 |
| Hemlock (*Tsuga* species) | Evergreen conifer | Short, soft needles and small cones; grows quickly to about 20', then slows down. Grows to 100'. | 4–9, depending on species |
| Oak (*Quercus* species) | Stately deciduous or evergreen trees | Glossy leaves, tassels of flowers, and acorns, with age. Grows to 100'. | 4–10, depending on species |
| Redbuds (*Cercis canadensis*, *Cercis occidentalis*, *Cercis texensis*) | Small deciduous trees | Purplish pink flowers stud the branches before the heart-shaped leaves appear; thin, flat pealike seedpods. Grow to about 20'. | *Cercis canadensis*, 5–9; *Cercis occidentalis*, 7–9; *Cercis texensis* (also known as *Cercis canadensis* variety *texensis*), 6–9 |
| Spruce (*Picea species*) | Evergreen conifer | Prickly, short needles; bears cones. Grows to 100' or more. | 2–9, depending on species |

fern stems for spring nesting material.

| USE | COMMENTS | OTHER BIRDS ATTRACTED |
|---|---|---|
| Catkins for food, canes, and insects | Another top choice for bird gardens; may be short-lived | Large and small finches, flycatchers, vireos, warblers, and other birds |
| Nest material | Useful as cover for ground-dwelling birds. Royal fern does best in moist to wet soil; great near a pond or birdbath. | Native sparrows, towhees, and thrushes |
| Canes, buds, insects for food, cover, roosting, winter shelter | A thing of beauty, even when young, and especially in snow. If woolly adelgid is problematic in your area, try a fir or spruce instead. | Large finches, grouse; many other birds, for roosting |
| Acorns and insects for food; nest sites | Valuable even when young. Try native species, which act as host plants for native moths and butterflies. | Grosbeaks, jays, orioles, tanagers, vireos, warblers, woodpeckers, and crows; grouse, quail, and wild turkeys |
| Seeds and insects for food | One of the best trees for a bird garden. The plain, unimproved species type is beautiful and bird-approved, and it grows fast. | Flycatchers, vireos, warblers, woodpeckers, and many other birds |
| Canes and buds for food; roosting, nesting, cover, winter shelter | Natural shapes are better for birds than contorted or dwarf forms. Try a spruce that is native to your area for guaranteed bird appeal. | Small and large finches (including cardinals); many other birds |

titmice (and brown creepers and kinglets— birds this family often pals around with).

When late winter rolls around and breeding season nears, chickadees have a trick up their sleeve: A pretty two- or three-note whistle, with the last note lower. Think "Three Blind Mice," or in shorter versions, "Three Blind."

I'm not naming names, but one bird-watcher I know very well was fooled for a while by this call, until she spotted the chickadee serenading his partner.

Titmice are often quiet at the feeder. But they whistle back and forth and keep in touch with thin, rapid, high-pitched calls when they're roaming about. Those call notes sound very much like the calls of chickadees, and also like that of the brown creeper, with which they often keep company in winter foraging flocks. In late winter, titmice add another song to their repertoire—a whistle.

## Hanging Out

Did somebody say party? Chickadees and titmice are social birds. They hang out in small flocks of their own kind or flocks that include compatible pals that share their habitat and eating habits. Only during nesting season do they leave the scene behind and focus on the family.

No dieting regimes for this family—their metabolism is set to "high." You'll usually see them in motion, foraging through the branches so quickly that it's hard to tell what they're doing along the way. These birds are real gymnasts, with a great sense of balance and feet and legs that are built for grasping and getaways. Way back when, when I was designing bird ornaments that I cut from a flat sheet of copper, my chickadee was posed in a typical posture: upside-down.

## Look Here

Chickadees and titmice are naturally at home in woods or around shade trees, but that doesn't mean they're always in the treetops. They often drop down to small trees, shrubs, or brush during their never-ending search for food.

Since this family is one of the most frequent visitors to feeders, you may think your yard is already prime territory. It very well may be, especially in winter.

Backyards are a favorite habitat of many species, so you already have a head start. An older shade tree or conifer is a super foundation that you can enhance with young trees and shrubs, to entice the birds down to eye level.

Any deciduous tree, especially natives such as oaks (*Quercus* species), maples

(*Acer* species), sweetgum (*Liquidambar* species), tulip tree (*Liriodendron tulipifera*), ash (*Fraxinus* species), and many others, will appeal to this tribe of eager eaters. Why, there are so many wonderful native species of maples and oaks alone that I've often thought about planting a whole side of the yard with a sampler of these species.

These birds find lots of food in conifers, too, so try to find room for a fast-growing spruce (*Picea* species), hemlock (*Tsuga* species), fir (*Abies* species), or pine (*Pinus* species). Evergreens such as these also offer the birds shelter during bad weather. In dry gardens, mesquite (*Prosopis* species), palo verde (*Parkinsonia* species), and western juniper (*Juniperus occidentalis*) will suit these birds.

## What's for Dinner?

It's a mixed menu for the titmice and chickadee family, with insects as the entrée and seeds, nuts, fruits, and berries filling the rest of the plate.

Hard to believe, but the little birds we think of as cute, friendly characters are actually the premier caretakers of our country's trees. These common, widespread birds do a fine job of controlling the insects that target trees. Just about any insect they find in the foliage is fair game, from tiny ants and aphids to caterpillars, moths, and beetles.

Even better for our trees, these birds are super-skilled at ferreting out insect eggs. Since an insect may lay from dozens to scores to hundreds of eggs, every insect egg

Which chickadees are in your yard? In the Pacific states and Northwest forests, it's the chestnut-backed chick-a-dee-dee-dee.

that a bird eats has a huge effect on future populations.

This family eats insects at any stage of development. Egg, larva, pupa, adult—it all goes down the hatch with equal alacrity. Winter doesn't mean the end of their insect food; they simply switch to more durable forms, such as cocoons.

The frenetic habits of these birds mean that each tree gets a thorough going-over. Watch the birds in your yard, and you'll see that they examine just about every possible hiding place for insect treats, including rolled-up leaves, stems, and both the upper surfaces and undersides of the leaves.

When seeds of trees and other plants ripen, this family grabs a big share. Ragweed is a favorite. So are seedpods of maples (*Acer* species), redbuds (*Cercis* species), and other trees. The birds also visit small cones, such as those of hemlocks

The fanciest of the titmice, the bridled species livens up the Southwest.

(*Tsuga* species) and alders (*Alnus* species), as well as larger pinecones. The seeds of pinyon cones (*Pinus edulis*)—the ones we cooking fans know as pine nuts—are a big hit, and no wonder: They're huge and meaty, and high in oil.

Acorns, beechnuts, chinquapins, and other nuts round out the list. Fruit isn't a big draw, although chickadees do indulge in hackberries (*Celtis occidentalis*), mulberries (*Morus* species and cultivars), and wild cherries (*Prunus* species).

Here's how to match those feeding preferences in your own backyard, both with plants and at the feeder.

## In the Yard

- These birds always welcome insects, so leave your trees, shrubs, and flowers unsprayed, and they will have plenty to offer.

- Plant conifers for winter food and cover.

- Follow my rule of thumb when it comes to this family: The more leaves and branches, the better. If your yard is mostly open lawn or flowerbeds, you can add small trees or tall shrubs to multiply the leafy garden of bugs for birds. Don't worry, you won't have to do anything special to encourage insects to move in!

- Choose plants that will bear seeds or nuts, too. Small trees, including birches (*Betula* species), alders (*Alnus* species), and ever-reliable redbuds (*Cercis* species), are pretty enough for any yard. A group of redbuds looks even better than a single tree.

- Invest in an oak for the future; in the years before it starts to bear acorns, and while you're waiting for it to grow old and stately, it'll harbor thousands of insects for birds to feed on.

- Plant the classic annual sunflower (*Helianthus annuus*); its seeds are popular with these birds. When sunflower seedlings spring up from seeds dropped by feeder birds, I let them stay. Even a puny flowerhead will buy a week of entertainment as the little acrobats pluck out the seeds, one by one.

## At the Feeder

- Sunflower seeds
- Peanuts and other nuts, coarsely chopped
- Suet

- Peanut butter and other nut butters
- Insect-enriched suet, mealworms, and other insect foods

## Extra Attractions

Here are a few more tricks you can use to gain loyal friends among the chickadees and titmice.

- Fresh water in all seasons is a huge draw for these birds. Add an immersible heater to your birdbath.
- These birds nest in cavities—and birdhouses. You won't even need to pull out the ladder; a location about 5 feet from the ground will suit them to a T.
- Offer a selection of fluffy nesting materials, such as fur, wool, dry sphagnum moss, cotton balls, or Spanish moss.

## NUTHATCHES

Nuthatches are familiar friends at feeder setups, visiting daily, especially in winter.

Whenever anyone who's fairly new to bird-watching asks me about an unusual little gray and white bird that showed up at their feeder in winter, I always ask, "Does it look like it's wearing a tuxedo?" If the answer is yes, I safely guess "white-breasted nuthatch."

The white-breasted nuthatch wears the most formal outfit, and he's the biggest of the bunch, but he's still pretty small among birds. The other nuthatches are irresistibly cute, like tiny toys.

Nuthatches look and act like no other birds.

- They cling tightly to tree trunks and branches but move quickly, with a hitching, jerky gait.
- They usually move down tree trunks head first.
- They often pose with their head and chest sticking out horizontally, sideways from their body.
- Their bodies are plump but streamlined, with a pointy beak and stubby tail.
- They have short little legs—all the better for clinging to bark, my dear. All four species are two-tone: a slate-gray upper side, and, usually, a white breast and belly. (The red-breasted nuthatch has to live up to its name, so it's rusty red below.)

The white-breasted nuthatch switches to an upside-down pose with ease.

# The Congenial Creeper

The brown creeper is often seen in the company of nuthatches—when it's seen at all, that is. This tiny brown bird blends right in against the bark, but you may spot it when it flies off to begin working on another tree. It will land near the bottom, ready to start the trek upward, probing the bark with its long, curved beak.

The creeper sticks tight to the trunks of trees, tirelessly scouring the bark just as nuthatches do. But with one big difference: Nuthatches go down, creepers go up.

The brown creeper ranges from coast to coast in winter and is becoming more common at feeders, joining nuthatches at suet and insect foods. One or two brown creepers often join a roving band of chickadees, titmice, kinglets, and nuthatches to forage for food from fall through winter.

But although the creeper is a tree-hugger like the nuthatches and shares some eating habits, it's in a different family: the creeper family. Next time you visit the British Isles, keep an eye out for this little guy; the exact same species as we host in our backyards lives there, too.

**A brown creeper is easy to overlook—its feathers blend right in with tree bark.**

- A brown or back cap is part of the costume for all species. All in all, it's a tidy, dapper outfit.

You have a good chance of seeing a nuthatch in any backyard in the country.

- The white-breasted stays around all year in most areas, but is absent in the far Southeast and a few other spots.

- The red-breasted is a wintertime treat in the eastern two-thirds of the nation and a year-round pleasure in the West, in New England, and in the Appalachians.

In some winters, red-breasted nuthatches come down from the frigid North in big numbers.

- The brown-headed nuthatch sticks to the Southeast year-round.

- The pygmy nuthatch is limited to parts of the West, where you can see it year-round.

Nuthatches usually visit yards or feeders singly or in pairs. But in winter, their presence often picks up, with more birds coming to seek a good meal at your place.

## Welcome Home

Wherever you find trees, you're likely to see a nuthatch. Forests are their usual habitat, but they also frequent parks, golf courses, and street trees, as well as backyards.

Bark-scouring nuthatches and brown creepers need trees to suit their feeding habits. Trees of significant size, with trunks about 6 inches or more in diameter, are the main targets of these birds. Young trees aren't as appealing, probably because the bark hasn't yet developed the furrows that attract insects.

- The white-breasted nuthatch and brown creeper seem to be the easiest-going of the bunch, when it comes to the type of tree. It seems like just about any kind of good-size tree, deciduous or conifer, will snag their services.

- You'll usually see the red-breasted nuthatch at conifers, but it visits oaks, maples, and other deciduous trees, too.

- The pygmy and brown-headed species generally stick to conifers, and pines in particular.

## What's for Dinner?

Insects, nuts, and conifer seeds are the three basics for nuthatches. Naturally, all are found in trees, conveniently close at hand for these tree-dwelling birds.

Nuthatches have long, sharp, strong beaks. They're built that way to pry insects out of deep bark crevices and to whack open nuts or extract seeds from pinecones.

Smallest of the nuthatch family, the pygmy checks in at just a smidgen over 4 inches from stem to stern—and that's counting its beak.

Beetles, moths, scale insects, spiders, pine needle spittle bugs, and other insects found in or on bark are standard fare for nuthatches. Caterpillars and insect eggs are on the list, too.

Another big menu item? Take a look at the name of these birds. Nuts! White-breasted and red-breasted nuthatches eagerly eat any nut they can get their beaks into—acorns, pecans, beechnuts, pinecones—whatever's ripe for the picking.

### In the Yard

- Conifer trees produce cones at an early age, usually just a few years after planting. At a nursery, you may even be able to find container-grown trees that already have a few cones on them. May as well plant a tree that has a head start!

*(continued on page 318)*

## Plants to Attract Nuthatches

Seeds and trees are what win a nuthatch's heart, so try one of these plants to increase the appeal of your backyard.

| PLANT | TYPE OF PLANT | DESCRIPTION | HARDINESS ZONES |
|---|---|---|---|
| Annual sunflower (*Helianthus annuus*) | Annual flowers | Grows 4–8' or taller | All |
| Firs (*Abies* species) and Douglas fir (*Pseudotsuga menziesii*) | Evergreen conifer trees | Short needles and dense branches; multitude of cones with age. Grows to about 100'. | 3–8, depending on species and cultivar |
| Hemlocks (*Tsuga* species) | Evergreen conifer trees | Short-needled and densely branched, hemlocks are graceful trees even when very young. Quick to bear cones. Grows to 100' with age. | 4–9, depending on species and cultivar |
| Maples (*Acer* species) | Large deciduous trees | Moderately fast-growing trees with beautiful fall color of yellow, red, or orange. Grows to about 80'. | 3–9, depending on species and cultivar |
| Oaks (*Quercus* species and cultivars) | Large deciduous or evergreen trees | Stately, slow-growing trees with catkinlike flowers and acorns. Grows to 80–100'. | 4–10, depending on species and cultivar |
| Pines (*Pinus* species) | Evergreen conifer trees | Long-needled, relatively open-branched pines produce a bounty of cones. Many species, from 25–100'. | 3–10, depending on species and cultivar |

| USE | COMMENTS | OTHER BIRDS ATTRACTED |
|---|---|---|
| Seeds | Classic sunflowers with a single large head are guaranteed to attract birds; other cultivars with fancier flowers or multiple flowerheads will also appeal. | Chickadees, doves, large finches (especially cardinals), small finches, jays, juncos, quail, native sparrows, titmice, and woodpeckers |
| Cover, insects | Appealing to birds even when young. | Bushtits, kinglets, grouse, and many others |
| Seeds, insects | Hemlocks have been decimated by wooly adelgids in some areas, including the Northeast. Your Cooperative Extension Office can tell you if hemlocks are a safe bet in your area. If the insects are a problem, try a spruce or fir instead. | Bushtits, juncos, kinglets, native sparrows, and towhees |
| Insects from bark | Investigate maples that are native to your area; many serve as host plants for caterpillars of moths and butterflies. | Chickadees, jays, orioles, tanagers, titmice, vireos, warblers, woodpeckers, and other birds |
| Acorns, insects, possible nest sites, cover | Scout your local nursery and you may find an oak that already has a few acorns on it, for a head start. White oaks have tastier acorns than red oaks and are highly popular with birds. | Chickadees, doves, small finches, flycatchers, jays, juncos, orioles, tanagers, titmice, vireos, warblers, woodpeckers, quail, and wild turkeys |
| Seeds, insects | Pines look gawky when very young, but they quickly grow into beautiful specimens. | Kinglets; grouse and wild turkeys eat buds, investigate fallen seeds; many birds use as nighttime roost |

Once a rare treat, the red-breasted nuthatch has become a regular winter visitor in many areas.

(*Pinus taeda*) in the Southeast, are always a good combination.

- If you live in pygmy or brown-headed nuthatch territory, you'll have good luck attracting these birds by planting a pine that's native to your area, such as loblolly (*Pinus taeda*) in the South or lodgepole pine (*Pinus contorta* variety *latifolia*) in the West.

- Oaks (*Quercus* species) are excellent choices, too, and another opportunity to try out native species instead of planting whatever the garden center has on sale. Shop local nurseries and you may turn up some gems. All oaks grow into stately trees, and they're vital to wildlife, including dozens of bird species. To find out which species are native to your area, ask the staff at a local nature center or native plant nursery, or explore the wonderfully detailed USDA Plants Database at http://plants.usda.gov.

- Thanks to feeders, nuthatches have become big fans of a nontraditional food: sunflower seeds. And not only do they seek the seeds at feeders, they've also learned to pluck them from sunflower plants in our gardens. It's always a delight to watch these agile birds maneuver on the seed-filled center of a tall sunflower (*Helianthus annuus*).

- Both short- and long-needled conifers appeal to red- and white-breasted nuthatches, so why not include a mix of conifers? Native species, such as black spruce (*Picea mariana*) in Minnesota, Douglas-fir (*Pseudotsuga menziesii*) in the Northwest, or loblolly pine

**winter secret** One of the most important nuts in a nuthatch's diet isn't a true nut at all, but a seed. The seeds hidden within pinecones and other conifer cones are vital to this family—so much so that a bad year for cones in the North may touch off a southward swell of red-breasted nuthatches. Pygmy and brown-headed nuthatches also rely heavily on pine "nuts."

They'll pick out the ripe seeds from around the outer edges and keep coming back for weeks, until those in the very center have filled out.

## At the Feeder

- Just follow the natural menu as a guideline, and you'll have no trouble attracting nuthatches. Sunflower seeds, chopped nuts, and suet—which mimics their soft insect food—are all you need as temptations.

- Nuthatches also eat peanut butter treats (see page 267 for a recipe).

- Nuthatches are wild about mealworms and other insect-based foods.

## Added Attractions

Nuthatches are cavity nesters, so that means you may be able to attract them with nest boxes and materials for soft linings.

- Nuthatches often quickly adopt a birdhouse that's just their size. Invest in two types: One for the tiny species, and one for the larger white-breasted. That way, you'll avoid territorial battles between small nuthatches and bird-house-seeking house sparrows. If you can't find nest boxes that are labeled for nuthatches, look for a birdhouse sized for house wrens or chickadees, to suit small nuthatches; a bluebird-size box will accommodate the white-breasted nuthatch.

- Mount the box on a tree, about 15 feet off the ground.

- Help nuthatches line their nests by setting out a supply of cotton tufts or balls (not synthetic), soft feathers, fur, and moss. Think "fluffy."

- Nuthatches will collect dog hair they find among the pavers on a patio or elsewhere in your yard.

# Sources

## Field Guides

Is that shy brown bird with the speckled white belly a hermit thrush or a wood thrush? Or could it be a veery? And which sparrow is that beneath the feeder, the one with the eye-catching white stripe by its eye? Here are some field guides I keep handy; you'll find these and many others at bookstores, wild bird supply shops, and online sources, too.

Peterson, Roger Tory. *Peterson Field Guide to Birds of North America.* Boston: Houghton Mifflin, 2008.

———. *A Field Guide to the Birds of Eastern and Central North America.* Boston: Houghton Mifflin, 2002.

———. *A Field Guide to Western Birds.* Boston: Houghton Mifflin, 1998.
The 2002 edition of the *Eastern and Central* guide is an update of a previous edition and is the book that Roger Tory Peterson was working on at the time of his death in 1996. Peterson guides started it all; they're the classics and are excellent basic field guides. The illustrations have handy arrows to alert you to distinguishing characteristics, which is a big aid to sorting out the birds.

The new version of the classic Peterson field guides is bigger and heavier than the books that we're used to slipping in our pockets. But it's easier to use, because range maps are now on the same page as the birds. It's also beautiful, with clear illustrations that make it easy to tell which bird you're trying to match up. And, most important, it's the most up to date field guide out there, with maps that include the latest info on ranges—and those ranges have definitely changed in recent years.

Robbins, Chandler S., Bertel Brun, Herbert S. Zim, and Arthur Singer. *Birds of North America: A Guide to Field Identification, Revised and Updated.* New York: St. Martin's Press, 2001.
A perennial favorite of mine because of the bits of plants included in nearly all the illustrations: They're a big clue to where you'll find the bird. Maps are included right beside each species, so you can see at a glance whether the bird is likely to show up in your area.

Roth, Sally. *The Backyard Bird Lover's Field Guide.* Emmaus, PA: Rodale, 2007.
Traditional field guides can be difficult to use, simply because they include every bird for very large regions. To make it easier to learn the birds, I narrowed it down to the birds you're most likely to see in your backyard in seven distinct areas of the country. You'll learn each bird's name, but you'll also find out when you might see it, where to look for it, what it will be doing, and what it likes to eat.

Sibley, David Allen. *The Sibley Guide to Birds.* New York, NY: Knopf, 2000.
An education in itself, this guide includes regional plumage variations and lots of fun tidbits about each bird. Too big to carry easily in your pocket, but smaller versions are also available.

## Internet Birdsong

www.naturesongs.com/birds.html

www.mangoverde.com/birdsound/index.html

http://animaldiversity.ummz.umich.edu/site/accounts/souncds/Aves.html

www.birds.cornell.edu/MacaulayLibrary/ (search function)

www.enature.com/birding/audio.asp

# Feeders, Birdhouses, and Roost Boxes

These sources sell a huge variety of feeders, nest boxes, and roost boxes.

**BestNest**
4750 Lake Forest Drive, Suite 132
Cincinnati, OH 45242-3852
(877) 562-1818 or (513) 232-4225
www.Bestnest.com

**Duncraft**
102 Fisherville Road
Concord, NH 03303
(888) 879-5095
www.Duncraft.com

**WildBirdingWorld**
The Kayes Group, Inc.
PO Box 3326
Mesquite, NV 89024
(845) 691-2452
www.wildbirdingworld.com

## Starling-Proof Feeders and Anti-Squirrel Feeders

You'll find a variety of designs to discourage certain feeder "friends" at your local bird supply store. Or you can check the catalog or online-only offerings at these sources:

**Duncraft**
102 Fisherville Road
Concord, NH 03303
(888) 879-5095
www.Duncraft.com

**RollerFeeder**
St. Paul, MN 55108
(800) 432-3602
www.Rollerfeeder.com

**WildBirds Etc.**
www.Wildbirdsetc.com

## Insect Feeder Foods

Look here for insect feeder foods, including some that are roasted or otherwise packaged to minimize the "eeww" factor.

**Duncraft**
102 Fisherville Road
Concord, NH
(888) 879-5095
www.Duncraft.com

**Worm Man's Worm Farm**
PO Box 6947
Monroe Township, NJ 08831
(732) 656-0369
www.wormman.com

# Birdbaths and Accessories

In addition to water garden shops, wild bird supply stores, and some nurseries or garden centers, you can shop by mail or online for misters, solar fountains, drip tubes, "water wigglers," and other devices that cause the water in the basin to splash or gurgle.

**BestNest**
4750 Lake Forest Drive, Suite 132
Cincinnati, OH 45242-3852
(877) 562-1818 or (513) 232-4225
www.Bestnest.com

**BirdBaths.com**
NetShops, Inc. Corporate Office
12720 I Street Suite 200
Omaha, NE 68137
(800) 590-3752
www.birdbaths.com

**Duncraft**
102 Fisherville Road
Concord, NH
(888) 879-5095
www.Duncraft.com

### Motion-Activated Cat Chaser

To find a device that hooks up to your hose to deter cats and other trespassers with a sudden blast of water, check bird supply stores, well-stocked garden centers, or suppliers such as these.

### Biocontrol Network
5116 Williamsburg Road
Brentwood, TN 37027
(800) 441-2847
www.biconet.com

### SafePetProducts.com
KMP Products LLC
1060 Zygmunt Circle
Westmont, IL 60559
(888) 977-7387
www.safepetproducts.com

### Native Plants

The Internet has been a boon for finding mail-order sources for unusual plants. Not so long ago, only a handful of nurseries specialized in native plants; today, there are scores of them, in every area of the country. Just do a search for "native plant nursery [your state]" and see what turns up.

## Mail-Order Plant Sources

You can find an excellent selection of native plants and other bird-attracting plants, including wildflowers, grasses, shrubs, trees, and vines, at trustworthy mail-order suppliers and native plant nurseries. Here's a very small sampling to whet your appetite.

### All Native Garden Center
300 Center Road
Fort Myers, FL 33907
(239) 939-9663
www.nolawn.com
Fabulous plants with tropical flair and natives that can take the heat and dry spells. More than 200 native Florida species of plants, many of them superb for hummingbirds and songbirds. No mail-order service currently, but worth the drive; the staff includes two National Wildlife Federation Backyard Wildlife Habitat Stewards, so you'll find plenty of information just for the asking.

### Blake Nursery
316 Otter Creek Road
Big Timber, MT 59011
(406) 932-4195
www.blakenursery.com
Specializes in plants for western gardens, including a terrific selection of hardy Montana natives that will thrive elsewhere in the West, too—or give that western touch to an eastern garden.

### Digging Dog Nursery
PO Box 471
Albion, CA 95410
(707) 937-1130
www.diggingdog.com
Get ready to fall in love with hummingbirds—this catalog has so many plants that hummers adore, you can fill your yard and your neighbor's with great finds. You'll also discover other interesting perennials, including native plants for songbirds. Specializes in plants for the Southwest, but many of these beauties will thrive elsewhere, too.

### Forestfarm
990 Tetherow Road
Williams, OR 97544
(541) 846-7269
www.forestfarm.com
Plant addicts, beware: One look at this chunky, jam-packed catalog and you'll be hooked. An unbelievably vast selection of thousands of plants, including natives from across America. Lots of favorite plants in my gardens have come from Forestfarm over the years, and I've been thrilled every time with their superior size and vigor.

**Hamilton's Native Nursery & Seed Farm**
16786 Brown Road
Elk Creek, MO 65464
(417) 967-2190
www.hamiltonseed.com
Seeds and plants for native grasses, prairie flowers, native shrubs and trees, and other great finds.

**High Country Gardens**
2902 Rufina Street
Santa Fe, NM 87507
(800) 925-9387
www.highcountrygardens.com
Want a nice low water bill? Explore the fabulous drought-tolerant perennials and shrubs in this enticing catalog. Many natives, including a huge variety of penstemons for hummingbirds, plus many other bird-beloved perennials, native grasses, and shrubs.

# Shop Smart

When you shop in person, you can be sure you're buying healthy, vigorous, good-size plants. To avoid disappointment when you shop by mail, try these tips.

• If the catalog does not prominently tell you, in plain English, how big a plant you'll get, you may want to shop elsewhere. How big is a "#1 plant"? I have no idea. But a gallon pot, or a 2½-inch pot—now that's my language.

• Before you buy, take a minute to read the fine print about shipping schedules and costs. Shipping costs are usually lowest if the source is near your home, and the plants from a nursery in your region may be better suited to your climate than those that originate far away.

• Look for a money-back guarantee, or at the very least, an offer to replace unsatisfactory plants. A reputable company will replace plants without requiring you to ship the plants back to them.

• Make your first purchase a small one. See what kind of plants and service you get before you spend a lot of money.

• I'm usually very happy with plants from mail-order nurseries whose catalogs I have to ask for, or which I find online. Makes sense: Those companies depend on the repeat business of satisfied customers.

• When I've ordered from the companies whose catalogs seem to arrive in my mailbox every few months—catalogs I never asked for in the first place—the plants have been outrageously small, sickly, or just plain dead. Now I toss those catalogs on the recycling pile right away, so that their low prices can't seduce my cheapskate side. It makes me wonder if companies that do mass mailings of unsolicited catalogs attract so many buyers that they can get away with selling poor-quality plants—it doesn't matter whether I buy from that company again, because someone else will.

• To find out what kind of experiences others have had with the company you're considering buying from, you can read reviews by actual customers on the Web site "Garden Watchdog" at http://davesgarden.com/gwd/. This site provides a great service, acting as a sort of Better Business Bureau for mail-order gardeners.

**Las Pilitas Nursery**
8331 Nelson Way
Escondido, CA 92026
(760) 749-5930
www.laspilitas.com
Discover wildflowers, shrubs, and trees for
Southern California, many of them natives.
This company emphasizes gardening for
butterflies, birds, hummingbirds, and other
wildlife, and you'll turn up all kinds of must-
have plants. If you can't visit either of the two
locations in person, you can browse and order
online.

**Prairie Nursery**
PO Box 306
Westfield, WI 53964
(800) 476-9453
www.prairienursery.com
Prairie plants are tough and adaptable, and
this company has supplied many of those in
my gardens. Reasonable prices and a
superinformative catalog chock-full of beautiful
grasses, coneflowers, perennial sunflowers,
and other wildflowers.

**Raintree Nursery**
391 Butts Road
Morton, WA 98356
(360) 496-6400
www.raintreenursery.com
Terrific fruit trees and bushes for people—and
birds! It's a treat to open a well-packed box
from this company and find big, healthy, high-
quality plants rarin' to go. You'll discover all of
the usual fruits and berries, plus a great
selection of varieties that are hard to find
elsewhere, such as mulberries and native fruits.

**Tripple Brook Farm**
37 Middle Road
Southampton, MA 01073
(413) 527-4626
www.tripplebrookfarm.com
Hundreds of fabulous plants—I need a bigger
yard!—including native viburnums and many,
many other natives.

**Woodlanders, Inc.**
1128 Colleton Avenue
Aiken, SC 29801
(803) 648-7522
www.woodlanders.net
One of the older native plant specialists (since
1979), Woodlanders offers mouth-watering
natives for the Southeast.

# Seeds

Planting a few handfuls of birdseed from your
feeder is the simple way to start a birdseed
garden. But lots of other plants supply excellent seeds for birds. Look for grains in the
vegetable section of catalogs. If you have a big
yard, check out prices for seeds in bulk. Here
are just a few of my favorites; you'll find
dozens of others online, and most sources for
prairie plants also sell seeds.

**Abundant Life Seeds**
PO Box 279
Cottage Grove, OR 97424
(541) 767-9606
www.abundantlifeseeds.com
Abundant Life Seed Foundation is famed for its
collection of all-organic heritage seeds from
around the world, many of them painstakingly
gathered from gardeners who shared their own
personal stock. Unfortunately, a devastating
fire hit the warehouse in Port Townsend,
Washington, a few years ago. To help out this
worthy cause, Territorial Seed of Oregon has
taken over the mail-order catalog, so you can
still find that wonderful selection of grains,
grasses, sunflowers, Indian corn, flowers, and
all the other treasures for which Abundant Life
is known. Enjoy and support a good cause—
the seeds that link us to gardeners of
generations before.

**American Meadows**
223 Avenue D, Suite 30
Williston, VT 05495
(877) 309-7333
www.americanmeadows.com
One of the very few companies that sells all-native mixes of wildflowers, instead of fattening the mix with inexpensive "filler" seeds. Also stocks many common annual flowers and wildflowers, plus regional mixes, both in small quantities and in bulk. Extremely reasonable prices—how about a pound of blue bachelor button seeds (*Centaurea cyanus*) for less than $10?

**Native Seeds/SEARCH**
526 North 4th Avenue
Tucson, AZ 85705
(520) 622-5561
www.nativeseeds.org
This fantastic small company offers a catalog of about 350 types of seeds, every single one of them suitable for farming in arid lands and many of them great for birds in any garden. From grasses to grains to sunflowers, these seeds will make birds drool. All are heritage types, handed down through the generations, including Native American varieties of corn and sunflowers, not to mention amaranth, millet, and others that are perfect for a birdseed garden—or a loaf of bread. Simply reading the catalog is an education.

**Pinetree Garden Seeds**
PO Box 300
New Gloucester, ME 04260
(207) 926-3400
www.superseeds.com
The first company I ever bought mail-order seeds from, and still going strong decades later. This family company offers a huge selection of interesting annual flowers at reasonable prices. You'll also discover a great collection of sunflower varieties at prices cheap enough to try them all, plus graceful millets, wheat, corn, and other grains for birds.

**Territorial Seed**
PO Box 158
Cottage Grove, OR 97424
(800) 626-0866
www.territorial-seed.com
You'll find a mix of interesting vegetables and bird-beloved annuals in this delectable catalog, including an unbelievable array of sunflowers. Look for grains and corn, too, including Native American varieties.

**Wildseed Farms**
425 Wildflower Hills
PO Box 3000
Fredericksburg, TX 78624
(800) 848-0078
www.wildseedfarms.com
A good source for fast-growing annual flowers with seeds that birds adore. Look for cosmos, zinnias, and many others, in packets or in bulk. You'll find low-priced wildflower mixes, too, but they're not entirely native. Personally, I don't mind red Flanders poppies (*Papaver rhoeas*) adding some zing to my flowerbeds, but if you prefer natives-only, you can make your own mix by buying seeds of individual plants.

# Photo Credits

Page 1 © Art Wolfe/Getty Images

Page 2 © Ethan Meleg/Getty Images

Page 3 © Dave Welling

Page 4 © Tom Vezo/Minden

Page 5 © J. Schumacher/Vireo

Page 6 © Doris Dumrauf/Alamy

Page 9, 12, 19, 46, 50, 53, 54, 55b, 57, 61b, 94, 102, 104l, 104r, 123, 124, 126, 132t, 132b, 135t, 140tr, 168, 173, 174, 179, 187, 188, 199, 200, 204, 205, 208t, 212, 213b, 213t, 214b, 215, 216, 218, 219, 222, 226l, 230, 236, 278, 289t, 289b, 292tr © Mark Dauble

Page 10 © A. Morris/Vireo

p.11, 45, 58, 73, 161, 180, 209, 221, 229, 277 © William Leaman/ Alamy

Page 13 © Robert Winslow

Page 16 © Bill Brooks/Alamy

Page 17 © Neil Holmes/Agefotostock

Page 19 © Blickwinkel/Alamy

Page 20 © Dr. M. Stubblefield/Vireo

Page 24 © G. Lasley/Vireo

Page 26 © Woodfall/Photoshot

Page 32 © Bob Stovall/ Bruce Coleman/Photoshot

Page 33 © Paul Miles, Jr/ Bruce Coleman/Photoshot

Page 35 © H. Page Smith, Jr./Vireo

Page 36 © R. Crossley/Vireo

Page 167, 175, 178, 214t, 294, 318 © Jim Zipp/Ardea.com

Page 41 © Nan Moore

Page 43, 44, 95, 122, 135, 139, 145, 147, 151, 159, 169, 186, 191, 193, 196, 281, 296, 306 © Richard Day/Daybreak Imagery

Page 48 ©B. Runk/S.Schoenberger / Grant Heilman Photography

Page 49 ©David Kennedy

Page 51 © Gay Bumgarner/ Getty Images

Page 52 © G. McElroy/Vireo

Page 55t © Mike Lentz

Page 59, 217, 224 © Steve Maslowski/Visuals Unlimited

Page 60, 140, 233 © Steve & Dave Maslowski/Photo Researchers, Inc.

Page 61t © Charles Melton/Visuals Unlimited

Page 64 © Larry R. Cartwright

Page 65t © Anthony Mercieca/ Photo Researchers, Inc.

Page 65c © J. Schumacher/Vireo

Page 65b, 87, 98, 182, 201 © R. Curtis/Vireo

Page 74 © B. Henry/Vireo

Page 82 © Gay Bumgarner/ Getty Images

Page 84 © Peter Bisset/ Stock Connection/Alamy

Page 85 ©Ron Mayberry

Page 88 © David Osborn/Alamy

Page 91, 161t © R.& N. Bowers/ Vireo

Page 97 © Wildscape/Alamy

Page 103 © Bob Gibbons/Alamy

Page 109 © Steve Littlewood/ Oxford Scientific/Photo Library

Page 110 © John Van Decker/Alamy

Page 114 © Robert Baker

Page 116 © Nikki Edmunds/Alamy

Page 117 © Tom Vezo

Page 118 © Phyllis Greenberg/ Animals Animals

Page 119 © Juniors Bildarchiv/Alamy

Page 125 © Ruth Cole/Animals Animals

Page 127 © Steve Maslowski/ Photographers Direct

Page 129 © Kate Preston

Page 131 © Ken Newcombe/ Photographers Direct

Page 140bl © Betty LaRue

Page 143 © Scott Leslie/ Photographers Direct

Page 146 © Johann Schumacher Design

Page 150 © Dave Welling

Page 151br © Rick & Nora Bowers/ Alamy

Page 158 © Robert McKemie/ Daybreak Imagery

Page 160 © Joe McDonald/Bruce Coleman/Photoshot

Page 165 © Tohoku Color Agency/ Getty Images

Page 166 © Gay Bumgarner/ Getty Images

Page 171 © Cyril Ruoso/ Minden Pictures

Page 177 © Tim Zurowski/Corbis

Page 184 © Simon Whaley/Alamy

Page 186b © John Daniels/Ardea

Page 193b © Peter Llewellyn/ Bruce Coleman/Photoshot

Page 196r © Joe Austin Photography/Alamy

Page 208b © Steve Maslowski/ Getty Images

Page 220 © Tim Gehring/ Photographers Direct

Page 222 © Jason Smalley

Page 223 © Adam Jones/ Visuals Unlimited, Inc.

Page 226r © Robert Smith/ Photographers Direct

Page 228 © Arthur C. Smith III/ Grant Heilman Photography

Page 238 © Raymond Gehman/ Getty Images

Page 240 © Hannu Hautala/ Getty Images

Page 274 © K. A. Niyo/Vireo

Page 275 © David Richard

Page 279 © Millard H. Sharp/ Photo Researchers, Inc.

Page 284, 288 © Nature's Images/ Photo Researchers, Inc.

Page 286tl © Arco Images GmbH/ Alamy

Page 286 bl © Michael Giannechini/ Photo Researchers, Inc.

Page 287 © Jeannie Burleson

Page 292tl © Dwight Kuhn

Page 298 © John Cancalosi/ Ardea.com

Page 299 © Richard R. Hansen/ Photo Researchers, Inc.

Page 301 © Daybreak Imagery/ Animals Animals

Page 307 © Glenn Bartley/ Rights Managed

Page 311 © Peter Llewellyn/ Peter Llewellyn Photography

Page 312 © Rolf Nussbaumer/ DanitaDelimont.com

Page 313 © Max Allen

Page 314 © Jim Zipp/ Photo Researchers, Inc.

Page 315 © Laure Neish/ Vireo

# Index

Boldface page references indicate photographs or illustrations.
Underscored references indicate boxed text, tables or charts.